The Patron-Driven Library

CHANDOS
INFORMATION PROFESSIONAL SERIES

Series Editor: Ruth Rikowski
(email: Rikowskigr@aol.com)

Chandos' new series of books is aimed at the busy information professional. They have been specially commissioned to provide the reader with an authoritative view of current thinking. They are designed to provide easy-to-read and (most importantly) practical coverage of topics that are of interest to librarians and other information professionals. If you would like a full listing of current and forthcoming titles, please visit our website, www.chandospublishing.com, email wp@woodheadpublishing.com or telephone +44 (0) 1223 499140.

New authors: we are always pleased to receive ideas for new titles; if you would like to write a book for Chandos, please contact Dr Glyn Jones on gjones@chandospublishing.com or telephone +44 (0) 1993 848726.

Bulk orders: some organisations buy a number of copies of our books. If you are interested in doing this, we would be pleased to discuss a discount. Please email wp@woodheadpublishing.com or telephone +44 (0) 1223 499140.

The Patron-Driven Library

A practical guide for managing collections and services in the digital age

DEE ANN ALLISON

CP

CHANDOS
PUBLISHING

Oxford Cambridge New Delhi

Chandos Publishing
Hexagon House
Avenue 4
Station Lane
Witney
Oxford OX28 4BN
UK
Tel: +44(0) 1993 848726
Email: info@chandospublishing.com
www.chandospublishing.com

Chandos Publishing is an imprint of Woodhead Publishing Limited

Woodhead Publishing Limited
80 High Street
Sawston
Cambridge CB22 3HJ
UK
Tel: +44(0) 1223 499140
Fax: +44(0) 1223 832819
www.woodheadpublishing.com

First published in 2013

ISBN: 978-1-84334-736-1 (print)
ISBN: 978-1-78063-402-9 (online)

Chandos Information Professional Series ISSN: 2052-210X (print) and ISSN: 2052-2118 (online)

Library of Congress Control Number: 2013941271

© D.A. Allison, 2013

Typeset by Domex e-Data Pvt. Ltd., India
Printed in the UK and USA.

This book is dedicated to my parents –
Duane and Geneva Allison

Contents

List of figures and tables

Figures

Tables

List of abbreviations

ACRL	Association of College and Research Libraries
AI	artificial intelligence
ALA	American Library Association
API	application programming interface
ARL	Association of Research Libraries
ASERL	Association of Southeastern Research Libraries
CPU	cost per use
DOI	Digital Object Identifier
DRM	digital rights management
DUR	density-of-use ranking
ERM	electronic resource management
GLO	general learning outcomes
ILL	interlibrary loan
ILS	integrated library system
IM	instant messaging
IP	Internet Protocol
IR	institutional repository
LC	Library of Congress
MARC	MAchine-Readable Cataloging

NFC   near field communication

NII   National Information Infrastructure

NISO   National Information Standards Organization

OA   open access

OCA   Open Content Alliance

PDA   patron-driven acquisition

PPV   pay-per-view

QR   Quick Response (code)

RDA   Resource Description and Access

RDF   Resource Description Framework

RFID   radio frequency identification

RI   Representation Information

ROI   return on investment

RUR   raw-use ranking

SERU   Shared Electronic Resource Understanding

SOA   service oriented architecture

VLE   virtual learning environment

VR   virtual reference

Acknowledgements

With thanks to the staff of the interlibrary loan unit at the University of Nebraska-Lincoln and the Computing Operations and Research Services Department, who demonstrate the values of a patron centered library every day.

About the author

Dee Ann Allison is Director of Computing Operations and Research Services and Professor at the University of Nebraska-Lincoln. Dee Ann is a graduate of the MLS program at the University of Hawaii and has been involved in special and academic libraries for more than thirty years. During this time she has participated in the technological revolution that has improved library services from card catalogs and mediated online searching to telnet, Gopher and the web-based environment that challenges librarians today. Her peer-reviewed articles cover a wide variety of topics including database selection, librarian turnover, indexing and patron search behavior, to her latest research interest in artificial intelligence for reference chatbots.

Introduction: patron centered libraries

Librarians are responsible for preserving knowledge. Others will take credit for inventing machines, building bridges or curing diseases, but it is the responsibility of librarians to be the keeper of the facts behind those achievements so that others can repeat the successes or avoid the failures.

This is the important mission that brought many into the library profession, and it is a singular purpose that will help librarians stay afloat while others drown in the bits of information flooding into homes, businesses and schools off the World Wide Web. It is the responsibility of librarians to assist people by connecting them to the right information, when they need it, and in a form they can use. In the past, librarians advocated for increased access to information technology as a means by which to expand services, improve productivity and reduce costs. No one could have predicted the sea change that occurred with the web, or how libraries would be struggling to remain relevant. In spite of these challenges, librarians can overcome the barriers facing the profession today, and technology can play a key role.

Any invention adds an element of the unknown and is a catalyst for change. The more technology is incorporated into life, the more it accelerates change. Technology is now changing at a faster pace than generational turnover, which is stretching the comfort level of individuals. In the past, when new technology was introduced, workers retooled their skills. Now, technology is being introduced at a rate that requires re-education, or that even causes workers to change careers. The current generation is using technology in ways that could not have been imagined by their grandparents. Young people are more disconnected from nature (Louv, 2008: 390), and at the same time are moving away from traditional social customs.

It is no wonder that librarians are struggling to serve the multi-generational needs of users. This book is intended as a guide for librarians to develop a new relationship with technology that preserves the core mission of libraries while responding to the needs of a new generation of library clients. At stake is the future health of libraries. Will the next generation of librarians inherit museums or libraries?

The following chapters will look at the challenges facing today's libraries and will summarize current research and experiments reported in library literature. Building on these themes, practical advice is offered on management, collections and services that will produce an organization that emphasizes the patron while preserving the ideals of the profession. This is a new age, when the success of a library will not be judged by the size of the collection, but by the quality of the librarians and services.

Part 1
Libraries and library users
changing with the times

From the White House conferences and the golden age of libraries to challenges for libraries in the age of digital information

Abstract: Librarians were excited about the two White House conferences in the late twentieth century. The increases in library funding from the conferences have slowed as the economy has declined, while the improvements to connectivity brought by the growth of the Internet had a dramatic and positive impact on libraries. Publishers and librarians are using information technology to deliver information in new formats, and both are struggling to create pricing models that will maintain the health of each sector.

Key words: big deal, e-books, e-readers, High Performance Computing and Communication Act, Library Services and Technology Act, recession, serial pricing, White House Conference on Libraries and Information Services (WHCLIS), budgets, digital divide.

Lessons from the White House conferences on libraries and information services

The late twentieth century may well be seen as the golden age for American libraries. Two White House Conferences on Libraries and Information Services (WHCLIS) brought national attention to the needs of libraries. The first was held in 1979, with additional momentum for library support added by the second conference in 1991. The preparation, discussions and ideas generated from the sessions brought excitement and hope, which energized librarians to engage with the issues of the time.

Pre-conferences for the first White House conference were held between 1977 and 1979 to gather input, define issues and vote on resolutions and recommendations. The first conference sought to improve information access through interlibrary cooperation and telecommunications, to advance public library services, to create leadership development opportunities, and to expand services for Native Americans. In addition to expanding services to under-represented groups, the conference highlighted the need to improve literacy.

In preparation for the second conference, pre-conferences were again held around the county to gather input from over 100,000 citizens and librarians. These pre-conferences focused on three areas – literacy, productivity and democracy – and resulted in a call for a national campaign for lifelong learning. The second conference also paid special attention to the development of the National Information Infrastructure (NII), which was defined in the High Performance Computing and Communication Act of 1991.

The key recommendations from this Act for network infrastructure with implications for libraries included free access to information, assurances for privacy and copyright (Walsh, 1994: 3). Librarians looked forward to improved network capabilities that would bring libraries closer together and provide library patrons with immediate access to information.

Libraries did benefit from the high-speed networks built to support defense, research and business interests. The genius of the NII was in building an infrastructure of "organizations, businesses and people who are not so much concerned with the technology as they are in being connected on an affordable basis and a fast-rising number of new businesses and services designed to add value to that connectivity" (ibid.: 18). The NII succeeded far beyond expectations. The expansion of network infrastructure combined with technological advances in computing power and price and size reductions in computers during the 1990s, made computing more economical and practical for commerce, libraries, research and, most importantly, home use.

It is hard to recall the world of 1991 when computers were an extravagance and librarians thought of the digital divide in terms of those who had computers and those who didn't. Librarians feared that children would be deprived of the educational benefit of digital information because their libraries and schools lacked basic infrastructure. The Library Services and Technology Act passed in 1976 was revised to focus on school libraries, and provided funding for literacy.

In the years since the White House conferences, library technologies have changed dramatically. Holdings were computerized and made available through integrated library systems (ILSs), direct patron searching replaced mediated searching by librarians and libraries offered public access terminals for general use. Increasing portions of library budgets were diverted to support new technology, and managers looked for ways to cut staffing expenditures because of the efficiencies brought about by technology. This was occurring at the same time as efforts were underway to connect libraries, schools and medical facilities via the NII infrastructure.

Today, Internet connectivity is as important to families as television, and open wireless networks are available in coffee shops and libraries around the world. When librarians speak about the digital divide today they mean the difference between those who have embraced technology and those who are uncomfortable with computers. Although the world today is very different from the world experienced by the participants of the White House conferences, there are messages from the conferences that are still valuable. In particular, the conference participants agreed that librarians should never take patronage for granted. In the years since the conferences many librarians have forgotten that message, but library promotion is more important now because information is everywhere on the web – libraries have competition.

It also seems that the US government has forgotten about libraries. In an article that appeared in the *New York Times* on 30 May 2012, "The new divide is such a cause of concern for the Federal Communications Commission [FCC] that it is considering a proposal to spend $200 million to create a digital literacy corps. This group of hundreds, even thousands, of trainers would fan out to schools and libraries to teach productive uses of computers for parents, students and job seekers"(Richtel, 2012). Librarians are trained and ready to supply these services so why does the FCC believe a new program is needed? This is an example of a growing disconnect between government and libraries as evidenced by reductions and eliminations of school and public libraries. Librarians need to address this trend through a combination of activism and proactive services which make the case for libraries through measurable benefits.

Rising costs and reduced budgets

Libraries experienced success with information technology that included sharing cataloging and resources, and improving overall efficiencies in operation, but those successes have not been rewarded with sustained budget increases. The federal government has an inconsistent approach to supporting library efforts to improve access to the web. The 2009 American Recovery and Reinvestment Act's Broadband Initiatives provides grants for projects that improve broadband services, including in under-served areas; however, the FCC, which released the National Broadband Plan, is proposing to finance the Connect America Fund by using the E-Rate Fund. The E-Rate Fund has been used historically to support Internet connectivity to libraries and schools (Jaeger et al., 2012) and reductions will impact the ability of libraries to provide network connectivity for patrons.

Public libraries are a good barometer of the health of the profession in general, and the news has not been good. Funding at the national level from the Library Services and Technology Act has been declining since 2002. Likewise, state support for library programs is falling as the recession, which started in 2007, continues to impact tax receipts. Libraries have entered a gilded age, where declining budgets are challenging academic, public, school and special libraries.

Once-supportive legislators look for programs to cut, leaving cash-strapped communities to make up the difference. In turn, mayors are asking public libraries to cut back on library hours, staff or library services as budget saving measures. Librarians faced with flat budgets but increasing expenses for materials and staff, or, worse, faced with budget reductions, have been forced to prioritize services and material budgets.

A 2009 survey conducted by June Power through the CIRCPLUS discussion list highlights some of the ways in which libraries were being impacted. These included lay-offs, reduced funding for programs and reductions in the number of programs, reductions in the numbers of student workers, positions that were not replaced, and cuts to state-wide consortiums (Power, 2009). Reductions in staffing were common in all types of libraries in the early days of the recession, with a preference for reduction through attrition.

The American Library Association (ALA), reporting on the state of public libraries in the US, noted that:

> data from the 2010–2011 Study present libraries grappling with a new normal of flat or decreased funding, paired with increased demand for public library technology resources. The result is a mix of the grim austerity, reflected in decreased operating hours and closed library outlets, in contrast with the robust delivery of technology resources that support workforce development, e-government services, and skills training for the competitive global marketplace.
>
> (American Library Association (ALA) Office for Research & Statistics and the Information Policy Access Center at the University of Maryland, 2011: 7–10)

The Future of Libraries report published in *CQ Researcher* in 2011 confirms the public library cuts, and reports similar circumstances for school libraries, "Libraries in urban school districts are facing numerous difficulties, ranging from staffing cuts to reduced operating hours. Less than 40 percent have at least one full-time librarian and 35 percent report decreased staffing levels over the past three years" (Mantel, 2011: 628).

Academic libraries are also suffering from a reduction in tax support and double-digit percentage reductions in endowment earnings because of declining stock value. Tuition increases to offset declining revenues are unpopular with students and parents. University administrators are becoming wary of raising tuition beyond the modest cost-of-living increases, while libraries struggle with increases on materials that exceed inflationary rates for other commodities. Academic libraries have reduced staffing and other operating costs and have turned to the materials budgets: "Among the strategies employed, journal cancellation was most common and used by 54%, followed closely by 41% reducing monograph purchases, and 30% eliminating databases. Since around the year 2000, libraries have moved from purchasing print and e-versions to e-only; and 21% used the strategy this year when it could reduce serial subscription cost" (Lowry, 2011: 45).

Rising prices for books and journals are straining all types of library budgets. As reported by *Library Journal* in 2011, serials prices are increasing without corresponding increases in budgets:

> During the recession there was a reduction in cost for most commodities and goods, with the Customer Price Index (CPI) dropping in 2009 and only increasing 1.6 percent in 2010. During that same period, serials prices continued to rise at well above the CPI (four to five percent), and, against the backdrop of decreased federal funding for libraries, price increases are very hard to sustain.
>
> (Bosch et al., 2011: 3)

This comes as no surprise to librarians who are making difficult choices to cancel print subscriptions. In a 2010 survey reported by EBSCO, a subscription management company, libraries are absorbing reductions by reducing staff and renegotiating license agreements (Collins, 2012). Additional tactics include dropping print in favor of electronic journals (86 percent), and looking for ways to save money by reducing or eliminating the duplication that comes with package plans (75 percent) (ibid.).

Book prices are increasing but not at the same rate as serials. Publisher income from book sales is led by the growth in e-book sales: "The growth in eBook trade publishing has grown from .06% in 2008 to 6.4% in 2010" (Tonkery, 2011: 36). The percentage of e-book sales for publishers is increasing consistently and is expected to continue to grow in light of the rising popularity and variety of reading devices.

Publishers have also impacted on library budgets through mergers and publisher acquisitions. Many librarians were concerned about the consolidation of publishers, and, in 2003, the American Association of Law Libraries, the American Library Association, the Association of College and Research Libraries, the Association of Research Libraries, the Medical Library Association, the Special Library Association and SPARC combined to form the Information Access Alliance, whose purpose was to tackle perceived insupportable increases in prices. In 2003, the Alliance issued a report, *Publisher Mergers: A Consumer-based Approach to Antitrust Analysis*, which highlighted the concerns librarians have about the consolidation of the publishing industry (Susman et al., 2003: 33). In spite of Alliance efforts, the consolidation of publishers continues, and some distributors are now entering the market as evidenced by EBSCO's acquisition of NetLibrary eBooks and

H.W. Wilson. In addition to publishers swallowing other publishers, there were also instances of a publisher selling a single journal to another publisher, which further consolidates subject titles with particular publishers.

Figure 1.1 illustrates a "map" of three publishers' acquisitions, and the companies that they absorbed or transferred between them. The publishers in circles were subsumed by the purchasing company they are linked to, which in turn was acquired by or merged with the publisher in the tinted box. The figure illustrates the trend towards publisher consolidations, a particular theme for the scientific and legal areas: "Elsevier is one of many journal publishers

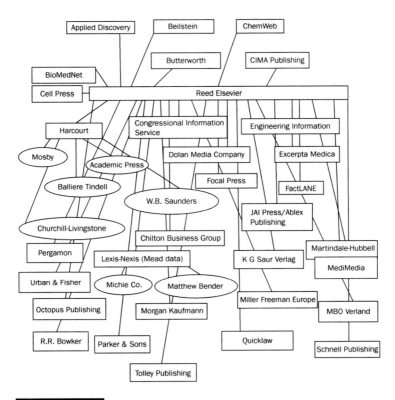

Figure 1.1   Reed Elsevier map depicting publisher acquisitions

that has digitized its full backfile, with the number of articles on ScienceDirect passing 9.5 million – about 25% of the total scientific, technological, and medical (STM) literature" (Hunter and Bruning, 2010: 148).

Publishers defend these acquisitions as efficiency measures that can reduce production costs, which in turn will result in lower costs to libraries. However, this argument is difficult to defend given the increases in pricing reported by libraries. The Association of Research Libraries (ARL), reporting on information collected from member libraries over the period 1986 through 2009, demonstrated that serial costs grew 381 percent during that period (Kyrillidou and Morris, 2011: 11). These unsustainable increases are causing libraries to rethink their purchasing decisions and collection policies.

One group of publishers that is suffering under budget reductions is university presses. University presses are among the smallest publishers and have a tradition of producing scholarly publications which generally do not have mass appeal. The principal customers for university presses are libraries, and sales from 2005–9 have been flat (Greco et al., 2007: 10). The current economic situation has added to this pressure and as the economic situation improves it is unlikely that university presses will be able to bounce back as well as the more diversified commercial publishers with which they compete.

Consortia: power in numbers

Libraries are increasingly forming consortia as a way to reduce expenditure for materials and forming alliances for other purposes. Librarians began forming consortia in the nineteenth century as they discovered the value of working together to achieve common goals. There are many types of consortia, and libraries frequently belong to more than one. Examples include geographic alignments, subject specialization or institutional affiliation. The main purpose of consortia is to accomplish collectively something that couldn't be accomplished, or would be very difficult to accomplish, by a single library. Consortia share expertise and stimulate creative answers to common problems. They also leverage buying power in deals with publishers, form nodes for resource-sharing through interlibrary loans (ILLs) and cooperate on collection development to provide access through resource-sharing agreements.

The Center for Research Libraries is a good example of a consortia founded by universities looking for ways to reduce storage costs (Harris, 1995). The purpose of the Center is to share costs associated with purchasing, borrowing and preserving newspapers, journals, documents, archives and other traditional and digital resources collected from around the world. By pooling resources, member libraries can borrow titles on an unlimited basis, and thereby can reduce storage and preservations costs at their institutions.

As budgets get tighter there is more incentive for libraries to join together on purchasing deals, and although there can be difficulties reaching agreements many libraries consider the benefits more persuasive than any potential problems (Torbert, 2008). Consortia members must agree on vendors, on the specifics of license details and on decisions on title inclusion. Resolving technical issues can also be difficult when a consortia is acting as a middleman between a participating consortia library and a vendor. However, the benefits of a strong alliance can expand significantly the buying ability of a single library and can offset losses in autonomy.

Big deals and rising serial costs

In 1996, Academic Press started a publisher trend by offering contracts for bundled serials to library consortia with price caps to control inflation. Publishers liked the idea of contracts calculated on a formula that used the number of participating libraries in a consortia and the amount of expenditure rather than individual subscriptions. These contracts, known as "big deals," provided more predictable revenue streams for publishers.

Consortia that purchased big deals did so in order to increase access to more titles for less than the individual cost per title. The number of titles included in a plan was based on formulas that included factors such as the size of the consortia, an annual price calculated on historical spend, access fees for additional titles included in the plan, and a guaranteed inflation cap for price increases during the contract period. However, within a few years big deals started to look like bad deals to some librarians and small publishers, as outlined in Table 1.1.

From the list of pros and cons in Table 1.1 it quickly becomes clear that there are two sides to every issue. Libraries might receive more titles, but if the additional titles are not used, the cost per use is higher. Publishers argue that the price per title is lower than what libraries would pay if titles were ordered individually, so bundling means that libraries are getting more titles for their money. However, when the overall cost of the plan is consuming a larger portion of the budget, the result is less funding for other materials. Discounts made to smaller institutions, which discriminate against larger libraries in consortia, are also being disputed (Van Orsdel and Born, 2009). Under such terms, larger libraries appear to be carrying a larger portion of the costs.

Table 1.1   Pros and cons of the "big deal"

Is the "big deal" a good deal?	
Pros	**Cons**
Contracts based on serial costs anchored in a specified year with a designated rate for inflation, typically 6 percent, running for a specified period of time, often three years, with the positive effect of a fixed expenditure for libraries.	The inability for librarians to select titles, which might result in a mixture of high use and low use with a high cost per use.
Libraries gain access to a larger number of titles, thereby expanding their holdings.	Inability for libraries to eliminate duplicates between plans resulting in multiple vendor access and higher costs per use.
Libraries might save costs through the consortia plans over individual library subscription.	Less flexibility in library budgets because of the large amount of funds necessary to commit to plans.
Libraries save staff time by transferring duties to vendors, and by eliminating time-consuming negotiations, or title-by-title selections.	Librarians spend more time tracking title changes in the plans, either actual title changes, or titles that get dropped and added.
Access to titles is shared among consortia libraries.	Some vendors change FTE calculations resulting in higher prices to the library.
Publisher receives higher profits by bundling specialized titles that typically have fewer subscriptions.	Smaller publishers, not part of a deal, are disadvantaged and librarians are often forced to cancel their titles to fund deals, jeopardizing the long-term viability of smaller publishers.
Known and fixed revenue stream for publishers.	Restrictions in ILL reduce the ability of libraries to share outside the contract.
Libraries can maintain print copies and get digital copies at a discount.	Depending on contracts, when a deal is cancelled, libraries can lose access to the issues they paid for while on the plan.

Table 1.1   Pros and cons of the "big deal" *(cont'd)*

Vendors provide accurate statistics for evaluating titles based on actual usage.	Titles that libraries do not need are included in the plans.
Vendors gain better control by eliminating subscription agencies.	The budgets encumbered to plans reduce flexibility for libraries to add new titles that are not part of the plan.
Libraries can cancel print copies in favor of digital copies and save money.	Cancellation allowances are often unfavorable or too restrictive for consortia members. When members drop out deals are threatened.
Consortia agreements save money over individual library subscriptions.	Extended contact time between renewals reducing flexibility in budgeting for libraries.
	There is no incentive for publishers to monitor quality of journals included in packages, and in fact there is some incentive to add titles so the package appears to be a better deal.

Thus, package plans are being considered more carefully as they come up for renewal and some are being pulled apart or discarded in favor of more targeted content. These decisions are being driven by concerns over costs, increasing momentum for open access and usage data that reveals that too many of the titles aren't being used (Boissy et al., 2012).

Technology is providing better information on the true cost of titles by combining usage data with subscription cost. Data on cost per use, impact factors and other bibliometrics are being combined with consultations with library patrons to identify critical titles for retention. The ability to collect statistics for usage and cost analysis is a necessity for library managers, and is another way in which technology can be incorporated into management decisions.

Librarians are also returning to the art of negotiation in order to improve the terms of their contracts. Vendors who repackage publisher titles are dependent on libraries for revenue, and librarians have power. Multi-year contracts are being renegotiated with options that are more favorable to libraries. These include shorter contract periods, leased vs. perpetual access, smaller subject-oriented packages, the ability to add titles during the contract period for reduced cost, and increased flexibility with regard to cancellations.

Alternatives to deal packages include title-by-title selection, pay-per-view for articles from journals that are less heavily used, or replacing plans with access through distribution services that provide citation databases with full-text access. ILLs are also being used to obtain articles that are not included in packages. Open source publications are becoming more attractive as a means for adding to or substituting purchased titles with equivalent content. PLoS ONE is providing a model for open source publishing within a peer-review framework, and some libraries are following this lead with their own peer-reviewed journals. Increased awareness within the academic community of the crisis in materials pricing is fueling an interest in alternatives to high-cost journals as evidenced by the "academic spring" movement in 2012 (*http://thecostof knowledge.com/*), when researchers protested against Elsevier's high prices for subscriptions, big-deal bundling and other efforts to restrict access to information.

Cautions against exclusive contracts

Some publishers sign exclusive contracts with aggregators so that their content is only available from one source. This makes it more difficult to negotiate new contracts but it also jeopardizes access. When a library is notified that a source is now exclusive there are several actions that should be taken:

- Determine how long the title will be exclusive with the source, and what guarantees exist for permanent access.

- Identify the cost for the title and verify that exclusivity will not result in higher costs to the library.

- Determine if there are possible consortia deals.

- Consider ILLs as an alternative for low-use titles.

- When a title is discontinued by the supplier, verify that access to back issues will continue.

Relationships between electronic publishers and librarians

Although publishers and librarians are often at odds, in reality they have a symbiotic relationship. Publishers rely on libraries for much of their business and librarians need the titles publishers produce for library collections. There are two other important elements in this relationship: authors and readers (see Figure 1.2).

When publishers add titles to their lists to increase their revenues, they may be serving the interests of authors, but not necessarily those of libraries or readers. Librarians don't need titles in which patrons have no interest, and readers only want what they want, quickly and without cost. When

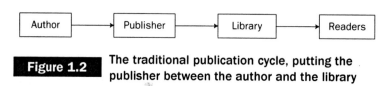

Figure 1.2 The traditional publication cycle, putting the publisher between the author and the library

librarians cancel titles because the content isn't used, this impacts on the publisher's revenue, causing publishers to look for additional sources of revenue, i.e., to add more titles. These new titles can be added into a package deal, which continues the cycle. This battle has come to the area of e-print, and it will cause additional friction if publishers and librarians can't come to agreement.

"Whereas 80% of sales were in print only in 1998, now print makes up only 38% of sales while electronic-only sales have gone from 4% of sales in 1998 to 50% of sales today"(Collins, 2012: 28). This remarkable statement from EBSCO is echoed by others in the publishing field who recognize the potential for increased revenue from e-print sales. Librarians are also looking to e-print, but as a less expensive alternative to print. In addition to lower access costs, librarians see advantages to digital formats in expanded accessibility, reduced life-cycle expenses for processing and lower storage costs (Okerson and Schonfeld, 2004). Libraries moving in this direction must give careful consideration to issues of long-term archiving, which may add some additional costs in the transition from print to e-print. It is clear that digital material will become an important part, if not a major part, of libraries' collections, making this a topic for ongoing discussion between publishers and librarians, each with a stake in the outcome.

There are several methods that publishers use for pricing library access to e-books. The models take into account methods for controlling access and protecting revenue. Some vendors restrict access to a single simultaneous usage of a title, or require the purchase of a second copy after a specified number of uses. In other cases, vendors provide multiple purchasing models including alternatives for concurrent access, pay per use, short-term loans, or a traditional one-time purchase with perpetual access.

When a library's e-books are managed by a distributor, the patron's experience mimics a print circulation. E-books are checked out, and in cases where there is no simultaneous license, holds can be placed. Titles can be downloaded to the e-reader device for a specified period of time, and are either deleted or become inaccessible after the checkout period expires. There are also options to read the material online using a web browser without any apparent checkout process. E-book provision through libraries is a great convenience for patrons who either can't afford to buy e-books or who simply don't want to spend the money for something they intend to read only once.

When publishers look at the library use of e-books as if they were print copies, they place restrictions on e-book usage based on a fear that library e-book usage will reduce consumer purchases. Some publishers are restricting sales of individual titles to libraries in a region if another library in the same region already has the title but has more strict lending policies. Some publishers are also removing e-books from their offerings through distributors, or increasing prices because of a fear that they will lose revenue because of e-book lending. However, there is evidence to show that the argument that having e-books in libraries will reduce publisher revenue is exaggerated. A 2012 study by the PEW Research Center indicates that, "Among those who read e-books, 41% of those who borrow e-books from libraries purchased their most recent e-book" (Zickuhr et al., 2012: 7). Likewise many e-books are already free, "free eBooks are a major component of the digital marketplace; in November 2010, the BISG reports that 48% of all eBooks downloaded were free; by January 2011, that number had grown to 51%. This data would seem to vindicate the contention of librarians that giving away material for free helps drive sales"(Coffman, 2012: 43).

Some e-book distributors are competing with libraries by experimenting with their own version of lending as an additional revenue stream. For example, Amazon now offers a lending library for Amazon Prime members with Kindle e-readers for borrowing e-books. As this conflict between librarians and publishers continues, it seems doubtful that library e-book lending will seriously impact e-book sales. The problem for libraries is that publisher restrictions on library lending will impact general public access to a growing market of information that is made accessible through e-books, and, potentially, only through e-books.

Consumers are also being affected by e-book pricing, as publishers rethink sales practices that have been used for years for pricing retail books. In April 2012, the US Justice Department filed a civil action against Simon & Schuster, Hachette, Penguin, Macmillan, HarperCollins and Apple because of a new *agency pricing* model. This model changes the way in which e-books are being priced, from a wholesale model where the retailer sets the customer price based on a profit margin to a system where the publisher sets the e-book price and the retailer or agent receives a percentage. This agency model is attributed to Apple, which was looking for a way to compete with Amazon's discounted e-books, and, according to the Justice Department, has resulted in higher prices for e-books – in some cases higher than the print copy.

In 2012, Amazon proposed a new agreement with the Independent Publishers Group (IPG) that would change the terms for e-books and presumably reduce the amount IPG receives. This dispute resulted in Amazon removing e-book titles. In April 2012, Google announced the end of a program that allowed independent booksellers to sell e-books through Google. This relationship between Google and the American Booksellers Association eliminated worldwide independent retailers from one source of sales. Google is also involved in a settlement dispute with publishers over claims that Google violated the copyrights of authors, publishers and others by digitizing titles, creating a database and displaying excerpts from books in Google searches without permission. These examples demonstrate the volatile nature of this emerging technology.

Although consumers are becoming a force in e-print purchasing and a direct revenue source for vendors, libraries remain the prime customers. According to the Association of American Publishers' data for 2010, there was a net revenue of $5.97 billion and unit sales of 143 million from purchases by libraries, government agencies and professional businesses (Association of American Publishers, 2010: 1). Although these amounts are less than retail sales, they indicate that libraries are playing a role in the health of the publishing community. It is important, therefore, that librarians continue to work with publishers and advocate for the population of readers who rely on libraries for access to quality information.

2

A culture of technology

Abstract: While scientists debate the evidence that technology-using behaviors are changing the way the brain functions, there is much evidence that the Millennial Generation has incorporated technology into their lives in a way that greatly exceeds the influence technology has had on past generations, and, in so doing, has created a culture of technology. Librarians face new challenges as they adapt to this generation while continuing to serve the interests of less technology-connected users.

Key words: culture, technology, Millennials, technology culture, technological innovation, plugged-in patrons, digital natives, collective intelligence, information literacy, social networking.

Culture describes the manner in which humans work and interact, and defines the rules for social interaction. During World War II the role of women changed when they started working in factories as replacements for soldiers. Afterwards, they returned to the tradition of raising children. Their daughters went to school in dresses and sat quietly while the teacher's attention was given to their brothers; after all, the girls were expected to grow up and keep house, while the boys joined the workforce.

In actual fact, the girls did not stay home, they went to work and fought for equal rights, nurturing their daughters in a different culture, and since the 1980s there have been more girls in US colleges than boys. Imagine the world today if the culture of the last thousand years had treated both sexes as equals? How many female Isaac Newtons have been lost? That is the power of culture.

Today a new generation, often called the Millennial Generation, is embracing technology with such force that a new culture of technology has emerged. This culture is defining how people communicate, collaborate and incorporate technology into daily activities. It is demanding more flexibility in the workplace and using technology to bridge family, social and work activities. It equates change with something "better" and is impatient with others who are slow to adopt new technology, or technology that isn't intuitive or reliable. For this generation, technology isn't a tool – it is more like a family member.

Millennials are different

Technology has moved beyond work and entertainment into the area of social interaction. Economics, technology and social factors all play a role in creating the variations that distinguish one generation from another. Although there is overlap between the birth dates associated with each generation, it is the similarities among individuals born in a specific age range that make them different from those who come before and after.

The six named generations are: the Greatest Generation, the Silent Generation, the Baby Boomers, Generation X, Generation Y and Generation Z. The Greatest Generation is composed of people who matured during the Depression and fought in World War II. Members of the Silent Generation, too young to fight in World War II, were influenced by childhood experiences of the Depression. The Baby Boomer generation grew up during the time of affluence after the war, and as teenagers engaged in an anti-establishment counter-culture. They were followed by Generation X, which was raised in two-income families, creating an independent and resourceful generation suspicious of authority. Generation Y, also known as the Millennial Generation, is now coming into adulthood and these young people are the first generation to grow to maturity having never experienced a world without computers. The ubiquitous presence of electronic gadgets has profoundly influenced this generation to the extent they have been called digital natives because of their ability to understand and manipulate technology in an organic way that is unfamiliar to older generations. The Millennials are followed by Generation Z, also called the Internet Generation because of their early exposure to the Internet and the convenience delivered through networks.

Beginning with the Millennial Generation the number of years between generations appears to be growing smaller (see Table 2.1). Some factor is, or some factors are, influencing people so dramatically as to create differences that are reducing the time between generations.

Table 2.1   Generational timeline

Generation	Birth date range		Number of years
Greatest Generation	1901	1924	23
Silent Generation	1925	1945	20
Baby Boomers	1946	1964	18
Generation X	1961	1980	19
Millennials	1981	1989	8
Generation Z	1990	1999	9

This trend seems to match the increasing speed of technology penetration within society, so it is not surprising that the Millennial Generation is taking the lead in a cultural revolution that includes technology. This generation uses technology whenever and wherever they want and they are as likely to send a text message at 2.00 a.m. as 2.00 p.m. They blend work, home and social lives into a seamless continuum, and technology is the glue that holds it together. They reject traditional classrooms and don't like being cooped up in an office. They also want to be judged on their performance, not on predictable office hours (Tapscott, 2009). They are comfortable figuring out new technology and love customizing their gadgets with wallpapers, ring tones and apps to notify them of updates from social media sites. Social networking enables this generation to collaborate in a manner that keeps them connected 24 hours a day. They collaborate through chat rooms, blogs, instant messaging and multi-user games, and they share everything from personal insights to challenges at work.

As confident as Millennials are in their technology culture, there are hidden dangers in their openness. Notifications come at all times of the day and night, and can be seen by others as interruptions. Living in a technology culture that is always on can result in a loss of freedom because of expectations that a person will always respond immediately. Further, there is nowhere to hide when technology is constantly updating a person's GPS location, turning privacy into an illusion. Privacy is a concern that deters many older generations from embracing the technology culture. They are worried about the amount of personal information available to the public and about how it is being used. E-book vendors are collecting a large amount of information on their users; everything from the average length of time it takes to read a book to how people browse is being collected without the knowledge of readers (Alter, 2012: 1). Although much of this information is gathered in order to analyze use for future publications, librarians see this data as an intrusion into personal space.

Older generations which have adopted aspects of this culture have not integrated information technology into their "DNA" as the Millennials seem to have done. Neurobiologists are just beginning to explore the effects early exposure to technology is having on brain development (Prensky, 2001). An experiment was undertaken by Gary Small using magnetic resonance imaging (MRI) to determine whether prior experience with technology influenced brain function. Those with prior experience of searching the web activated different parts of the brain than those with no experience. This experiment involved a small sample of 24 subjects aged 55–78, and "despite such limitations, our findings point to an association between routine Internet searching and neural circuitry activation in middle-aged and older adults"(Small et al., 2009: 125).

It will be interesting to see if this experiment can be replicated, but the possibility that exposure to instant answers and web search results is altering brain functions is startling. If our thought patterns are being modified by experience with technology as is suggested, then it is important to understand those changes. Otherwise, the more we rely on search engines as our guide, the more our intelligence will be shaped by technology. The filtering of information by search engines must be questioned through a process of critical thinking.

This is the new frontier for literacy, and it is an opportunity for librarians to renew the spirit of the White House conferences. Twentieth-century librarians must help readers interpret information and discover the significance of the research. This is something search engines can't do, and is often masked behind large result sets.

Millennials as plugged-in patrons

Millennials are plugged-in patrons, born into the technology culture; they bring different perspectives about the library that librarians can use to improve services. Millennials like participation and they expect their voices to make a difference. They make ideal participants in focus groups where they can mingle with peers, bounce ideas around and provide opinions on library operations. However, they are not likely to wait patiently for improvements so librarians need to be prepared to move quickly when a particular direction is apparent.

Not only are Millennials willing to provide input, but they will do so without being asked. As a consequence, librarians should be listening on social networking sites for their brand name in order to monitor what people are saying about their library. Best practices developed for commerce can be adapted to the public sector to provide a model for a new emphasis on the user experience in library services.

Librarians should not underestimate the important part Millennials can play in fund-raising. Research indicates that this is a generation which places a high value on civic-mindedness and which demonstrates a commitment to volunteerism (Myers and Sadaghiani, 2010; McGlone et al., 2011). Any library campaign which requires volunteers for manpower should look for ways to reach this generation. These could include contacting local schools and colleges, and distributing flyers around Millennial hang-outs. When Millennials believe that their efforts are serving a greater good they will return, so it is important to emphasize the contribution they make rather than the assigned task. If Millennials believe they are being used as free labor without a social value, librarians will lose their support. Millennials are also likely candidates for volunteer work in order to learn new skills; in this case a connection must be made between the work they are volunteering for and the skills they are learning that will help them further personal goals.

When planning library programs librarians should expect a large number of drop-ins because Millennials are less likely to register in advance, and they should expect to share their attention with mobile devices. Getting the attention of Millennials will require new methods. Librarians should consider going to where Millennials hang out, including coffee shops, malls and other social attractions. Game nights in the library might attract Millennials, and a video-editing booth will capture their interest and keep them coming back to the library.

It can be difficult explaining the principle of copyright to a Millennial who believes information should be free. There is a growing divide between their generation and older generations that have benefitted from the protection of copyright. New laws are needed to define copyright in an age where digitization makes it possible to remix an original into something new. When does a video remix become a new video and how does copyright relate to both? Current interpretation of the law would prohibit any alteration of a protected item without permission, but the web has many examples of creative music and video editing that seem to violate the law. When it comes to digitized textual material there are provisions for fair use, but the Millennial Generation appears to have difficulty understanding these requirements and instructors often complain about plagiarism.

As researchers, Millennials are self-reliant and expect a single search to give them the results they need (Sweeney, 2005). In the British Library and JISC report, "Information behaviour of the researcher of the future" (University College London, 2008: 35), it appears that Millennials search in a serendipitous manner, jumping from link to link.

If they start on a library page they may leave it and never return. Millennials are an impatient generation; deadlines, ease of use and quick access to full-text sources are of prime importance in their research (Young and Von Seggern, 2001; Connaway et al., 2011).

Millennials are adept at filtering information but they are not skilled at evaluating the quality of the information (Taylor, 2012). Their skills for analyzing and examining logic appear to be underdeveloped, and they are more likely to accept information without questioning the source. They evaluate the quality of information only when they see a value in spending extra time doing so. For example, they understand the need to evaluate sources for a classroom paper but see little use in spending time assessing resources for a personal search (Gross and Latham, 2009). A second trend among Millennial researchers lies in the importance of reputation, or prior experience with a resource in evaluating the credibility of sources. For example, the reputation of the search engine that brings up a link may be enough to make that link credible (Hargittai et al., 2010). Millennial researchers often express a bias for a favorite site, and for selecting the first listed citation among search results (Porter, 2011).

Millennials are insatiable consumers of information from social networks or *collective intelligence*. Collective intelligence is a phrase used to describe the process of a group of people collaborating on an opinion or project. It is a helpful process for generating ideas and can be used to divide work; however, more attention should be given to the relative value and safety of this activity (Poore, 2011).

Research on the Millennial Generation described the challenges of teaching this generation (Worley, 2011). They learn better through a participatory process including, for example, games (Werth and Werth, 2011). Millennials find personal relationships a powerful resource, so librarians who take the time to develop these contacts will be more successful in teaching the research skills needed for critical thinking: "Students prefer to seek help from people they already have an established relationship with, but they may also solicit help from strangers who appear available to talk and approachable" (Gross and Latham, 2007: 343).

Information literacy is a valuable skill, and when Millennials learn that librarians are willing to share knowledge that will help them succeed they will be welcomed into social networks. Knowledge builds credibility, and credibility is the foundation of social networks. Librarians must devote the time necessary to build the credibility that will attract Millennial followers.

Commercial companies are finding ways to do business almost entirely through social networks. For example, Threadless, a company that was founded in 2000 by Jake Nickell and Jacob DeHart, is based on a community of users who submit designs for T-shirts (Brabham, 2010). Like Wikipedia, which has user-supported content, Threadless has a community that both contributes and votes on designs. This new trend in collective intelligence can be applied to the library through patron acquisitions, ratings, reviews and other crowdsourcing activities.

Communication is vital to building relationships with a generation ensconced in participation. Technology will provide one means for collecting information about what Millennials want and need, but an informal high-touch approach will also work. This can include blogs, focus groups or simply "walking around" or being available for consultation in a place where Millennials gather. Librarians should be careful with blanket e-mails or forced communication, which aren't appreciated. Millennials, like most generations, want control over the information they are receiving.

According to the Pew Research Center the recession has impacted this group more than older generations: young adults aged 18–24 have an employment rate of 54 percent, which is the lowest since 1948 (Taylor et al., 2012). Many have taken multiple jobs and are working in non-traditional workplaces. Libraries can be a welcoming setting for these nomadic workers by providing comfortable spaces for working and wireless connectivity. Library programs directed at assisting Millennials to find jobs or acquire work skills will also bring good publicity to the library, either through word of mouth or conventional media.

Millennials as librarians

When a Millennial is hired as a librarian, s/he comes to the library with her/his social network. This can help a new librarian with problem solving and idea generation. Companies are beginning to recognize the importance of social networking as an aspect of performance. Not only do social networks assist workers in problem solving by tapping into collective intelligence and information-sharing, but they are also a factor in helping workers adjust to change. Social networking analysis is a tool that can be used to develop a map of relationships between workers to identify individuals who are isolated from organizational processes, or identify where bottlenecks may be occurring (Knoke and Yang, 2008; Landis, 2010). By analyzing these relationships, libraries can enhance their organization to better energize staff to face the challenges of technological change.

Millennials also expect their employers to be contributing to the improvement of their communities. In a 2006 survey by Cone, "A majority of respondents (78%) believe that companies have a responsibility to support social and/or environmental causes" (Cone, Inc., with AMP Agency, 2006). Millennials' technology skills will be helpful in developing programs to teach others about the web or library resources, and their social orientation makes them likely candidates to visit nursing homes or other centers to promote the library.

Millennials are a natural choice to evaluate technology and make recommendations for when and how to add new devices to the library. They can shepherd technology through the stages of implementation from introduction to adoption (Blackburn, 2011). When funding is an issue they should be encouraged to explore grants and other funding possibilities. The MacArthur Foundation's Digital Media and Learning Program (*http://www. macfound.org/programs/learning/*) is an example of one program that offers funding for technology projects in libraries.

Millennials are direct, and they speak out when they believe something isn't fair to either themselves or their co-workers. It is important that supervisors of Millennials talk openly about areas of disagreement. Millennials expect their working environment to evolve at a fast pace so good communication is vital. They will challenge the library to move in new directions, and this can be a source of friction with older colleagues. As a result, transparent decision making is especially important to maintaining good relations between management, older generations and Millennials.

It comes as no surprise that a generation accustomed to free access to information on the Internet and a lifestyle of collaboration would be a strong supporter of the open source movement. Open source is a hallmark of the technology culture and is in direct opposition to corporations guarding copyright and trade secrets. Although this can be a problem for companies, it can be an asset for libraries building open source applications as long as copyright boundaries are respected. This requires managers to discuss issues of copyright with new employees.

Managing the generation gap

Millennials may be different from other library users only in the degree to which they have been influenced by technology. Older generations are not excluded from the technology culture as the Accenture (2012) consumer electronics products and services usage report indicates. Older generations may be later adopters of new technology, but they still own more devices when compared with those below the age of 35, and they are using the same web services. These include cloud-based e-mail, movie streaming, photo storage, back-up services, file sharing and calendars. Not surprisingly, older people use online games less than Millennials, but both generations are adopting mobile devices in increasing numbers.

Technology is making it easier for libraries to move away from print-based collections to e-print collections that are accessible from anywhere at any time, providing the instant access the technology culture loves. However, it will be some time before e-print replaces a library's print collection, and, until then, libraries will continue to support both print and e-print.

Public libraries are leading the way in efforts to promote e-print by supplying e-readers and e-books for checkout. Academic libraries have been slower to adopt e-books, but they are increasingly adding e-books to their collections. Some academic libraries are also experimenting with e-textbooks; for example, a 2012 pilot between the University of Minnesota and McGraw-Hill offered e-books at discounted prices to students registered for courses. School libraries lag behind both public and academic libraries, but according to a 2011 report, *Ebooks the New Normal: Ebook Penetration & Use in U.S. School (K-12) Libraries*, school purchases of e-books are increasing (Library Journal, 2011).

Technology is also providing new methods of communication between library clientele and librarians. While technology conservatives discuss the value of social networking, others are quick to embrace new social media sites. For the latter, social networking is an integral part of their lives and the number of enthusiasts is growing: "While the youngest generations are still significantly more likely to use social network sites, the fastest growth has come from internet users 74 and older: social network site usage for this oldest cohort has quadrupled since 2008, from 4% to 15%" (Zickuhr, 2010: 3). Millennials also appear to respond to social networking efforts that promote consultation with librarians (O'Connor and Lundstrom, 2011).

When people come into the library they should have a positive experience that blends technology with traditional methods for research. Access to resources, word processing, statistical and other applications are prerequisites for modern research. In addition to computers, libraries should provide resources such as scanners, large format printers, multimedia equipment, and, most importantly, the staff to help people use the equipment.

While older generations expect libraries to be solid, dependable sources of familiar books, Millennials are willing to experiment when databases are enhanced or web pages are redesigned, as long as these are intuitive. This requires librarians to carry out usability testing with a variety of groups in order to balance the demands between generations.

Table 2.2 compares library services with generational appeal. All but one of the services that would attract Millennials are also beneficial to older generations.

Table 2.2   Generational preferences for library services

Library activities	Millennials	Older generations
Advocacy	x	x
Assessment	x	x
Discovery tools	x	x
E-formats	x	x
Engaged librarians	x	x
Extended services	x	
Future of reference	x	x
Information literacy	x	x
Interactive help	x	x
Learning spaces	x	x
Marketing services	x	x
New spaces for new services	x	x
Non-traditional or off-site locations	x	x
Open source	x	x
Repositories	x	x
Social networking	x	x

The culture of technology is causing librarians to rethink services and collections. Millennials are demanding new services; for example, electronic games (once considered children's toys) are now learning objects: "We already know that gaming skills improve the performance of surgeons; that gaming environments are showing up in R&D laboratories; and that gaming is proving to have positive military, safety, educational, and learning benefits" (Abram, 2006: 101). A modern library may well have a gaming room with the dual purpose of providing entertainment and education. A library that emphasizes service over collections will look very different, as rows of stacks are replaced with dynamic special-purpose areas.

A final word on the influence of technology

In 2012, four universities – the University of New South Wales, Purdue University, the University of Melbourne and the University of Sydney – announced that they had developed a single-atom transistor: "The single-atom transistor could lead the way to building a quantum computer that works by controlling the electrons, and thereby, the quantum information, or qubits" (ASM International, 2012: 16). The advantage of a qubit is that it can be a "1" and a "0" at the same time, whereas an ordinary computer is just "1" or "0," i.e., on or off. This ability greatly speeds up mathematical computations and, by extension, the creation of data.

No one can predict what further inventions will come from this single development (or even if it is a practical development), but there is no shortage of engineers who will try, and if they succeed, software developers will follow. This is a key problem, because inventors can't predict what ideas will emerge from their invention, nor how people will use and adapt them for unpredictable uses. For the immediate future, it is likely that technological innovations will continue to pour onto the market and affect every aspect of life. The question that remains is how much technology will change the behavior of people. What is certain, however, is that technological change will continue to be a force in our lives, and librarians must be prepared for a murky and untidy future.

Part 2
The rise of the librarian: service over collections

3

A focus on readers

Abstract: Modern libraries are transitioning from a collection-centric view to one that emphasizes the needs of patrons. Collection development is not important in an era where information is available over the web, and readily provided through ILLs – access is the new collection development. Librarians are building digital libraries with content and tools that are available everywhere and at any time. Social networking is being explored as a way of making connections with users that improve library experiences. Cloud computing, mobile computing and collective intelligence are all available to the digital library where websites are designed for users with user involvement. The key to a modern library is an engaged librarian who puts the needs of users over organizational issues.

Key words: digital library, social networking, mobile computing, cloud computing, website design, collective intelligence, engaged librarian, embedded librarian, augmented reality browsers, e-kiNETx, patron-centered service.

Libraries are competing with other entities for the time and attention of people. Individuals, whether from the general public, or affiliated with an institution, need a reason to visit the library when the library is no longer the first choice for information. This chapter will introduce the challenges and opportunities for libraries in today's digital environment, themes that will be explored in more detail in following chapters.

Technology is making it easy to create, discover and deliver full text. Digital copies can be simultaneously delivered over the web for multiple access from wherever the patron is located. Print materials and digital copies of articles are routinely transported between libraries through ILLs or pay-per-view. In the past, arguments were made about the importance of staff, but the primary focus has always been on the collections and the prestige given to libraries with large collections. Today, with the wealth of material available over the web, it is no longer necessary to have copies in the library stacks. The visibility of the library through the contributions of librarians and staff members is the new measure of the quality of a library.

Libraries must move from a print-centered view of collections to one which focuses on the needs of a specific user community. When librarians change the focus of their activities from the collection to patrons, the collection becomes secondary to meeting the needs of library users. A vibrant library will not necessarily have a large print collection, but it will have access to information that is delivered in different ways, and an emphasis on meeting patrons' needs will require librarians to spend more time engaging patrons and less time managing items.

Enhancing the user experience

The provision of a welcoming facility that is safe and well equipped with computers, wireless access and snack facilities is attractive to patrons and will increase building counts, which is an important metric in evaluating service, and, in the case of academic libraries, useful for recruiting new students. Some librarians have been reluctant to allow food and drink into libraries because of concern over damage to computers and materials, but the elimination of this restriction has brought about a positive view of the library that far exceeds any negative impact (Foster, 2008). Library regulations that emphasize *what might happen* are not useful in a world where building counts are declining.

Academic libraries are also expanding library hours with minimal staff. Concerns about security can be addressed by policing arrangements and the installation of security cameras (Smith, 2007). The availability of a safe environment for study and collaboration is important for many patrons looking for a third space away from the distractions of the home and workplace. Library facilities can provide this environment, which can feel like a retreat from daily pressures.

Libraries can do much more than simply house materials; they are becoming dynamic spaces that facilitate and stimulate learning. This requires weighing the relationship between function, use and aesthetics. Libraries which are built in the present-day should take as their starting point the user not the collection, and should focus on the needs of the institution or community served by the library. Certain building projects include "green" features to reduce costs and appeal to energy conscious communities, and are being designed for user needs (Fox, 2011; Reviews, News and More, 2011). The University of Chicago's Mansueto Library was designed around a student survey and combines the need for high-capacity stacks with a functional area for students (Albanese, 2008).

Some public libraries are reducing hours or closing branches because of budget shortfalls. Research indicates that proximity to a library increases use so this practice could discourage less-advantaged groups from using the library (Sin and Kim, 2008). If a library must reduce its hours because of budget problems, its librarians can continue to provide access to full-text materials and services by providing technology that is available when the library is closed.

Information technology is also useful for expediting routine business such as texting alerts about hold availability or courtesy notices about upcoming due dates, as well as for reference chat services provided through cooperative agreements with other libraries. Where these services are available, it is critical for the library to market them so that less-advantaged groups will know about their availability. It is no longer sufficient to build a service; without aggressive marketing patrons are less likely to use the service.

Digital libraries

Librarians use the phrase "digital library" to encompass the e-collections and e-services that are provided to users. However, this phrase has been commandeered by various groups to include the code for software applications, scholarly or popular digitized print, collections of thoughts from blogs, data sets, and information repositories of all types. When the term "digital" is applied to a library, the meaning requires a context in order to understand what "digital library" really means, and in today's world that context is supplied from the viewpoint of the user.

A quote by Norman Cousins in the *ALA Bulletin* provides some wisdom for librarians struggling with the changing concept of a library:

> The library is not a shrine for the worship of books. It is not a temple where literary incense must be burned or where one's devotion to the bound book is expressed in ritual. A library, to modify the famous metaphor of Socrates, should be the delivery room for the birth of ideas – a place where history comes to life.
>
> (Cousins, 1954: 475)

It follows that a digital library must include information available over the web, and requires a redefining of the research process in order to recognize the commanding role of library patrons; so librarians must provide what patrons want, not what librarians believe they need.

The shift from print material to digital information has many benefits for library patrons. They enjoy the time saved searching for and retrieving information, 24-hour and remote access, and immediate availability to the latest research. However, not everyone prefers digital content, and patrons report confusing navigation, no support for natural language searching, and too many different interfaces (Liu and Luo, 2011). Other reasons why people stop using digital resources include a perceived lack of necessity and technical issues (Consonni, 2010). Libraries are addressing these issues with simplified user interfaces and discovery tools that provide a single search platform for books, articles, multimedia and full-text material. Ways to reduce user frustration include using OpenURL resolvers to connect citations with full text, and better authentication using Shibboleth and the Central Authentication Service (CAS), which eliminate multiple logins.

Libraries are also becoming publishers of information and partnering with content experts in the creation of scholarly information. This is a good fit for librarians who have developed skills in the organization of information through metadata coding, and who are committed to the long-term preservation of information. Librarians are involved in other ways, too, as they move out of the traditional library setting into data centers, where they are partnering with technology specialists in the best practices for data management and assisting researchers in the development of data management plans.

Librarians are also involved in projects that convert print into other formats to reinvigorate the information for a new generation. For example, Southern Cross University in Australia has a project to convert documents into audio formats (Wallin et al., 2012). The goal of this project is to provide an alternative to text that will encourage the exploration of scholarly literature, and that will add value to the experience through new functionality for personalization.

Some librarians are going beyond digitizing text and are adding new features to create new knowledge. For example, librarians at the University of Nebraska-Lincoln are involved in developing tools for analyzing text. In a 2011 article, Bernholz and Pytlik Zillig reported on a study using the Levenshtein metric to compare texts of the Senate-amended Treaty of Fort Laramie with Sioux for discrepancies between versions of the treaty (Bernholz and Pytlik Zillig, 2011). Text analysis and data mining are two examples highlighting how librarians' skills are proving useful for research and the creation of new information.

Mobile libraries

The mobile library isn't a bookmobile driving between locations; rather, the mobile library refers to library services and materials that are available 24 hours a day on any type of device. Applications, or apps, are an emerging technology that is impacting libraries. Apps work differently than websites. A web application is accessed using a web browser such as Internet Explorer, Firefox or Safari, while an app is specific to an operating system and is downloaded to a device that connects directly to a service. Apps are developed to work through the Internet and outside the web. Many library vendors have developed, or are in the process of launching, their own apps that work with their services. Apps eliminate competition from search engine discovery, and provide fewer headaches over browser and operating system compatibility. Although there is no general agreement about the future of the web vs. apps, apps are becoming more numerous as tablets and mobile phones increase in popularity. App development is predicted to outpace software development for PCs (Anderson and Rainie, 2012).

Libraries have several challenges with apps: they further silo information sources, pose authentication issues, and reduce the visibility of library branding. Libraries must work with vendors to develop apps that work across library resources and clearly brand the library. These "discovery apps" will be critical for library marketing, and without a viable app for their favorite device, many patrons may turn away from libraries.

A mobile device provides a different experience than a desktop computer and requires more than a resized screen. In particular, mobile device users are often in a hurry, and are looking for targeted information, thus only the most frequently-used links should be presented. It is particularly important to provide links to mobile versions of popular databases, options for reviewed or rated sources, and, when possible, a link for real-time help. When libraries support mobile computing they may have to develop several different websites for a variety of devices. There are many types of phones and tablets, some will have touch screens, others won't, and they will have different support levels for JavaScript, Java and style sheets, all of which need accommodation. Web logs provide information on mobile device usage and can inform decisions about priorities for website design.

Cloud computing

Libraries have accessed resources that have been stored and managed off-site for many years; this method of storage has come to be called *cloud computing*. These services have the advantage of being delivered over the web and frequently include functionality for collaboration. Other cloud services include storage for user files, or access to resources and services. Some of these are free or low cost, others charge on an annual basis via subscription, maintenance fees or usage. When libraries use cloud services they are not responsible for maintaining the servers, operating systems or applications that run the service. This is a prudent solution for libraries with excellent network connectivity and a lack technology staff or hardware for running applications on-site. With a growing number of cloud providers for data storage and server support, more libraries are expected to contract out for these services.

There are several models for cloud computing, including Software as a Service (SaaS), Platform as a Service (PaaS) and Infrastructure as a Service (IaaS). SaaS provides application and server support, so the library doesn't need to manage the systems. Some libraries have used SaaS to outsource their catalog or discovery tool. PaaS is used by librarians who want to manage their own application development on an infrastructure they outsource to a vendor that manages the server and operating environment. The IaaS model is used when a library subscribes to a vendor that provides basic services that can be scaled as the need arises. The most common use among libraries is for data storage.

Most cloud providers maintain a robust production environment where the servers, applications and data are replicated to minimize downtime or data loss. There are other differences between providers besides costs; they may have different policies and procedures for archiving, security, interoperability and migration for the beginning and end of service. They also have privacy policies, which librarians must evaluate, and, depending on the sensitivity of the data, will dictate acceptable locations for data storage. Providers which offer a free service may have some restrictions or conditions that librarians may be reluctant to accept, for example advertising or less privacy for users. Even when the library is contracting to a fee-based service there may be some loss of control. Good license agreements can mitigate some of these concerns.

The contracts for cloud computing will include many of the same terms as library vendor contracts, for example clauses concerning applicable law and jurisdiction for disputes, definitions for acceptable use, liability, technical support and terms of availability. In addition, a contract should include provisions for data integrity, preservation, privacy and storage location. Bradshaw et al. (2011) compared the contracts of 30 cloud service providers and noted a wide variance in disclaimers for liability, warranty and service level agreements (SLAs). A final consideration for librarians involves weighing loss of control, the importance of preservation and risks for outsourcing against the savings in administrative outlays and improved architectural environments for collaboration.

Publishers are also turning to cloud computing to manage business operations. The growth in e-print has created significant challenges to publishers who are themselves responsible for maintaining systems with 24-hour access to their products. Likewise, there are independent author-publishers using cloud-based sales like Lulu, Amazon and Smashwords. The opportunities to reduce overheads by outsourcing system management for inventory, production and other functions will change the publishing field (Hill, 2012). Perhaps the cost savings from cloud computing will be passed on to customers in order to reduce the need for price increases. Given the close relationship between libraries and publishers these developments are worth watching.

Website design

The library website is one measure of the degree to which a library is patron centered. If the website is designed to reflect the organization of the library and not the user perspective it sends a message that the library is more important than the patrons who use the library. Websites should be as flat as possible so that every link is no more than three clicks deep.

One particular 2012 survey of how researchers find citations compared 2005, 2008 and 2012 data and revealed a downward trend in using the library website to locate citations (Gardner and Inger, 2012). Preference was shown to Google Scholar, journal home pages and subject databases ahead of the library. This emphasizes the need to brand all access points for library subscriptions, and highlights the importance of having a recognizable presence on the aforementioned sites so that patrons understand that the library is providing access.

There are several measurements for user satisfaction with a website, including perceived usefulness, system quality, intention to return to a site and information quality (Schaupp, 2010). Factors that contribute to user satisfaction include ease of use and relevancy to the perceived need. Subjective measures of user satisfaction require a research methodology that includes direct contact with users that goes beyond counting link clicks to why particular links are selected. Direct methods include surveys, focus groups and single-user testing. Usability metrics will be discussed in greater detail in Chapter 7.

Searching motion and image: the next generation of indexing

The next generation of search engines will move beyond the limitations of fixed key word searching to provide a more natural format-based retrieval. Augmented Reality Browsers are being explored which will significantly add to the user experience by providing a hybrid that has features of a browser but operates like an app. Visual and/or sound information is captured through a mobile camera or microphone, and is processed through the browser to deliver mediated information with which users can interact. An example of a library app could include a patron using his camera to scan a library media center, which brings up the software loaded on specific computers as they are captured through the camera. Apps are already in use in the Victoriei train station in Bucharest (*http:/ /2d-code.co.uk/qr-codes-at-victoriei-station/*) which allow patrons to capture a QR code from a display picture of a book available as an e-book or audio file, which is then downloaded into their mobile device.

Another example of research into new methods for storing and retrieving information is e-kiNETx (Embodied Knowledge Integration in Networked Experiences), which is being developed at Arizona State University (*http://dance.asu.edu/ research/collections/e_kinetx.php*). This concept integrates dance theory with technology so that dance information is organized in ways that are more intuitive to dance performers, scholars and students; to retrieve information, a searcher will use movement rather than entering search terms.

Collective intelligence

Collective intelligence and crowdsourcing are terms that describe a participative process whereby people can contribute opinions, advice or content. Wikipedia is a successful example of content submitted and revised by the general public. The fundamental assumption behind all collective intelligence is that participation by a group of individuals will add value because they have new information to contribute that improves the product.

This crowdsourcing activity is being used to create information through the work of many hands, just like a quilting bee where each individual adds a piece to the whole. Characteristically, these collaborative projects are in a perpetual state of flux – new information is added, outdated or incorrect information is removed, and revisions happen in real time. Contributed information from crowdsourcing activities is sometimes revised by an authority, but in the case of blogging opinions, ratings and reviews, revision is minimal.

Crowdsourcing is a useful tool for historians and archivists who use it to identify unknown persons in photographs or videos by drawing on the collective memories of users to supply missing information. Time can be a critical element because information is lost when individuals with knowledge pass away. Librarians are enriching projects such as the Omaha Indian cultural heritage project (*http://omahatribe. unl.edu*) which provides images and accompanying information on members of the Omaha Indian Tribe, and the Omaha Ponca language dictionary (*http://omahaponca. unl.edu/*) which is preserving an endangered language.

Tagging, reviews and ratings have become important components on business sites, and many consumers have come to expect and use the information before they make purchases. Another feature of online catalogs is a listing of "people who read this also read," which assists people in identifying related books. Research demonstrates that Millennials are influenced by what others say and that they generally supply useful commentary when they add opinions (Mangold and Smith, 2012). Some librarians fear this activity will result in abuses and cause additional work, but these assumptions are unproven (Spiteri, 2011). Tagging, reviews and ratings are now part of the collective experience of library patrons; it is time now to trust library patrons and focus on how library services can better meet user needs.

The engaged librarian

For many years librarians were seen as curators of collections, and most library operations were focused on the collection and on teaching patrons how to use the collection. The idea of an engaged librarian isn't new, rather it is an extension of the embedded librarian concept. Embedded librarians can be physically located away from the library where their patrons are housed. They co-teach classes, partner with faculty on research projects, develop web pages, tag and link records, publicize group activities, serve on committees, and make connections.

David Shumaker started a blog about embedded librarians at *http://embeddedlibrarian.com/* in order to provide a forum on the challenges of working as an embedded librarian. He provides a running commentary on issues of the day and serves as an advocate for embedding librarians into user communities:

> *The Embedded Librarian* blog is dedicated to exploring the development of embedded library and information services in organizations of all types. It starts from the

perception that the trend of moving librarians out of libraries, both physically and organizationally, is growing, can be of great value to the organization, and can be very rewarding to the librarian – if done well.

(Shumaker, 2013: "about" web page)

Most definitions of embedded librarianship relate to subject specialists, or liaison librarians serving within the activities of an academic department:

In the case of the librarians embedded in the Center for Global Studies at the University of Illinois at Urbana-Champaign (Illinois), these other duties include outreach to K-12 teachers, participation in workshops developed by the Center, teaching courses, representing the Center at conferences, involvement in writing grants, and participating in staff meetings and board meetings.

(Rudasill, 2010: 84)

The concept of an engaged librarian expands the idea of an embedded librarian to include all librarians at the institution, not just public service librarians. The needs of the patron become more important than operational concerns for all librarians. It flips the operational structure so that activities center on patrons' needs. It applies equally to librarians in public service and technical service areas. Everyone serves as advocates for collections, programs, research, information delivery, information technology and interface design in order to enhance the library experience.

All engaged librarians use information technology as a tool to connect with patrons and focus on what the library can do, rather than what the library can't or won't do. The library organization is moved into a secondary position, behind the needs of users, making flexibility more important than control. Figure 3.1 shows the differences in approaches between the librarian as curator and the engaged librarian. The librarian as curator is focused on the collection and on teaching patrons how to use the collection – emphasizing

Librarian as curator

Collection focus

- Instruction and compliance
- Focus on library resources
- Passive communication and wait for response
- Waits for patrons to come to the library

Core values

- Collection first
- Librarians know best
- Process matters

Engaged librarian

Reader focus

- Co-pilot with patron
- Uses web and library resources
- Uses social media to connect with users
- Goes to where patrons hang out

Core values

- Service first
- Collaboration
- Outcome matters

Passive patron

Library is for school

- Sees the library as a formal setting for school work
- Follows directions to get the best grade within the time allowed
- Doesn't use services because he/she doesn't know about them
- Sees librarians as authoritative figures

Engaged patron

Librarians have credibility

- Sees the librarian as ally and mentor
- Understands inquiry is research and sources must be evaluated regardless of how they are discovered
- Has a librarian as "friend" on social networks
- Connects with librarians outside the library

Figure 3.1 Differences in approaches between the librarian as curator and the engaged librarian

how the library works. The engaged librarian is focused on the patron so that interaction is from the perspective of the patron's needs – the patron is not assumed to be in an inferior position.

One of the problems with teaching people how to use the library is that users are more likely to see the library as disassociated from their typical research patterns, and to see it as a place that is only consulted for school purposes or as an afterthought, when the answer isn't readily available from a favorite application or web search engine. Therefore, it is important for librarians to partner with researchers and support their goal, not to teach the "library way" or lecture the user.

When librarians are engaged in the research process they collaborate with patrons to achieve the patrons' goals, either directly or virtually (Kesselman and Watstein, 2009). Technology can assist in this process so that remote patrons who can't take advantage of on-site opportunities for instruction also receive support (Matthew and Schroeder, 2006). However, technology shouldn't replace personal contact completely because research demonstrates that contact with a librarian increases the librarian's credibility with patrons (Connaway and Radford, 2010). A friendly and knowledgeable librarian will be more approachable for future contact and may turn a non-user into a library patron.

Unfortunately, many libraries today are seen by community members as book depositories and not as active centers of learning nor places to access information. Many people do not know that libraries provide computers, wireless access, e-books or full-text materials that are accessible from home. It is the responsibility of librarians to engage information seekers directly and change that image.

The key to making this change is *engagement*. Some ideas for engagement are:

- Start a LocalWiki (*http://localwiki.org*) – create a crowdsource for sharing media and information about the local community, school or academic institution.

- Advertise library programs through community channels. Most cities, media outlets and institutions have events calendars – locate these and turn them into a list that guarantees that library events are listed.

- Get on the map – verify that the library is listed in Google Maps (*http:// maps.google.com*).

- Ask book clubs to review books on the library website or catalog.

- Work with a local TV station and media or business club in a high school to create a library advertisement for TV – better yet, turn it into a contest.

- Rent a billboard and put up advertisements.

- Have a local performing arts group work an event on the library grounds to bring attention to the library.

- Identify a group for increased library usage and target one specific demographic – for example, adolescent boys, working mothers, seniors in nursing homes, undergraduates in engineering. Then focus on ideas for reaching that group.

- Set up a blog for library workers and volunteers to contribute what they like about the library.

- Create a discussion blog for a popular TV show – set up a TV in the library for a public viewing followed by a discussion.

- Move a librarian to off-site locations either temporarily or permanently.

- Display the library office hours at a consulting desk in a local business.
- Host a blogging site for reference questions and answers.
- Volunteer to help with activities that will build a connection outside the library.
- Provide individual tutoring or instruction customized for the individuals in need.
- Co-sponsor a service with another department, by providing space or staffing assistance.
- Create a team to come up with marketing and program ideas that will either bring people into the library or take library staff off-site to the community.

Social networking sites

Social networking sites like Facebook and Twitter have a place in library services because they are familiar to many patrons. Twitter can be effective in promoting activities and programs that are occurring in the library (Krabill, 2009) and Facebook has been used by libraries and librarians alike as a means to connect with users.

Individuals create a Facebook *profile*, which is different to the Facebook pages used by libraries and other organizations. Profiles allow individuals to request and manage friends but are not intended to be used for professional advertising. Librarians should not "sell" products or use a profile for commercial purposes. This does not preclude librarians using Facebook to communicate with patrons, but it is important that personal posts from friends and family are kept off any profile being used to communicate with patrons.

Libraries which create *pages* are easier to manage because friend requests are automatically accepted. A Facebook page for a library is owned by a legitimate representative of the library for the purpose of communicating with fans. There is no access to fan profiles, but page updates are sent automatically to all fans. Pages allow libraries to establish roles for managing the site, which include: the administrator, content creators, a monitor (who manages the daily routine of watching for comments and responding), and someone to create advertisements and manage the insight analytics that provide metrics on pages. The ability to create polls is another feature available for pages, and libraries can use these to engage users.

Facebook also supports the creation of groups for communication between people who share common interests. These are being used to organize people into groups, and to share information, photos or event information. They can be public or private, and updates are transmitted automatically to members.

The ability to interconnect social media also makes it easier to coordinate communication. Social media dashboards provide management services for connecting multiple networking sites, and provide analytics on use. HootSuite (*http://hootsuite.com/*) has a basic plan at no cost. These services provide a way to keep sites organized, which is important because librarians will have separate personal and professional sites. It is also possible to connect sites in such a way that an addition to one site is automatically added to other sites. For example, a video can be posted to YouTube, and automatically added to Facebook, and is then distributed to all followers. Other useful tools include the URL shortening websites that shorten long URLs. Tiny (*http://tiny.cc/*), bitly (*https://bitly.com/*) and Ow.ly (*http://ow.ly/url/shorten-url*) are services which shorten URLs to more user-friendly sizes, which is helpful for tweets and posting to social media sites.

Virtual Interest Groups (VIGs) use social media to create groups based on interests for the purpose of collaboration. LinkedIn (*http://www.linkedin.com/*) is an example of a social media site that facilitates the development of interest groups. There are other ways to create groups including using blogs, which is what two hospitals in Calgary, Canada, did to provide training, information consultation and consultations between researchers and librarians (Lin and Kathryn, 2012). In addition to blogs, the librarians used chat and Delicious (*http://www.delicious*.com) to answer questions and share information. Participants reported less fear about using social media tools, and noted that they found blog posts to be most helpful.

HASTAC (*http://hastac.org/*) is another network for individuals and institutions to provide learning and collaboration through networked research that bridges the disciplines of humanism and technology. This group is particularly useful for academic librarians working to create new digital information.

Diaspora (*https://joindiaspora.com/*) is a private, open source social network. Diaspora was developed to address privacy concerns related to social networks like Facebook. Users establish their own server to host content, and these servers or pods can then interact with each other to share social information. By creating a private network of sites, people have more control over access to their information than on other social sites that frequently have defaults for more open access.

Social media must be updated on a regular schedule, and the information should be interesting and worth reading, otherwise patrons will not sign up. A 2011 survey of the ARL provides some discouraging results (Wan, 2011). While over 90 percent of the libraries had Facebook pages, 35.8 percent had fewer than 200 fans, and 19.5 percent hadn't updated the page in the month of the study. These statistics imply that ARL libraries do not have a clear direction, or much enthusiasm for their pages, which may explain why they have so few fans.

Practices, policies and privacy: three Ps for social media

Many libraries are struggling with policies to govern the management of social media. The ALA has information on developing privacy policies (*http://www.ala.org/offices/oif/ iftoolkits/toolkitsprivacy/libraryprivacy*) which includes information about minors. Chris Boudreaux, who is a leader in the area of social media practices, also maintains a database (*http://socialmediagovernance.com/policies.php*) with social media policies categorized by industry. However, this writer believes that libraries which opt for too much control over the activities of individual librarians are missing opportunities. Social media is all about personal expression, and control, when needed, should be applied in the context of the social media. The individual is ultimately responsible for his or her actions, and the group following that individual will be holding him or her responsible. The only time it should be necessary for institutions to get involved is when a librarian violates an administrative policy regarding behavior. The one caveat – and it is an important one – is privacy.

Librarians continue to have responsibility for guarding patron privacy. Libraries should not post any personal information on a public site. However, greater discretion is given to adult patrons who are responsible for posting their own opinions and reading habits: "Libraries have never tried to regulate whether patrons could voluntarily give up their own privacy ... we don't really care if someone keeps a public list of the books he's read, as long as it is his list" (Griffey, 2010: 35).

Libraries should establish guidelines for any site to which patrons contribute information and where identify might be revealed. It is good practice to include a privacy policy on all library sites so that patrons understand what information will be revealed to others, and how it might be used. Libraries should be especially cautious about posting information that might come from patrons under 18 years of age without evidence of parental approval. In this circumstance it is good policy to have a warning on the site that posting is for adults only.

Some public and school libraries have elected to restrict access to social sites in the library in order to protect patrons. Although there are moral, legal and institutional policies that justify these actions, it seems that librarians are failing to recognize social media as a legitimate means for exchanging information. Free speech is important in a democracy and social media is an increasingly useful tool for communication. It seems short-sighted for librarians to be reluctant to argue against restrictions, especially when freedom of information is a cherished value to the profession.

Librarians should embrace social networking and recognize that conversations happen in both public and private spaces and they should guide conversations accordingly. Social media is not without boundaries, people are free to set limits on who can access their site. It is necessary to be "invited" into social sites, which is not unlike the protocol in real-life settings. Discussions about privacy are legitimate topics, and librarians should not be hesitant about providing opinions.

Now is the time for testing old assumptions – impulses for order and control will restrict experimentation just when it is most important for librarians to be exploring new methods for reaching library patrons. Librarians are hired for their expertise, they are on the front line working with patrons every day and if they can't be trusted with managing a Facebook page, how can they be trusted with face-to-face interaction? With background technical support for editing and formatting, and guidance for managing the library brand, librarians can become skilled at handling a social media account.

Not all social media experiments will prove beneficial. For example, there was much enthusiasm about Second Life (Ralph and Stahr, 2010), but interest in it has been declining over the past ten years. However, the inability to predict outcomes is not a reason not to experiment. The only way for librarians to understand the dynamics of social media is to experiment.

Librarians who are new to social media should experiment with personal sites before hosting a public forum. Each social site has a set of netiquette conventions or e-manners that govern polite behavior. These include practices that most librarians already use with e-mail or listservs, but with a social site it is also important to become familiar with group dynamics before engaging in conversations. Experienced social networkers ask questions that are directed to the group, and don't waste time asking questions that an individual could answer. They add value to conversations, avoid humor or other message tones that could be misinterpreted, and never respond to messages while angry.

Hosting a site requires a few additional skills because social networking is a democracy where the leader exercises gentle guidance or risks losing participants. Table 3.1 highlights a number of guidelines for a new host.

Table 3.1   Guidelines for hosting social networking sites

Guidelines for hosting social networking sites
Articulate the purpose of the site
Set up any "rules" from the beginning – this is important for classroom sites where there is a possibility that some students may be too critical
When issues arise respond to the offender via e-mail, not in the open forum
Be cautious when including minors on a public site – establish parental permission
Facilitate – let the group communicate
Start conversations with open questions
Acknowledge contributions
Instruct through the conversation

Other nonprofit organizations are experimenting with social networking sites to help promote their organizations. A 2008 study of humanities, education, healthcare, human service, religions and allied organizations revealed some interesting trends on Facebook usage: 74 percent used discussion boards; 56 percent posted images; 54 percent linked to news stories; and 24 percent posted videos (Waters et al., 2009). This same study also suggested that nonprofit organizations were struggling with Facebook and were not utilizing some of the interactive features, perhaps because of the time required to manage the sites. Any organization must allow staff time and resources to support ventures into social media if they are going to be successful. It takes time and patience to build a user community, and that requires support from managers and administrators.

4

Information literacy and social networks

Abstract: Instruction on information literacy and social networking go together in the modern world of the web. Social media and web searching have changed the way people do their research, and librarians need to adapt their information literacy instruction to recognize and incorporate new research patterns into training. Instruction tools developed using Web 2.0 technology can aid in delivering instruction but they won't replace personal attention from librarians and staff members who can do the most to reduce library anxiety and encourage library use for lifelong learning.

Key words: information literacy, collaboration, Cyber-Navigator, digital divide, social media, online tutorials, learning object, lifelong learning, library instruction, research, Web 2.0, learning activities, library anxiety.

A new model for research

The World Wide Web offers an endless supply of facts and opinions, but it does so with minimal quality control. Traditional library instruction for research methods has focused on teaching patrons the different approaches needed for searching individual databases. This type of instruction ignores the natural behavior patrons typically use when they search the web. Teaching patrons how to search the "library way" is a linear, step-by-step process that emphasizes searching features within library databases, and it pays little attention to resources available on the web or to the purpose of the research.

This instruction does not work well with a generation that starts every search on the web, and that includes social networks as sources of information (OCLC, 2002; Weiler, 2005). There are also questions as to whether this type of instruction will develop the searching and evaluative skills necessary for critical thinking (Currie et al., 2010), and critical thinking is the foundation of information literacy.

A typical web search can return thousands of results. Although search engines are developing algorithms to improve the results so that the "best" results appear first, the danger remains that researchers lack the skills necessary to identify quality resources. By emphasizing the research process over sources, librarians can contribute a missing piece in the path to critical thinking. The new challenge for literacy is information literacy, which is the ability to think critically about the search process and linked information.

The Association of College and Research Libraries (ACRL) defines an information literate person as someone who can:

- determine the extent of information needed;
- access the needed information effectively and efficiently;
- evaluate information and its sources critically;
- incorporate selected information into one's knowledge base;
- use information effectively to accomplish a specific purpose; and
- understand the economic, legal and social issues surrounding the use of information, and access and use information ethically and legally.

(ACRL, 2000: 2–3)

These principals for instruction are as valid for Millennials as for any generation, however because Millennials appear to have a more scattered approach to research, special attention should be given to judging information effectively and efficiently (Holman, 2011). To generate lifelong learning, research instruction should be adapted to accommodate the serendipitous discovery method, with particular attention given to an evaluation of information that also respects the value of social networking in the research process.

In a linear approach to research the process is highly controlled with clear steps. Figure 4.1 depicts the steps, which begin with topic formation and refinement and proceed through location of resources, beginning with books from the catalog, followed by articles. Evaluating the quality of sources happens as sources are gathered, guiding the researcher to the best sources until everyone is quoting each other, which leads to a conclusion and, finally, a paper backed by citations. This is the model usually taught by librarians.

Figure 4.1 Linear research methods

Increasingly, however, this is not the method used by those from the technology culture. They are accustomed to finding information on the web using hypertext (Holman, 2011), which allows them to jump around based on interest and curiosity in a non-linear fashion. The linear process feels unnatural to this group, and forcing them to use this traditional model of research will not translate into permanent habits; it is time for a different approach that respects serendipity.

Figure 4.2 demonstrates a non-linear approach that includes the hypertext linking preferred by younger researchers: "Horizonal information seeking, a form of skimming activity, where people view just one or two pages from an academic site and then 'bounce' out, perhaps never to return. The figures are instructive: around 60 per cent of e-journal users

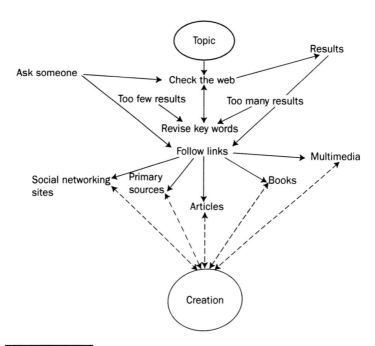

Figure 4.2　**Non-linear research methods**

view no more than three pages and a majority (up to 65 per cent) never return" (Nicholas et al., 2008: 294).

Research demonstrates that Millennials prefer to begin their research on a general site such as Wikipedia (Porter, 2011). Starting with a general information source like Wikipedia, an e-encyclopedia or a social site provides an overview of the topic. The researcher follows the links which eventually lead to the discovery of the full text. It doesn't matter where the process ends, whether it is with books, articles, multimedia or primary sources. The sources can be found in the library or anywhere on the web, it doesn't matter to the Millennial researcher.

Millennials are also likely to consult social media sites along the way. As the process of tracking links unfolds, the researcher begins to formulate a hypothesis and the creative process begins. Sources are evaluated by degree of credibility as they are encountered, so critical analysis simultaneously informs the hypothesis and creation output. It isn't important when it occurs, just that it occurs early enough in the process to ensure quality research.

Much of the evaluation process takes place during the creative phase after links are followed, as represented by the dotted lines in Figure 4.2. This model emphasizes communication as an integral part of the process and recognizes the social interaction that occurs naturally during the research process. Particular attention should be paid to judging the credibility of resources, and to recognizing themes that arise as the research is conducted.

Instruction on research methods should help patrons build confidence in their abilities to conduct research. Huvila identified four characteristics of the process of research:

- Make information creators think about the readers (or listeners or spectators). Emphasize information creation for a community of users and as part of that community.

- Focus on simple tools in order to achieve as much as feasible, no more.

- Emphasize the ways in which information creators themselves can benefit from better-created information.

- Emphasize citing, reusing and linking to existing information as virtuous habits, and the creation of new information as desirable only when a particular kind of information does not seem to exist.

(Huvila, 2011: 237–45)

This method can be seen in a 2012 article reporting on a group of 15–18-year-olds who applied information as they participated in a digital community (Harlan et al., 2012). During this study, participants used social connections and web searching to gather information to collaborate and create content that included social media: "Thinking practices reflected engagement with information, integrating information into existing knowledge so that it could be used in the creative process" (ibid.: 577). Throughout the research process, the participants used information to learn as they worked towards the final creation.

Librarians should incorporate social media into the process so that students develop improved skills for evaluating social media as it relates to a particular question. One of the more valuable skills students can learn in today's environment of information abundance is the point at which they can reasonably stop searching. This particular issue is further complicated when patrons wait too long to start their project or when they want answers immediately. Instruction that presents research in a familiar, non-linear process will help patrons expedite their research to produce an acceptable product.

The new digital divide

Librarians face challenges from the diversity of patrons' technology abilities, with some patrons lacking basic computer competency. A multifaceted approach is needed to first identify the skill level and then supply the necessary help. Chicago public libraries employ CyberNavigators to assist people who need more help with using computers (Williams, 2012). This program was developed to respond to users seeking help for specific purposes such as job hunting. Patrons who need help "just in time," will remember the assistance they received and are likely to return. As one CyberNavigator responded after helping a patron, "By the way, she started signing up for my basic Internet class" (ibid.: 64).

Teaching the web

Teaching users how to evaluate web resources isn't very different from teaching patrons about library sources; in fact, many library resources are available on the web through Google Scholar. Web search results give some preliminary information: title, URL and a snippet describing the content. Teaching a critical evaluation of web resources begins with the identification of the source of the website. Top-level domain names provide one clue: education (edu), organization (org), government (gov), network (net), commercial (com) and codes designating the country of origin. All domain names ultimately resolve to a single IP number which consists of three numbers, e.g., 123.123.123.123. The top-level domain names are being expanded through registry sales and will soon include a variety of brand names that are specific to a vendor, not just the familiar edu, gov, com, org and country abbreviations.

Identifying the author and the date on which the website was last updated provide important indicators of the quality of the information. Outdated websites may have old information. The author may also be misinformed or may have a biased opinion. The author's reputation can be checked using citation indexes, or a software tool like Harzing's Publish or Perish (*http://www.harzing.com*). Another tip requires searchers to follow the sources listed on a page to see where they lead.

There are network tools that can assist in the verification process. Network Tools (*http://network-tools.com*) traces hostnames and IP numbers to registry information. It gives the name of the institution or organization that "owns" the hostname, and contact information for reporting abuses. Another tip for evaluating sites is to see who is linking to the site by entering link://[hostname] in the browser. This will list the sites that are linking to the resource in question, which gives an indication of the credibility of the site. There is no doubt that the web is a useful source of information, and fortunately it also includes sites that help evaluate the websites it hosts. Showing users how to use the web and library resources to verify the credibility of sources is another way to teach information literacy skills that will help them become better consumers of information.

Collaboration and collective intelligence for learning

Collective intelligence is a phrase that describes information generated through the cooperative efforts of many. The information may or may not be verified or vetted by an authority in the field. Most educators are teaching students to avoid using sites created in this fashion for their research projects and most students are responding. Students understand that they can't quote Wikipedia for a school paper, but that doesn't stop them using it as a starting point, or using it for personal decisions. Making a case for different evaluative criteria between school and the remainder of life doesn't serve students well. After all, learning doesn't stop when someone graduates, and inaccurate information should never be used for work or personal decisions. It is time for librarians to include social networking sites in instructional sessions, and to prepare students for a time when they may not have access to the same resources they have while in school.

Many forms of technology have been used to create learning dialogs between librarians and patrons, including e-mail, chat, bulletin boards, or a course management system as in a pilot project at one university (Hawes, 2011). A virtual learning environment (VLE) was designed through collaboration between the library and the Faculty of Business and Law at the University of Queensland (Stagg and Kimmins, 2012). This project resulted in quick, five-to-seven minute tutorials designed to answer a single question that related to the teaching curriculum. The designers used screen capturing software to create mini-tutorials that were stored in their course management system. Measurements of student usage of the tutorials indicated fewer views at the beginning of the semester, but these increased in relation to those months when assessments were due. This suggests that the project was successful in meeting "just-in-time" instruction.

An approach that blends research, teaching and authorship using open source is being explored at Columbia University, internally referred to as "Small p Publishing." Blogs are used to publish material that supports academic and professional communication, and an informal review process is included (Martin and Hughes, 2012). This model was developed by the Teacher's College as a network of blog sites, where posts are linked to the contributing authors, and readership is restricted by network membership. Students and faculty exchange posts, interact with posts, and, through linking and reposting, demonstrate the growing influence of an idea. It is an interesting hybrid model which removes some of the psychological barriers that inhibit beginning authors.

Collaboration is a powerful tool in information literacy training. When librarians support research from the patron's viewpoint, or cooperate with faculty to support classroom activities with targeted instruction, they are more in sync with patrons' interests. This is fundamental to the transfer of learning that reaches outside the "bubble" of formal education.

Web 2.0

Web 2.0 is being used to make library services more interactive and collaborative: "The attributes of these new software tools make possible a new wave of online behavior, distributed collaboration, and social interaction, and they are already having a transformative effect on society in general and education in particular, triggering changes in how we communicate and learn" (McLoughlin and Lee, 2008: 12).

Characteristics of a Web 2.0 application include:

- Available everywhere and whenever needed.
- Interactive, so users can control and change the flow of the application based on input.

- Functionality for collective intelligence that allows users to contribute to as well as use an application.

Librarians are increasingly including Web 2.0 functionality such as reviews and ratings into library resources. Blogging, bookmarking sites, Facebook, Twitter, YouTube and wikis are also being used to promote libraries and allow users to interact. These applications are easy to learn and use, and support learning by sharing ideas and opinions. Blogging builds a feeling of community, and research suggests that this may be linked to positive learning outcomes (Top, 2012). Further, blogging can be a powerful tool for reinforcing learning because blogs can provide commentary on information and reflective thought about a subject that demonstrates critical thinking. A good blog will inform patrons about library services and resources and should use terms that will be picked up by search engines to drive traffic to library pages.

Libraries are using YouTube (*http://www.youtube.com/*) for a variety of reasons including professional development, promoting the library or library events and instructional purposes. The University of Kansas developed a great promotional video, *Lord of the Libraries* (*http://youtube/ CdTAv4dCZMg*), which was written and directed by then student, Christopher Martin, who has since been recognized for his work on films and television. Local communities have many talented individuals who can be recruited by libraries to produce quality productions.

Many libraries are allowing users to post comments on their videos. For the most part, the comments are either positive or neutral (Colburn and Haines, 2012) but libraries should not be afraid of negative comments because they provide valuable feedback for assessment.

Online tutorials

Tutorials are a useful means of augmenting face-to-face training. Web-based tutorials come from many sources, some are librarian-created and some are developed by vendors. Vendor-produced tutorials provide quick on-demand training for users needing more information on databases or software products. The tutorials produced by librarians explain local services and augment vendor tutorials with information on research. Regardless of the source, effective web-based tutorials are short, single concept and provide user control. Many are being made available on the web through YouTube, iTunes University (*http://www.apple. com/education/itunes-u/*) and other sites.

When tutorials are incorporated into a face-to-face classroom session they should be an interactive part of the class and not a passive show; for example:

- use pauses to explore concepts and verify students' understanding;
- use a video to introduce a topic, and build experience using an activity that complements the video;
- use tutorials to create anticipation for an activity; and
- use a community exercise to review the tutorial, divide the group into teams and have the students create their own version.

There are a number of software packages that facilitate the process of creating tutorials (see Table 4.1). There are differences in pricing and functionality between the packages so careful consideration should be given to the purpose and infrastructure for supporting tutorials before making a purchase.

Table 4.1 Online tutorial providers

Adobe Captivate	*http://www.adobe.com/products/ captivate.html*	Charge
Adobe Presenter	*http://www.adobe.com/products/ presenter.html*	Charge
Articulate	*http://www.articulate.com/*	Charge
CamStudio	*http://camstudio.org/*	Free
Camtasia	*http://www.techsmith.com/ camtasia.html*	Charge
Classtools	*http://www.classtools.net/*	Free
Composia	*http://www.composica.com/*	Charge
CourseLab	*http://courselab.com/db/cle/E746 101340F8075FC32571690042CB 16/doc.html*	Free/charge
dominKnow	*http://www.dominknow.com/index. cfm*	Charge
Knowledge Presenter	*http://www.knowledgepresenter. com/assets/products.htm*	Charge
Lectora	*http://lectora.com/e-learning- authoring-software*	Charge
MadCap Mimic	*http://www.madcapsoftware.com/ products/mimic/uses.aspx*	Charge
Multimedia Learning Object Authoring Tool	*http://www.learningtools.arts.ubc. ca/mloat.htm*	Free
RapidIntake	*http://rapidintake.com/overview*	Charge
Raptivity	*http://www.raptivity.com/elearning- product*	Charge
ReadyGo WCB	*http://readygo.com/main.htm*	Charge
ViewletBuilder	*http://www.qarbon.com/ presentation-software/ viewletbuilder/*	Charge
Wink	*http://www.debugmode.com/wink/*	Free
Xerte	*http://www.nottingham.ac. uk/~cczjrt/Editor/*	Free
Xical	*http://xical.org/*	Open source

Before librarians create a new video, they should see if another library has a video that would be suitable for use at the local institution. Since 2006, ACRL has provided a clearing house of tutorials through the PRIMO project. The project is managed by a committee of the ACRL Instruction Section that "promotes and shares peer-reviewed instructional materials created by librarians to teach people about discovering, accessing and evaluating information in networked environments" (American Library Association, 2012). The database is searchable, and a record typically includes the author, title, URL for the tutorial, category, audience and date, and a link to a survey of author-supplied information about the tutorial. Tutorials must be approved before they carry a PRIMO logo.

Games that teach information literacy are also being explored by libraries. Librarygame™ (*http://librarygame. co.uk/*) incorporates aspects of social networking into a game that librarians can use to teach and access information literacy skills. It works through integration with the library catalog and provides a competitive environment for exploring the library. Students earn points by returning or checking-out books, visiting service points, and other activities.

The librarian as learning object

A learning object is usually defined as "a reusable instructional resource, usually digital and web-based, developed to support learning" (Mestre et al., 2011: 237). In this definition it may seem unusual to include librarians as learning objects; however, as a model it can be useful as a new way to envision the role of a librarian in the learning process. Moving the focus from a set of objectives developed from the instructor's viewpoint to the student's perspective is more likely to engage the student in the learning process so that they can apply what they learn to other circumstances. One example can be found in the program at Drexel University (*http:// www.library.drexel.edu/personal-librarian*), where personal librarians are assigned to freshmen in order to help them succeed in the critical first year at university.

So, the face-to-face format for instruction may not be as important as once thought; students can learn as well from online instruction as they can from face-to-face sessions (Anderson and May, 2010). A hybrid approach that consists of both face-to-face and online instruction has the advantage of providing the efficiency of high-tech with the personal touch that makes patrons comfortable with librarians as research guides.

Efficiency is much valued in today's society, and that includes people completing research. Librarians should provide researchers with all the tools they need to complete their research as efficiently as possible. Librarians should never assume that patrons have this information already or can find the information on the website. Important shortcuts include:

- citation managers for keeping track of references, incorporating citations into word processing and building bibliographies;
- alert services from the catalog and databases for new articles and books;
- profile availability for saving searches and search results;
- document delivery options;
- permanent URLs that make referrals easy;
- resolvers for locating associated information and full text; and

- aggregate searching and discovery tools which can reduce the number of databases that must be searched, or which assist in finding the best database for searching a particular topic.

Research indicates that Millennials are connected into collective intelligence for advice and recommendations (Gross and Latham, 2007). A librarian who participates in social networking can become part of the crowd – an engaged librarian who is a living learning object. Here are some guidelines for individuals who wish to participate in social networking sites:

- Sites are judged by their "friends," so invite library users – this sends a message that the librarians are here for them.

- Establish profiles that are designed for library users.

- Join sites where library users gather; leverage time to get the most benefit for the least expenditure of effort.

- Look for subject communities to join. These can include sites or groups within larger social sites, e.g., Twitter and LinkedIn. Create a new community using a service like Ning (*http://www.ning.com*).

- Differentiate personal and professional sites – don't mix content.

- Don't be controlling – let the "friends" contribute and judge the success of the site by the level of activity.

- Take time to learn about all the features included in the site, and experiment.

- Keep management informed of activity, when a site is set up the librarian is representing the library as much as him- or herself.

- Be aware of context; although social networking sites are usually informal in tone, it is important to keep the postings courteous. Never post anything that shouldn't be seen by the general public.

- Be prepared for new technology; librarians who use social media need to learn about CSS, HTML and other coding systems in order to have attractive sites. Most sites provide tutorials and other documentation to get started.

When an account with a site is established be prepared for advertising, since most free accounts include advertising. Someone has to support the site and that is typically accomplished through advertisements paid by businesses. Take the time to read the privacy statement and any other conditions before accepting an account, because the conditions may be unacceptable. Table 4.2 provides a list of some popular sites.

Social networking sites can be a valuable way to keep a conversation going after a formal instruction session has ended. Patrons can ask advice on topics, key words for searches and databases options, as well as which websites offer quality information on their topic. Patrons have these types of conversations with each other and there is no reason why librarians shouldn't be included.

Microblogging tools like Twitter are useful for short answers in real time. Blogging sites offer additional options like file sharing, streaming options and data storage. Edmodo (*http://www.edmodo.com/*) is a blogging service developed for schools and provides some of the same functionality as a course management system. "The more librarians teach with these tools to improve information and social media literacy skills, the more likely students will understand best practices in using these tools" (Hricko, 2010: 689).

| Table 4.2 | Social networking sites for finding and making connections through technology |

Social networking sites	URL	Group
Academia	*http://academia.edu*	University and college faculty and students
ALAConnect	*http://connect.ala.org*	Librarians
Badoo	*http://www.badoo.com*	Everyone 18+
Blogger	*http://blogger.com*	Blogging
CafeMom	*http://www.cafemom.com*	Mothers group
Call for Creativity	*http://www.callforcreativity.com*	Photography, art
Classmates	*http://classmates.com*	Connect with classmates 18+
Delicious	*http://delicious.com*	Sharing bookmarks
deviantART	*http://www.deviantart.com*	Shared art interests 13+
Facebook	*http://facebook.com*	Everyone 13+
Engagedpatrons	*http://engagedpatrons.org/*	Integrated social networking site for public libraries
Famiva	*http://famiva.com*	Geneology
Flickr	*http://flickr.com*	Photos and videos 13+
Google Plus	*http://plus.google.com*	Everyone
Kincafe	*http://kincafe.com*	Geneology
LawLink	*http://www.lawlink.com*	Law
LibraryThing	*http://librarything.com*	Book lovers 13+
LinkedIn	*http://linkin.com*	Shared interests 18+
LiveJournal	*http://www.livejournal.com*	Community groups
MeetMe	*http://www.meetme.com/*	Everyone
Meetup	*http://meetup.com*	Find people with shared interests 18+

MyLife	http://www.mylife.com	Social site manager
MySpace	http://myspace.com	Teens 13+
Orkut	http://www.orkut.com	Everyone 18+
PatientsLikeMe	http://www.patients likeme.com	Medical 13+
RareShare	http://rareshare.org	Medical
Tagged	http://www.tagged.com	Everyone
Twitter	http://twitter.com	Microblogging
WordPress	http://wordpress.com	Blogging
YouTube	http://youtube.com	Videos

Incorporating social networking into library instruction may be a way to reduce anxiety about libraries. Anxiety about the library itself has been reported as a barrier to using the library for research (Mellon, 1986). When librarians convince students they are a credible source of advice by providing a friendly and supportive climate, students will become less anxious about doing research. Studies indicate that research instruction is one way to reduce library anxiety (Gross and Latham, 2007; Bell, 2011).

It seems obvious that one of the goals for instruction is to make the library less scary by incorporating library services as part of the assignments. By becoming familiar with the services, patrons are more likely to feel comfortable. The following list provides some guidelines for creating a "safe" environment for learning about the library:

- Require students to go to the reference desk for an assignment – the goal is to reduce anxiety about asking questions.

- Include an electronic reference question as part of an assignment – introduce students to reference anywhere, anytime.

- Include an assignment that requires use of the ILL service – this demonstrates that any item can be obtained through the library.

- Include an assignment where students create a project that uses at least three services – this introduces multiple ways to use the library.

- Provide opportunities to tour other libraries – giving students an opportunity to see what other libraries can do for them.

- Let the students select the topic of interest – this gives them a chance to explore an area of interest, and they are more likely to learn.

- Design options for learning on their own, or as part of a team – some people prefer working alone and others prefer working in a group.

- Allow students to use personal technology whenever possible – using their own devices will personalize the experience and make the library available in a familiar way.

- Connect instruction to real-life needs – this demonstrates that critical thinking will help them in the future whenever they need to find answers.

- Provide a safe environment for risk taking and exploration – make the consequences for failure low, learning is what is important.

- Provide assignments that support a trial-and-error method for exploration – which demonstrates that mistakes are part of the learning process.

- Incorporate opportunities for peer-led instruction – this provides an opportunity to learn from peers, which reinforces learning for Millennials.
- Recognize the importance of emotion and attitude in a successful learning outcome.
- Provide visual clues in learning activities.

One item missing from this list is the lecture or PowerPoint format. This format is "old school," and it is difficult to hold the attention of people who are sitting passively or otherwise distracted by mobile computing. Even simple classroom or audience-response technology which allows students to interact with the instructor using their own device or a clicker can grab and keep the audience's attention. Response systems use infrared (IR requires direct line of sight and is limited in distance), radio frequency (RF does not require line of sight) or WiFi (network) to communicate between the user and the instructor station. Some versions allow the polls to be distributed to social networking sites so that people outside the classroom can participate.

Reducing library anxiety appears to be a singular task for people, and not an area where technology will be of much help. A study undertaken by Van Scoyoc in 2003, comparing computer-assisted instruction and instructor-led sessions, revealed that students from the instructor-led session had a greater reduction in library anxiety as measured on the Library Anxiety Scale than those who had either no instruction or computer-aided instruction (Van Scoyoc, 2003). Although sweeping conclusions shouldn't be based on one study only, it does seems logical that reducing library anxiety is one area where high-touch could have better results than high-tech.

Everyone who works here is a teacher

If instruction is important in reducing anxiety about library use, then it would seem beneficial for every staff member to act as if he or she were an instructor. Instruction doesn't require a formal presentation – it is the simple connection between two people for the benefit of the patron at the point of need. This concept is known as social marketing, and the goal is to change patron behavior so that the patron learns something. Whether it is a circulation clerk checking out a print item and informing a patron about an upcoming program on the topic of the book, or a reference librarian answering a question and pointing out a related resource, or a staff member in ILL fulfilling a request and providing a tip about a nearby library – all are involved in instruction through service. Staff members associated with "back office" activities like cataloging or technology support are also involved in training as they meet user needs and answer questions that will make research more stress free. Every communication between a staff member and patron is an opportunity to teach something small, which is easy to master and remember.

This also applies to student workers hired for positions in which they have contact with library patrons. Most Millennials have extensive experience with social media tools and could make good assistants for an instant messaging (IM) reference service (Langan, 2012). After initial training on reference practices, ongoing supervision and supplementary training can be provided through IM logs. The logs should be analyzed in a safe environment where all the student assistants can benefit from the learning experience.

Student and patron workers are also great advocates for the library. They are liaisons between the library and other patrons and can encourage an ongoing dialog that bridges generational and cultural differences. They can articulate the patrons' viewpoint and help determine priorities, and through participation they gain a sense of ownership (Miller, J., 2011). They are also a good source of ideas for reaching people who are not using the library.

Managers can facilitate the cultural shift towards a patron-centered environment of collaboration by promoting the exchange of ideas that inform activities throughout the library. These include breaking down any departmental silos that encourage staff to have a narrow view about their work and role in the organization. Open communication between library staff and patrons is essential for an operational climate that centers on patrons.

The case for lifelong learning

What is the cost to society if its citizens have poor skills in locating and evaluating information? It isn't hard to imagine the complications that may arise from decisions based on poor information. One estimate is that poor quality information can negatively impact organizations and cost from 10 to 20 percent of revenue (Editorial, 2004). The ultimate impact on individuals caused by incorrect or inadequate research is impossible to measure, as are the pleasures that come from learning. In addition, advances in technology bring new discoveries that can invalidate previously accepted facts. Questioning with an open mind uncovers these developments, which can result in new behavior. These are a few of the reasons why lifelong learning is critical in a modern society.

Collaboration on the development of instruction programs between school, public and academic libraries, with the goal of embracing lifelong learning, would have been applauded by the participants of the White House conferences. Lifelong learning is necessary for anyone who strives for information literacy in a technology-rich society. Any library setting can be used as a learning environment with supportive librarians. "Vital elements of informed learning in scholarly contexts include: reflective learning, which promotes inquiry, reflection, and problem solving; thoughtful and effective management of information and resources; self-directed learning individually and in teams; research-based learning that activates and extends prior learning; and curriculum" (Bruce et al., 2012: 535–6).

Learning can take many forms, and it is important for instruction to be flexible and designed with the motivations of students first. In a public library this can take the form of a book club, where discussions about fiction and other genres can stimulate learning (Blackburn, 2010). In a school or academic library it can be embedded into curriculum activities, with each session building on and reinforcing concepts taught in other settings. As Constance Mellon states, "academic library instruction cannot be planned and delivered in a sphere totally separated from school or public library instruction. A collegiality needs to be developed among librarians whose concern is educating the library user" (Mellon, 1988: 139).

Technology can assist in developing educational material for information literacy programs. Much of the material produced for students in academic or school settings can be made available to the general public through social media sties. The sharing of material through social networking sites is a cost-effective way of providing learning materials across locations and sharing expertise between different types of libraries.

The web is a grand experiment in democracy which tests the limits of free speech by providing anyone with a platform for sharing information. However, much of the information is not checked for accuracy and can become outdated. Children and adults need to understand that surfing the web isn't a trivial activity. All web searching requires critical thinking; there are risks concerning fraud, computer viruses and incorrect information. Product advertising is often disguised as fact. Researchers who do not question the veracity of information can be misled. The web is a crucible for learning where ideas and opinions are presented, challenged and accepted or rejected.

These are important life skills that a strong partnership between teachers, faculty and librarians could instill. "If we accept the proposition that embedding information literacy into the curriculum is necessary for preparing students to be lifelong learners, then faculty-librarian collaborations that exist on many levels and in many forms can provide us with an infinite array of possibilities for building experiences" (Frey and Fiedler, 2001: 169). Regardless of the type of library, it is important that all librarians play a role in assisting patrons to find and interpret information, even as it changes and evolves on the interconnected networks of the world today.

5

Collaborative collections

Abstract: "Just-in-time" purchasing is replacing "just-in-case" collection building as librarians evaluate usage statistics and adapt technology to deliver information to patrons more efficiently. Patrons are directly involved in the acquisition process by clicking on records in the catalog, or indirectly through ILL requests. Librarians can use social media to solicit information for purchases, and by working with consortia they can expand the collection beyond the library walls. Negotiation is a necessary skill for building collections, and best practices for negotiating will result in contracts that benefit libraries and vendors. All contracts and open source licenses include language that should be examined.

Key words: patron-driven acquisitions, evidenced-based selection, social media, consortia collections, negotiation, contracts, open source licensing.

A collection is a gathering of items into an identifiable group, and a collaborative collection is a group assembled through the efforts of many. A collaborative collection may contain items that are directly purchased or recommended by readers, materials ordered through an ILL request, and materials made available through consortia lending agreements. Collaborative collections also include vendors who assist by providing collections for patron acquisitions and added services to expedite processing. Collaborative collections are a natural by-product of information technology. Technology is making is easy to quickly provide information as it is needed, reducing the necessity to build collections because patrons might want the information someday.

Patron-driven acquisition (PDA)

Traditionally, librarians have been responsible for building collections based on an understanding of past, present and future predictions of use. This type of collection development has been called *just-in-case* selection, in the belief that patrons will use the materials sooner or later. Unfortunately, libraries are reporting a high percentage of titles that never circulate, ranging from 40 percent (Spitzform, 2011) to 70 percent (Sharp and Thompson, 2010).

There is also a high degree of duplication of titles between libraries. If libraries shared access to titles, money could be directed to purchasing unique titles that would expand the shared collection. An OhioLINK study estimated a 70 percent duplication rate among recent imprints that were available for lending between consortia members, which increased to 75 percent during the time period of the study (Kairis, 2003). These facts make it difficult to justify just-in-case collection development to administrators looking for evidence-based management decisions.

Patron-driven acquisition (PDA) is a new practice among libraries, where patrons make the decisions about what to purchase without the mediation of a librarian. The methods for these *just-in-time* purchases include the patron clicking on a record in the catalog, initiating a purchase, or ILL, so a title is purchased instead of borrowed from another library. Libraries do not generally publicize PDA because they want the selections to happen organically, and not be forced by any individual attempting to over-select titles for their use.

PDA begins with the library working with a vendor to create a profile of the types of records to be loaded into the catalog as potential purchases. The profiles are defined by subject content and publication criteria (date, publisher, etc.), and generally include price considerations. These profiles can include printed books or e-books depending on the library specification. The vendor prepares records which are loaded into the local catalog, awaiting discovery. Titles selected by patrons come under the contract details. Libraries can lease or purchase titles once specified conditions are met. The conditions will vary depending on the publisher contract, for example:

- After a specified number of clicks the purchase is made.
- A pay-per-view charge with purchase and ownership after a specified number of clicks.
- After a specified amount of time "reading" an e-book a purchase is made.
- A collection of titles is used for a specified period (for a fee) and the library makes permanent retention decisions based on usage statistics provided by the vendor.
- The additional requirement for the purchase of another e-book copy when a specified number of uses is reached.
- A pay-per-view model, where a fee is paid each time a title is viewed, but the library doesn't own the title.
- A subscription model, where the library loses access to titles when the subscription ends.

After the contract period is completed the records for titles that were not purchased are deleted from the catalog. While the contract is operating, readers don't know they are making a purchase, for them it is a seamless process that results in a book being delivered. In the case of printed books, the publisher ships the book according to the contract, which can include *shelf-ready* processing where the book arrives with all processing complete ready to be put on the self. The University of York, reporting on a 2009–10 PDA project, loaded 3000 e-book titles; 433 titles were purchased and another 648 titles were not purchased because they were viewed only once (Sharp and Thompson, 2010).

Another variation on PDA by Elsevier uses an evidence-based model with a slight modification in the program (*http://www.info.sciverse.com/sciencedirect/subscriptions/evidence-based-selection*). With this model, there is an initial fee based on a percentage of the total value of content selected by the library, with access for 12 months, after which time the library decides which titles to purchase and keep in perpetuity. These titles are priced up to the value of the initial content investment and based upon usage of the entire content. This is a hybrid system where patrons gain access to many titles, but the library retains control over what is actually purchased.

Patron ordering appeals to libraries moving away from just-in-case collection development to a system that is more patron centered. By loading records for titles based on profiles, librarians are able to provide access to many more items than could be purchased using either approval plans or just-in-case librarian ordering alone. The University of Arizona redesigned their acquisition system with the goal of providing the e-book first, and when e-books weren't available a print copy was delivered to the shelf within five days (Jones, 2011). Studies for the PDA model show that titles are being used repeatedly (Thompson, 2010), and this lower cost per use holds true for both print and e-books (Schroeder, 2012).

According to a 2012 EBSCO survey of librarians and publishing professionals, 56 percent of the librarians said they intended to use PDA for books or pay-per-view (PPV) for journals (Powell, 2012) as a replacement for big deals. This is a new trend among libraries – to move towards more patron initiated purchasing as a means to save money while improving user experiences.

ILL purchasing

Patron initiated ordering began as an experiment to reduce interlibrary costs. Those in favor of buying instead of borrowing point to lower total costs than librarian mediated or just-in-case selections, because patron selected titles receive more circulations and therefore have a lower cost per circulation (Tyler, 2011).

Purchasing books rather than borrowing from other libraries reduces the workload of ILL staff and reduces the time it takes to supply titles. Libraries using this technology may need to revise workflow by including circulation and subject librarians in the workflow and feedback loops (Herrera and Greenwood, 2011). This retooling often employs technology like the Getting It System Toolkit (GIST) (*http://www.gistlibrary.org/*) which was introduced into OCLC's ILLiad (*http://www.oclc.org/illiad/*) ILL application. It has a feature which allows patrons to easily suggest titles for purchasing, making the process seamless for users. It combines information from users and sources to provide data on local availability, web versions and cost (Pitcher et al., 2010), which simplifies the workflow between acquisitions and ILL.

A successful project requires coordination between the ILL staff, the technical services staff and subject librarians. While the ILL staff members monitor the process, technical service staff members manage the cataloging and ordering, and subject librarians promote ILL. Depending on the organization, the ILL staff may do the actual ordering, and in some cases the subject librarians can influence the purchasing decisions, generally by influencing the criteria for purchasing decisions.

Libraries which purchase rather than borrow titles establish clear guidelines about what is appropriate when purchasing rather than borrowing. These guidelines complement the collection development policies used to govern just-in-case selections. Considerations include maximum costs, genres and media that are not acceptable, and publication date ranges. A consideration often used during pilot programs is the status of the patron, so undergraduates and children may be excluded.

One of the main reasons for purchasing books, instead of borrowing books through ILL, is that purchased books circulate more often so they have a lower cost per use. Research indicates that purchasing these just-in-time materials may initially cost more than titles acquired through approval plans, but not significantly more (Tyler et al., 2011). Analyzing the increased circulation data makes purchased titles a bargain for libraries because they circulate more than titles obtained by other means, which may never circulate. This is true whether value is measured by cost per transaction (Perdue and Van Fleet, 1999) or whether percentage expected use values are used (Tyler et al., 2011). Even when comparing regularly purchased titles that had circulated with those purchased through ILL, the ILL purchased titles had a better price per annual circulation (Tyler et al., 2010).

Patrons surveyed after an ILL purchase express a high degree of satisfaction with the process (Ward et al., 2003; Hussong-Christian and Goergen-Doll, 2010). Librarians also report satisfaction, and indicate that, overall, the materials being added are relevant and enhance existing collections. Finally, it is more cost effective to obtain titles through the ILL program than to change approval plans to match what patrons are requesting (Anderson et al., 2002).

There are circumstances when borrowing appears to be a better option than purchasing printed materials, especially for titles with a low circulation. Such is the case of books from overseas publishers which are delivered faster via ILL than through purchasing (Chan, 2004), which also incurs higher postage rates, requiring the titles to circulate more times before they are cost effective. This may be true for printed books in general when the lifetime costs for maintaining a print book are included (Van Dyk, 2011).

As with any library service, an analysis of the goals of the program against the total operational costs is necessary in order to evaluate the return on investment (ROI) of the service. Processing, staffing and conservation practices vary between libraries and change over time, so simply researching what other libraries have done isn't sufficient to evaluate a library service. It may be more cost effective to borrow print materials through ILL and purchase e-books through a patron ordering system. Librarians considering a patron-driven acquisition program – whether through an ILL program or via direct patron ordering – must develop clear policies on the scope of the program and on how to evaluate its success. The bottom line should be improved service for patrons that is cost effective.

The role of social media in acquisitions

A recurring theme in this book is the use of social networking to connect with users, so it should come as no surprise that Facebook and Twitter (among others) can be used for suggestions of titles for purchase. The advantage of a social site is that it builds on the library's presence in that social network, and by doing so reinforces the relevancy of the library. Librarians are now monitoring their sites for comments so that they can provide a personal response almost immediately. Response times from typical input forms or e-mail can take longer, and when these suggestions are anonymous there is no response at all.

With social media it is easy to distribute a message soliciting requests, but it works best in relation to a larger marketing plan (Petit, 2011). The easiest way to explore social media for purchasing is to start with a modest plan that ties the request to a specific activity. This could be as simple as a book club, a special interest group or a bibliographic instruction session for students. The librarian will want to establish eligibility criteria from the beginning, and must be prepared to purchase or to respond to suggestions when the title can't be purchased.

The economics of shelf-ready

Library vendors now offer "shelf-ready" services that provide all the necessary processing to take books from the shipping box to the shelf. The vendor can provide the MARC (MAchine-Readable Cataloging) record, binding (as appropriate), labels, ownership stamps and barcodes or RFID tags. However, because of the processing it is usually impossible to return incorrect titles.

Librarians and vendors must agree in advance on the labeling specifications, the identification of titles to be excluded from shelf-ready processing, and any adaptations of cataloging standards because of local practices. Records are exchanged between vendors and libraries using electronic data interchange (EDI), which specifies the structure for data transmission between systems; EDIFACT is commonly used for this purpose.

Shelf-ready is used to reduce the staffing costs associated with processing and to improve the time it takes to get books to the shelf. However, there have been complaints about the quality of bibliographic records coming with shelf-ready plans that cause librarians to spend extra time processing bibliographic records (Jay et al., 2009). Likewise, when libraries have lower staffing costs and efficient processing the benefits of shelf-ready will be reduced. Reasons for adopting shelf-ready will involve an examination of several factors including the amount of money saved, reductions in processing time, and the benefits that come from these savings (Schroeder and Howland, 2011; Ballestro, 2012). These benefits include identifying other work that could be performed with the time that staff members save when processing materials.

Building consortia collections

In a world in which the reader is the center of library operations a consortia has an important part to play. In the past, librarians looked at the collection as the storehouse for scholarship. That is no longer true; the web is a distributed network for finding and accessing information. Libraries should look at the internal collection as part of the scholarship, with the remainder available over the web.

Through collections shared among many libraries, scholars will be able to obtain resources regardless of the size of the home library.

Successful collaborations have some common characteristics that include understanding the local library, the chemistry between institutions, and compatibility (Kanter, 1994). Understanding the local library means understanding more than the politics of decision making; it also means understanding the degree to which the library is excited about a project. Chemistry is the similarities between partners that indicate a willingness to persevere through challenges. Compatibility describes a shared vision that will endure over time. When all factors are in place, a consortia is likely to be successful for the long term.

OhioLINK (*http://www.ohiolink.edu/*) is a state-wide consortium of the Ohio State Library and college, university and community colleges that collaborate on: resource sharing, a combined online catalog, a digital repository, digital textbooks, e-books and licensing for the member libraries. The consortium has been able to save on licensing costs and has limited resource inflation to two to three percent annually while providing state-wide access (Advisory Board Company, Education Advisory Board, University Leadership Council, 2011).

There are several consortia projects underway, or in the proposal stage, for digitizing texts and making them available to a wide community of users. These projects address issues of copyright and the sustainability of digital collections into the distant future. The Open Content Alliance (OCA) (*http://www.opencontentalliance.org/*) is a collaborative project by a worldwide group of cultural, technology, nonprofit and governmental organizations working to digitize text and build a permanent archive of publicly accessible content that is available through the

Internet Archive (*http://archive.org/index.php*). The archive includes video and media content as well as text material that is out of copyright.

The HathiTrust (*http://www.hathitrust.org/*) differs from the OCA in that it includes a combination of material in and out of copyright. The material in copyright is only available through membership while the items out of copyright are available to all. The HathiTrust digitizes book and journal articles from member libraries. In 2011, HathiTrust member libraries voted for the establishment of a distributed print archive of monographic holdings that corresponds to the digitized content available through HathiTrust. It provides usage statistics to members through Google Analytics.

The Alliance for Information Science and Technology Innovation (AISTI) (*http://www.aisti.org*) supports research into the application of information technology issues facing librarians. AISTI projects include data mining and e-print delivery for institutional repositories.

The Western Regional Storage Trust (WEST) (*http://www. cdlib.org/services/west/*) is a print repository program for archiving journal backfiles. WEST has agreements for retention, holdings and access. It is funded on a cost-sharing basis which includes criteria for collection sizes. "Under the WEST program, participating libraries consolidate and validate print journal backfiles at major library storage facilities and at selected campus locations. The resulting shared print archives ensure access to the scholarly print record and allow member institutions to optimize campus library space" (California Digital Library, 2012).

LYRASIS is the product of a merger of three consortiums – SOLINET, PALINET and NELINET – for the purpose of "building and sustaining collaboration, enhancing library and technology operations, and increasing buying power" (LYRASIS, 2012). LYRASIS has over 1000 participating members who receive continuing education courses and advice on digitization, preservation and reciprocal borrowing through ILL.

The California Digital Library (*http://cdlib.org*) provides a variety of services including support for digitization projects, vendor licensing, open source publishing and preservation. It was formed by University of California Libraries in 1997 to encourage and facilitate information technology in the university system.

The Council on Library and Information Resources (CLIR) (*http://www.clir.org/*) manages a facility for over 150 member libraries that preserves and provides document delivery to low-use primary source materials in the humanities, social sciences and sciences. The goal of CLIR is to supplement local holdings by the acquisition of new resources through an elective process of member libraries.

Taking Academic Law Libraries Online (TALLO) is a proposed consortium model for sharing the costs of digitizing and maintaining collections within the framework of current copyright. Library copies that have been obtained through purchase or gifts would be digitized and made available to member libraries. "It contemplates circulation only of the number of copies owned, would not damage the author's ability to continue selling copies in the marketplace, and would be available only to library users, in a manner similar to licensed databases" (Wu, M.M., 2011: 549). This model differs from the other library initiated digitization projects of HathiTrust and OCA because it advocates greater access to copyrighted materials for potentially lower costs to member libraries.

The National Repository Library in Finland ensures that less used and older print material is preserved and made available to other libraries. It is an example of a state-supported library, where the ownership of materials is transferred to the library, which encourages libraries to remove duplicates (Vattulainen, 2005). By reducing the number of copies, all participants save shelf space and lower their costs. Likewise, participants are assured that their library will continue to receive governmental support, that it will continue to grow as needed, and that patrons will have access to the materials they need.

The art of negotiation

Collaboration and cooperation are elements of all social structures, and individuals at all levels of a society engage in negotiation. Librarians are likely to enter negotiations in a variety of circumstances. They will negotiate with superiors, vendors, colleagues and patrons, so it is important for librarians to develop good negotiation skills. Skilled negotiators understand their own strengths and weaknesses and have learned to listen to an inner voice that provides insights into the nuances of the negotiation session. This inner voice will tell librarians when to stop talking and listen, which will provide insights into the real needs of the other party rather than their expressed positions. The goal of every negotiation is to reach an agreement that respects the needs of both sides. One-sided negotiations will eventually create enough ill will to cause a disruption in the relationship that impacts the quality of the library and the services provided.

Best practices for contract negotiations with vendors

Contract negotiation can be defined as the process by which multiple parties reach a solution that meets most of their needs. Negotiation can be approached like any other library activity and requires preparation. This starts by learning the institutional framework for negotiating with vendors and by having a clear understanding of what is needed, of the product alternatives, of the staff's ability to accept a new product, and of the needs of users.

Understanding the rules for contract negotiation established by the institution or governing agency that the library is part of is a must for every librarian involved in contract negotiations. These policies are the foundation for any contract and will prescribe how agreements are reached. There may be a legal office which is responsible for the negotiation or for contract approval. Many institutions have specific requirements based on dollar amounts, which may require multiple quotes from different vendors, or they may have a formal process of Request for Proposal (RFP) or Request for Quote (RFQ). Failure to understand or follow the policies and procedures will have negative consequences for the librarian and the library.

Making deals

It is important to have a clear understanding of the strengths and weaknesses of the library. What are the priorities for collection development? What are the technological challenges that are impacting patrons most? What are the most important areas for improvement? Librarians may want to complete a SWOT analysis, which identifies strengths, weaknesses, opportunities and threats. Asking questions is the quickest way to get information from vendors, patrons and library staff. Using e-mail to communicate with vendors will save time and will be less threatening to librarians. Hypotheticals and scenarios are additional ways to collect information in a non-threatening way that may generate new ideas.

Identifying the best possible alternative to a particular deal is a good technique for determining the point at which it is best to walk away from a negotiation. It is easy for beginning negotiators to get caught up in the negotiation process and lose sight of the goal. The point of negotiation is to reach an agreement, but there are always alternatives to any deal. Understanding the consequences of any failed negotiation is powerful, and gives librarians leverage in discussions. Failure to reach an agreement can be due to a price point, to the titles that must be included in a package, or to definitions of the number of simultaneous users – anything that will have an unacceptable impact on users. Knowing the acceptable alternatives makes it easier to walk away from a negotiation, or to walk towards a different deal.

Researching products

Having an awareness of product alternatives provides leverage during negotiations. This requires having an understanding of the products under consideration. The web is a great place to start the research by comparing products on vendors' websites. This should be followed by contact with customers, and most librarians are happy to share their experiences with specific products. This research can be carried out using mail or online surveys, listservs or social networking.

When possible, ask colleagues if their system can be used for a brief trial; there is no substitute for user experience on a production site. This is particularly helpful when evaluating systems that require login accounts and when multiple functions are being evaluated. Article database testing through a vendor trial may be sufficient to evaluate the interface but be cautious when a vendor won't provide title listings. All vendors should be able to provide a list of titles included in their package, which should also provide information on full-text availability. Vendors should also be able to supply records for the catalog, and coverage information. Without this information it is difficult to compare plans. When testing a vendor's product, try to test the product using the library's authentication system, which will identify any incompatibilities.

Don't overlook possible collaborations with other institutions. Consortia agreements may be more cost effective for a library than going it alone. They also provide a platform for additional collaboration at a later date to improve collections and services across institutional boundaries.

When librarians are researching a general product like a laptop or projector they can send a tweet that starts with #help, #question or simply #h followed by the product question, which will provide suggestions for products from a broader community. Librarians should also check the product reviews that are provided on many product sales websites. However, be suspicious of reviews that seem overly positive or negative as they could have been written by company employees for their own advantage.

Understanding the library staff

Get to know the library staff and their willingness to explore products under consideration. There is great potential for conflict between staff and management when new products are acquired or familiar products are replaced by something new. Figure 5.1 depicts the polarizing influence of resistance

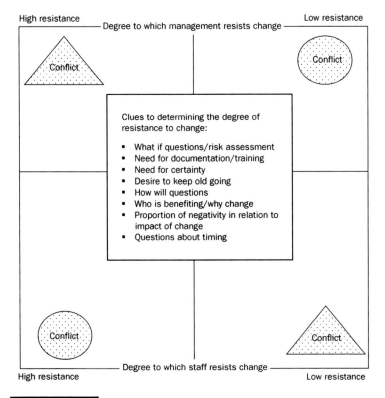

Figure 5.1 The polarizing influence of resistance to change

to change. Conflict will arise when management is conservative and resists change but the staff expresses a high degree of interest in exploring new systems. The same will happen when management is eager to adopt new technology but the staff is reluctant to abandon the familiar. Conflict is likely to result when there is a disagreement between management and staff about adopting change. In Figure 5.1, the matching conflict zones indicate where disagreements are inevitable, and the stronger the polarization, the more service areas will be impacted. Thus, attention should be paid to answering concerns by providing supporting information and gentle affirmation about the change.

Listening skills and clear communication about goals and the need for change are key to overcoming fears about change. Likewise, one of the best ways to overcome resistance is to involve staff in the selection process. Form a team to develop product requirements and carry out product comparisons. Once a product is selected, staff can also plan the implementation and test the product against contract requirements, and they can conduct post-implementation user assessments. The implementation team is the locus for training the staff and it can develop marketing ideas for launching the new product or service to library patrons. (Change management will be covered in more detail in Chapter 11.)

All negotiations will benefit from a strong team with varied backgrounds and strengths that can contribute to the process, therefore careful consideration should be given to selecting members and their respective roles within the group. Everyone should understand why s/he is a member of the team. Video and audio conferencing can be useful for bringing together team members at distant locations for briefings and meetings. Sharing documents via an intranet or the web is another way to encourage collaboration.

Knowing the needs of patrons

Perhaps the best advice is to know the needs and characteristics of the library's patrons. Online surveys and blogs help to identify what users are asking for, and any problem areas or changing demographics or interests. Library staff members are also good sources for identifying problem areas or changing circumstances. Asking staff to look out for such problems and report ideas to their managers is important and staff should be rewarded for looking after the interests of patrons. However, knowing what patrons need is the first step, the next step is to identify any training and marketing needs. There will always be a group of patrons who want to maintain the status quo and a group who will embrace change, so it is important to target marketing to each group.

Some patrons will embrace new technology eagerly; for this group an informational campaign that informs users of the new product is all that is needed. Extra training will be needed for groups who are less enthusiastic about new technology. Face-to-face training is probably the best way to convince this group, with examples of how the new technology will improve or simplify their activities. When new technology is introduced it should be rolled out with some fanfare, exposing all staff to the technology so that they understand how it fits into library services and impacts his or her job.

Cold calls from vendors

Sales representatives sometimes approach librarians in order to sell something the librarian hasn't considered but is, in the words of the representative, "a great deal." Having a priority list of products or needs will assist the librarian in deciding how to proceed with these cold calls. There is nothing wrong with listening to a sales talk to get more information, or to learn about new products, but that shouldn't result in a new best friend for life. Don't be influenced by deadlines set by the sales representatives to meet sales quotas or year-end deals.

The key to negotiating under this pressure is to keep the discussion on the librarian's terms, and to not be afraid to say no. Although it is certainly okay to be firm with a sales representative, it is also important to stay on good terms any company representative. Don't criticize a good sales representative to the representative's senior management if you want to have good relations in the future. The reverse is also true; sales representatives should never bypass the designated librarian in order to make direct sales pitches to administrators or patrons. That is unethical, and will create a bad reputation for that representative among librarians.

Negotiating with library administrators and staff

Negotiations with colleagues have many similarities to vendor negotiations. Start with an understanding of the problem and the best possible outcome, be prepared for alternatives and really listen for their needs. It may be necessary to sacrifice some ground early on in order to secure a better position for the future, and remember that there is no substitute for goodwill with both administrators and staff because both are necessary for managing a progressive library.

In some circumstances it may be necessary to gather support from patrons and other library supporters. Social media can be useful in gathering input and support to counter a move that would seriously harm a library program; an example can be seen in efforts to close the library school at Louisiana State University (LSU), where students initiated a campaign to save the school using social media (*http://savelsuslis.wiki spaces.com/*). Their campaign included a Facebook site that encouraged letters to administrators, and an online petition.

The program is currently still active with no indication that it will be closed. The passion behind that effort can be measured by the number and location of participants from beyond Louisiana, and the media attention that befell the university. Another example involved efforts to consolidate the Western Massachusetts Regional Library System, which was opposed by a group that formed a *We Love Western Mass Libraries* Facebook page. This resulted in a letter-writing campaign that inundated the Massachusetts Board of Library Commissioners. After demonstrations and counter-offers, the conflict ended with a compromise of a satellite office in Western Massachusetts (Poulin, 2011). Both of these cases demonstrate how social media can benefit libraries.

When negotiating through tense disagreements with patrons it is very helpful to refer to policies specific to the particular situation. The policies, which have been approved by officials, then become the focus of the discussion and provide a less emotional platform for it, and may show the path going forward. National library associations provide advice on developing policies but it is important that librarians do not hide behind policies when confronted with legitimate concerns by administrators and patrons. The primary concern of a library is to meet the needs of users, when those needs change policies will need to be revised to reflect the new environment.

Overcoming the fear factor in negotiations

The best way to build confidence is with practice. Librarians who are nervous about negotiating with vendors can improve their skills by knowing their own strengths and weaknesses first. There are several personality inventories that will assist in identifying personal characteristics that impact negotiations. Wells Fargo has a short test for negotiation style which may provide some insight (Wells Fargo, 2011). It is difficult for others to take advantage of a librarian who understands his or her own weaknesses.

Another technique for reducing anxiety over negotiations is to use a boilerplate for the standard clauses that the library wants to include. These are frequently available through the institution's legal office. Fiona Fogden provides advice on standard language for key areas that is easy to insert into contracts (Fogden, 2011). Contract clauses are useful to cover instances such as: substantial changes in content for a database; redefinitions of a product which remove or add components that will require additional costs to the library; definitions about who is allowed to use the product inside and outside the library walls; ILL use; changes in pricing models that disadvantage the library; mergers or buyouts; and cancellation. It is also useful to include a change clause with provisions for change orders in contracts that are likely to be in place for a number of years.

Institutions have different practices regarding this process and approval by a legal office may be required. For librarians, there are a few points that are particularly important in contracts for digital material:

- How are users defined? Is it necessary to authenticate walk-in users, or will the contract permit on-sight usage even if the reader isn't affiliated with the library?

- What are the provisions or restrictions for ILL?

- What is the length of the contract and what are the conditions for renewal?

- Can the price be changed? Under what circumstances?

- What are the provisions for cancellation? How much notice does the library need to provide?

- Look for restrictive wording that includes a penalty or liability on the part of the library for performing a specific activity that is contrary to policy. Do not agree to binding or mandatory arbitration.

- Where will disputes be adjudicated? This should typically be the local court jurisdiction.

- Verify that everything agreed upon in the negotiations is reflected in the contract.

- Check for areas that are "silent." These are items which are not included in a contract which will require additional negotiation or a new contract if the circumstances arise.

- Check for nondisclosure clauses, which make it difficult to share information with other librarians.

- What happens to access if the contract is cancelled?

- What are the vendor's provisions for long-term content preservation?

- Check for clauses about who owns the data. Verify that the vendor isn't claiming ownership of your data. This alone can be a reason for rejecting a contract because it will lock the library into a particular vendor for other products, or may even prevent you from using your data for another purpose.

Provisions for contract changes

Librarians should incorporate all the important factors into the contract before it is signed. However, over the lifetime of a contract it may be the case that either the vendor or the librarian may want to change some aspect of the contract. This often occurs when technology advances are such that either the vendor or the librarian wants to add new technology to a project. Other reasons for a change to a contract may include discoveries about the library environment or work processes that were unanticipated. A change clause in a contract spells out when a vendor can reject a request or re-quote a price for substantial changes. These clauses are important, particularly in expensive technology contracts, and it is beneficial to involve lawyers (Taylor and Davies, 2012). A change order authorizes a smaller change in the project and is co-signed by the vendor and librarian. Change orders include modifications that do not substantially impact the project, and project clarifications that are mutually acceptable. More substantial changes may require a new bid process. The mechanics for managing changes and the types of acceptable changes should be included in the contract's change clause.

If the contract is for a database vendor and contains exclusive titles, make sure to add a clause for perpetual access to the subscription. Exclusive contracts may expire or may be transferred to another source; when this happens a library can lose access to the content. Asking for a clause relating to permanent access or the transfer of rights for access will protect future use. One of the sticky issues with regard to digital content is the question of ownership. Most publishers are well aware of these issues and are making agreements with archiving sources. Many publishers are using Portico (*http://www.portico.org/digital-preservation/*) to archive back issues of titles. Portico manages permanent access to e-journals, e-books and e-collections, ensuring that libraries will have perpetual access to titles when vendors drop access.

SERU licenses for copyright and ONIX-PL for efficiencies

Shared Electronic Resource Understanding (SERU) (*http://www.niso.org/workrooms/seru*) is an attempt by the National Information Standards Organization (NISO) to define a best-practice approach for e-resources. SERU promotes the removal of licenses in favor of using copyright law. It does not remove price negotiations from the process, only negotiations around license agreements under the principal that all litigation can come under the umbrella of copyright law. Both libraries and publishers can register on SERU and join in efforts to standardize access along principles that are mutually beneficial. SERU can dramatically simplify licenses, but it only applies to subscriptions. "Recognizing this type of business need, the SERU Working Group is currently in the process of updating the NISO Recommended Practice to cover non-journal e-resources, such as e-books, and additional types of acquisition and use models" (Marshall, 2011: 21). With SERU, there is hope for the future simplification of all types of licenses for digital content.

ONIX-PL (*http://www.niso.org/workrooms/onixpl*) is a joint project of NISO and EDItEUR which is attempting to standardize the elements of licenses to make it easier for libraries and publishers to share license elements. The license terms are expressed in XML format, to be loaded into electronic management systems. The license agreements can then be displayed to patrons through the catalog, making license analysis easier for staff.

The open source choice

Open source materials frequently have licenses that should be examined before accepting. Open source licensing is defined by the Open Source Initiative under the terms of many different types of licenses approved by the group (*http://www.opensource.org/licenses/index.html*). Creative Commons Attribution is a generic license that many web contributors use to protect their rights when an item is available for distribution. It requires redistributions of the source to include an attribution specified by the author or licensor to the work.

Open access (OA) is a separate category of "free material." OA provides unrestricted access to scholarly articles, and, increasingly, to theses, dissertations and books. There is no single source definition for OA, but many organizations have issued definitions (Graduate School of Library and Information Science at Simmons College, 2012). The common requirement for all OA distributed material is that authors (distributors) have the legal right to disseminate the information. This can be complicated when authors want to contribute articles that were previously published with commercial publishers, and that have limitations on redistribution outside the original publication. Librarians who manage institutional repositories need to be aware of the publishers' policies on the redistribution of content. Some publishers embargo submissions into institutional repositories for a specific period of time, others will allow submission after the print copy is distributed, some require fees, and others will allow submission as long as the copy is an unpublished, or author's, copy.

OpenAIRE (*http://www.openaire.eu/*) was created to support open access in Europe by promoting and supporting an infrastructure for the open access policy of the ERC Scientific Council Guidelines for Open Access and the open access pilot of the European Commission. Among the features of OpenAIRE are: a European helpdesk system;

national and regional liaison offices in 27 countries; a portal and infrastructure for the repository networks; and a repository facility for researchers who do not have access to an institutional or discipline-specific repository.

6

The librarian as advocate

Abstract: Marketing and advocacy are becoming more evident in job responsibilities for librarians at all levels. The librarian as an advocate for the library promotes the library and the library services to the community. Marketing involves promoting specific services or resources and creating library promotions that match community interests. Branding the library is an important feature of marketing and, unless something significant changes, the characteristics of a brand should be maintained to build patron loyalty. Information about resources should be specific and should target classes of users. Designating a position of chief storyteller – someone who is responsible for coordinating marketing ideas, assisting with the development of content and educating fellow staff about marketing principles – will help develop a climate that encourages everyone to participate in marketing and advocacy.

Key words: advocacy, marketing, library guides, LibGuides, social media.

The concept of advocacy isn't new to librarians who have been promoting libraries for many years, but these activities are often seen as the responsibility of the library director, so many librarians in non-administrative positions have not been concerned about being an advocate for the library. Conditions are changing, however, and advocacy should be a common practice for librarians at all levels of the organization.

Marketing and advocacy differ in that marketing is the promotion of a resource or service to a target group, whereas advocacy is promoting the library as a whole. When libraries change from being collection focused to being patron focused the most valuable resources in the library become the people who work in the library and serve its patrons every day. It follows, then, that librarians at all levels in the organization are advocates for the library, and every librarian who has contact with patrons is involved in marketing. The same is true for everyone who works in the library, from the students and volunteers who shelve books to the library's director, and when everyone sees the patron as the driving force of their activities their behavior changes. This patron focus must be in place before any marketing and advocacy plan can be successful. A friendly, welcoming environment is the foundation for advocacy and marketing; in the absence of that environment, no effort to improve the image of the library will succeed.

Job descriptions for librarians are being revised to include responsibilities that involve user support, marketing and technology adaptations that improve user experience. Table 6.1 lists a sample of librarian positions listed in July 2012 from the job list of the ALA. The job titles are increasingly non-traditional titles that require new skills for interacting with patrons, including such skills and terminology as: technology assistance, partnership, outreach, embedded librarianship, engagement, digital, assessment, social networking, data management and emerging technology.

New technology and increasing expectations of service from patrons and administrators of parent organizations have created an environment that challenges traditional approaches to service. "These technologies have also changed the role traditionally played by academic librarians (providing research information, collecting of stock, classifying,

Table 6.1   Job advertisements emphasizing engagement, outreach and technology skills

Extract	Job title
Passion for teaching and learning and for leveraging emerging technologies to *provide user-centered services*.	Education and Reference Librarian
Actively engages the community and *ensures service aligns with local residents' needs*; oversees collection; interacts with and provides direct library services to customers.	Branch Manager
Develop collaborative grant proposals to further research in library instructional design, provide leadership for additional collaborations, shape new directions for services that support student learning and faculty research and scholarship, serve as a *role model for outreach and campus engagement that expands connections and builds partnerships*.	Assistant Head of Scholarship and Education Services
Leads collection-based projects, the continuing transition to online journals and an aggressive movement to e-book acquisitions, including a *demand driven acquisitions model*.	Collection Development Librarian
Works with other librarians to determine appropriate content for digitization or licensing. Provides research services for access to all collections, as part of a team. Also works closely with other groups to provide content and access to content. *Acts as a liaison with other library departments to ensure acquisitions, cataloging and collection management functions match service needs.*	Collections and Outreach Librarian
Participates in community events and works with community groups in order to promote the library and its initiatives; must have a definite commitment to public service within an urban library setting. Persons who speak Spanish or other foreign languages are encouraged to apply. Experience working with diverse populations is a plus.	Assistant Branch Manager
Candidates should have experience identifying, implementing and assessing technologies to support the curricula in the schools for cognitive and natural science; *an imaginative approach to outreach to students and faculty*; and an understanding of the rapidly changing model of scholarly communication in the sciences and a commitment to fostering ways for students to participate. Candidates should be experienced with *embedded librarianship and other new models of reference services, and demonstrate ability to use technology to connect users with library resources*, including web design, social media, etc.	Interdisciplinary Science Librarian

Table 6.1   Job advertisements emphasizing engagement, outreach and technology skills (cont'd)

Description	Title
They have a key role as *general communication links between the library and the academic departments to which they are assigned through the library's liaison program*. They are often called upon as a resource to assist other librarians engaged in the library's instruction, *outreach, and scholarly communications efforts* (including digital initiatives). They are expected to develop expertise in emerging technologies and lead and/or participate in innovative library projects.	Chief Bibliographer for the Humanities
Responsible for envisioning the information architecture, *coordinating user experience and evaluation activities, and* collaborating on the implementation of the web technology for the libraries' web presence.	Digital Access Librarian
Ensure technical access to the library's electronic resources and services, facilitate the integration of library resources into the college's teaching and learning environment, *and develop and maintain a statistical dashboard to support the library's continuous assessment/continuous improvement environment.*	Electronic Services Librarian
Opportunity to evaluate and improve search engine results for one of the world's largest Internet search engine companies.	Search Engine Evaluator
Increase the library's ability to collect, preserve and provide access to scientific data, and will act as a resource for students and faculty grappling with issues of data curation, digital methods for scientific research, and emerging digital resources; contribute to the development of data management plans for funded projects, and will assist in data extraction, reporting and monitoring compliance with established data management protocols; contribute to the Digital Repository by helping to develop the requirements and work flows necessary to support research; *by advising teaching faculty on the management of data and providing technical support for use of analytical tools; and in serving as an agent between researchers and the library's repository.*	Scientific Data Curator
Responsible for enhancing the functionality and effectiveness of the library website, overseeing content development and design. Coordinates access to web content and virtual services across all library departments. Creates modules on virtual technologies and participates in delivery of library services. *Engages in usability testing and other assessments of web-based services; experience in assisting users with online resources; background in developing database-driven dynamic websites.*	Virtual Services Librarian

Envision and implement the library's E-Science initiatives and serve as faculty liaison for the new institutional repository. Reporting to the head of the Reference Unit, the E-Science librarian will *provide research assistance, instruction, collection management and outreach services for students, faculty and staff in the physical and biological sciences.*	E-Science Librarian
Support library software serving the member libraries of the Consortium in support of Digital Collections and other services, work with management and staff, as well as *with member library staff to plan and implement new services, to develop and present continuing education programs, to organize consortia meetings and to coordinate problem analysis and resolution.*	Library Services Coordinator
Management, coordination and quality assurance *of cataloging, metadata systems and materials processing for books and other formats;* must participate in the library instruction and academic liaison programs, provide reference assistance and research advising, and meet departmental faculty standards.	Coordinator of Cataloging and Metadata Services
Creative, forward-thinking, experienced and *user-focused individual* to be the primary technology architect and planner for the library. The individual will have direct supervisory responsibility for three areas: Application Services and Design, Discovery Services and IT Operations	Assistant Director of Library Technology

Source: Extracts from job advertisements for the 21st Century Librarian: *http://joblist.ala.org/July2012.*

archiving and preserving documents) and proposed new ones for them as consultants, mediators between information creators and students, suppliers of international databases and structures, assistants in publishing, and educators helping users become information literate" (Pupeliene, 2011: 1).

One of the themes in these descriptions is the need for the librarian to be an advocate for the library through engagement with patrons. Every patron encounter with a librarian is an encounter with the library. When the experience is bad, the library is perceived as bad, when the experience is good, the library is perceived as good. The library is being judged through the eyes of the user and their experience of it. Creating a good user experience requires a climate in which assessment and performance measurement become ingrained in everyday activities. Librarians should look for opportunities to measure their activity and document the "return on investment" that comes from being engaged with patrons. Advocacy, assessment and marketing are tools for improving and expanding the user experience, which is at the heart of patron centered libraries.

There used to be a librarian for that at *News of the World*

A 2008 article in *Library & Information Update* reported that James Murdoch was eliminating most of the library positions in the News International research library in efforts to save money by transferring research activity from library staff to reporters. One of the library staff members was quoted as saying: "the decision suggests that News

International newspapers the *Sun* and *News of the World*, the main users of the library, don't particularly care about accuracy – or litigation" (Newspapers, 2008: 5). In July 2011, the *News of the World* (NOTW) was closed down – despite a large circulation – because of a scandal involving unethical news gathering practices.

Although the problems at NOTW – which involved phone hacking – started before the research library reductions, there is little doubt that staff cutbacks in the library reflect an organizational climate that undercuts research. In a world of information glut it is easy to lose sight of the importance of critical thinking and ethical behavior. The case of NOTW demonstrates the risks of ignoring thoughtful research and social values. It highlights the hard work ahead for library advocates, because librarians are not advocates for collections but for library users, and all that the library represents: critical thinking, lifelong learning, access to information, research methodology, information literacy and the ethics of scholarship.

Although there are challenges for those entering the library profession, this is also an exciting time to be an information professional, and the opportunities are as great as the challenges. The traditional responsibilities of referencing, cataloging and collection development are being replaced by more dynamic roles that center on the user experience and include marketing and advocacy.

Training in marketing is available for librarians through a variety of sources. The Public Library Association offers a free six-week online course in advocacy, Turning the Page (*http://www.ala.org/pla/education/turningthepage*). The ALA also has an extensive website on advocacy and legislation (*http://www.ala.org/advocacy/advleg/*). Other public awareness information includes Geek the Library (*http://get.geekthelibrary.org/*), Edge Benchmarks Initiative (*http://www.libraryedge.org/*) and Impact Survey (*http://impactsurvey.org/advocacy*). The last two sites cross the line between assessment and marketing by providing tools for assessment, and promotion ideas for reporting impact. The Edge Benchmarks Initiative was developed to measure public libraries in three areas: community value, engagement of the community and decision makers, and organizational management. Impact Survey has a survey instrument with training videos and documents that assist public librarians in communicating the survey results along with the impact value for the library.

Advocacy and marketing

Advocacy and marketing share characteristics that include: embracing the mission of the library, being enthusiastic about the offerings in the library, and having pride in being part of the library. Robinson (2012: 5) suggests that librarians who are developing marketing plans should adapt Peter Drucker's five questions:

1. What is our business?
2. Who is the customer?
3. What is value to the customer?
4. What will our business be?
5. What should it be?

This is a good starting point for the development of a marketing philosophy which can guide daily activities. The goal of marketing in libraries is not to "sell" the library per se but to position the library as an intellectual center for community activity. Marketing is not a series of flashy brochures but an ongoing conversation that is targeted towards the immediate needs of users. It can be accomplished with formal and informal conversations, blogs, Facebook profiles, or other means, anything that demonstrates the ability of the library to meet the immediate needs of the user.

If making connections with users is the goal of marketing, for public libraries, then, programs are one strategy that contributes to that end. Programs that involve the community on many levels will attract the most attention. Sze's "Taking ideas to the next level" (2012) lists ideas that engage both library users and the community in library activities of current interest. Poudre River Public Library took a theme from the ALA's reading day and combined it with a popular flash mob event. Palmyra Public Library worked with local churches to host an after-school youth center. Half Hollow Hills Community Library combined a book discussion group with a television show for a group discussion. Farmington Public Library worked with a local movie theater on a food drive called "Hunger is not a game." Salem-South Lyon District Library partnered with TipTop Entertainment to present an interactive program based on the sinking of the RMS *Titanic.* Jacksonville Public Library held a book drive with Feld Entertainment to make sure that *no book is left behind.*

Each of these events demonstrates a connection with the local community that builds on a headline, and draws on the enthusiasm already present in the community. Dougherty (2011) reported on advocacy lessons learned from the 1991 Rally for America's Libraries. These lessons included: explain how libraries serve; media coverage can help tell the story; criticism will happen; and keep the message positive and unified. It is important to try different approaches, to identify what works and to share that information with other libraries so that they can repeat the successes.

Memorable brand names

The library website is a collection of resources and services connected through the library's main page. These services are like a constellation among the universe of information sources, and branding is one of the tools that will keep the constellation recognizable. Kotler and Lee (2008: 131) identified six characteristics of a brand:

1. Establish the brand's purpose for your organization.
2. Identify target audiences for the brand.
3. Articulate your desired brand identity.
4. Craft the brand promise.
5. Determine the brand's position relative to the competition.
6. Select brand elements.

Brand elements include anything associated with the name, including colors and graphics. To be successful a brand must be used consistently across all distribution channels. Inconsistent usage leads to confusion and reduces the effectiveness of a brand.

Studies show that young people pay particular attention to brands in their information seeking behavior, and brand recognition helps them decide credibility (Hargittai et al., 2010). It is important to remember that brands are for patrons, not for library staff. Sometimes it can be difficult for staff to agree on a name for a library product or service, but once a name is picked it should be kept. Just because it seems tired or old-school to the staff doesn't mean it isn't enduring to patrons who will continue to ask for it by the old name. However, if there is a substantial change to the product, a name change may be required to grab the attention of patrons. Only change a brand if something substantial has happened to make the new name meaningful.

Content marketing

Content marketing is a concept that has been used in libraries for many years. It is an umbrella term that includes pathfinders, videos, tutorials and, more recently, LibGuides (*http://libguides.com/community.php?m=i&ref=libguides. com*). These are the means by which librarians tell the story of library services. Librarians could take some lessons from commercial marketing. Pulizzi (2012: 116–23) identified six characteristics or behaviors of great marketers:

1. Focused, educational content.
2. Opening up new content/media markets.
3. Chief storyteller.
4. Leveraging employees in content creation.
5. Removing the brand from the story.
6. Building a community by leveraging outside experts.

Focused, educational content is traditionally created by librarians for the purpose of instruction. It is directed to specific patrons and provides limited information so that the message doesn't get lost. Target resource guides for a specific audience; for example, faculty and undergraduates have different needs and require different approaches. Content that stresses the resource over the needs of the users will dilute the impact and will not be as effective as content developed for specific users.

New resources or changes to resources present a new opportunity for branding that is compelling to patrons. For example, when many libraries began launching discovery tools that searched across different resources including the online catalog, they needed a new name for the old online catalog that would differentiate it from the new tool. The name *classic catalog* caught on and many libraries are now using that brand name for their old catalog.

The chief storyteller, or communications coordinator, is a new position in many libraries and is responsible for managing the communications being delivered through the various channels. The story is a way of describing the benefits patrons receive from using the library. It is a personal approach to marketing that emphasizes the user experience. Part of a chief storyteller's job is educating staff on the principles of marketing, and assisting librarians with the creation and review of library guides. Communication librarians promote content that will engage users, and encourage staff to create the content that "tells the story of the library" and tells how the library meets the needs of the users every day.

Removing the brand from the story is a way to bypass stereotypes of the library by separating the library brand from the content. This technique attracts patrons who normally avoid the library because of preconceived ideas that discourage them from using libraries. Promoting Google Scholar as a discovery tool for researchers, while supporting it through Google preferences and resolver services, is an example of removing the brand. Patrons use a familiar tool, Google Scholar, but benefit from library subscriptions.

However, it is important for libraries not to remove their brand completely because by doing so they risk losing recognition. Databases and full-text resources must have library identification so that patrons understand that the resource is being provided by the library.

Few libraries have the funds to outsource marketing to commercial companies but they do have other resources they can draw upon from their community of patrons. Academic libraries have the advantage of business and advertising programs that could assist with content creation. Public and school libraries can draw on young people in the community through contests. Local media businesses may also be willing to assist with advertising for local programs.

Message in a bottle

Library guides that are poorly constructed are like a message in a bottle; thrown out on the web, they float in a sea of information in the hope that someone will discover them and find them useful. Content that targets a particular group, written in a language that will appeal to that group and delivered through familiar sources, is more likely to get used. Short is better than long. Reinforcing the benefits of using the content will draw in the reader; for example, a user guide entitled "How to write a successful paper in five hours" will appeal to busy students, whereas one entitled "How to use database X" could be overlooked.

Marketing through social media

Social networking sites can serve as a foundation for a marketing campaign. Most libraries are attempting to use Facebook as a marketing tool but not all are effective. Jacobson (2011) conducted a study of library Facebook pages but found it difficult to select candidates for the study because many sites hadn't been updated in six months, and, among the sites studied, many lacked evidence of engagement from fans. If a library has a Facebook page or any other media site that can't be maintained it should be removed. For libraries with the level of staffing necessary to manage a site, social media has much potential for creating opportunities for patron engagement.

As of June 2012, the Library of Congress Facebook page (*http://www.facebook.com/libraryofcongress/likes*) lists 70,114 "likes," 1945 "talking about this" and 8726 "were here" statistics. When a Facebook user looks at the page it lists all of that Facebook user's friends that have liked that page. On Twitter, the Library of Congress (*https://twitter.com/#!/librarycongress*) has over 390,000 users. The numbers are similar for the British Library (*https://twitter.com/#!/britishlibrary*) which has nearly 300,000 followers with 2432 tweets (June 2012) and a Facebook page (*http://www.facebook.com/britishlibrary*) with 48,675 "likes," 1414 "talking about this" and 16,490 "were here." Most libraries will not come close to these numbers, but a coordinated program using social media can increase participation in library programs and services, and, more importantly, build a loyal following of supporters.

All social media activity should direct users through the library website and not launch patrons to sites outside the library. When a link goes to a library resource, that resource should have identifiable branding so that users understand it is part of the library system. Facebook and blog pages should be regularly updated; there should be no reason to land on a page with the same information as appeared on it a week or a month ago. There is much competition for people's attention so information must be useful or interesting. Libraries with lively sites and interesting content are most likely to build engaged followings.

Marketing ideas

Marketing ideas can begin as a "brainstorming" session with staff, volunteers or patrons discussing the following open-ended questions:

1. What do people want? What are the outcomes they want to see in their lives?
2. How can we help them achieve this – where does the library fit into their goals and hopes for a better future?
3. How do librarians reach people, even those people who are not using the library?

These questions may seem personal, but information needs are personal, and when librarians work with patrons from their own perspective, and not the patron's, they miss the opportunity to create a partnership that will bring that patron to the library.

What follows is a list of sample marketing campaigns or ideas, not all will apply to all types of libraries but they may generate other ideas.

Augmented services

These are additional features which add something the patron didn't expect, maybe even a surprise. They can be added services or limited-time offers that target specific audiences. Added services are privileges that a select group receives, or customized services like saved searches and alerts of resources that match their profile. Limited-time offers include amnesty days for fines, free coffee or donuts during finals, stickers for reading books, and other incentives and rewards.

Banners/flyers/bookmarks

Banners or flyers or bookmarks which highlight library resources or services that will resonate with patrons can be beneficial advertising. Timing is critical for this type of marketing, and it should be used when people are engaged with the supported activity. Examples include: advertising library help when term papers are due; extended building hours before finals; assistance with data management plans advertised before grant deadlines; after-school programs that coordinate with school terms and classroom activities; and special programs that supplement or coordinate with local events.

Community activities

These provide the opportunity to highlight connections with the community. Librarians can provide awards, space or incentives for activities. Providing a space for a local group activity can be a way to introduce people to the services and resources in the library. Providing background reading and book displays is another way to support local groups and their events.

Fairs and book sales

Fairs and book sales which attract volunteers and patrons can also include kiosks or signs with library "ads" that inform visitors about services and resources, and introduce facts that demonstrate the value of the library. This is an opportunity for young people to create posters about the library and what it means to them; add a local celebrity who can serve as a judge and the crowd will get larger. Booths can be a useful way to attract people to a library display. They should be eye-catching, they should have clever items that visitors can take away to remind them of the library, and they should include an activity that will entertain and instruct.

Holiday celebrations

These can draw patrons into the library for information and entertainment. For example, staff can dress in costumes for Halloween, with a trick or treat at the reference desk to introduce patrons to reference services; if the patron asks a question the librarian can't answer, they get a treat.

Library stories

Library stories contributed by patrons on the library Facebook page, or through Twitter, describing their experiences when visiting the library are a form of word-of-mouth marketing that can be a powerful influence. Awards could be offered for the best story, or incentives for the xth numbered contribution. These stories can be re-purposed for other venues including local newspapers, billboards and tabletop displays.

Monitor media sites for criticism

Monitor media sites for criticism and respond with information that addresses the issue in a positive way. This is something that commercial sites do all the time and it helps to counteract a bad review that might prevent other sales. It also sends a positive message that someone cares about the user experience.

New and emerging technology

This provides opportunities for engaging library patrons. Develop a mobile app for the library, or develop a contest like that run by the British Library during the 2012 Olympics in London. The web-based "race for knowledge" challenge incorporated information about the library into the game, and included a survey to gather information about library use. Twitter and Facebook were used to advertise the game and garner more players.

Surveys

These can provide marketing opportunities even when the purpose of the survey is to discover why people aren't using the library. Go to where people hang out and have them complete a survey on why they don't use the library. The information gathered can reveal new insights that can be turned into action items. This also provides an opportunity to discuss how the library might be different to people's perception of it, which opens up the possibility of recruiting new patrons.

Tabletop brochures

When distributed in the library seating areas, these are another way to grab patrons' attention and spotlight services or resources. Check with local restaurants for the possibility of using their tables as well.

Video displays

Video displays that catch a patron's eye are another good advertising trick. Elevators and other places where people tend to congregate are possible locations for library information; anywhere people spend enough time to absorb the information. Avoid service points like reference and circulation desks because people shouldn't be encouraged to linger there long enough to read the screen. It sends the unfortunate message: "look at this while you wait."

Sponsoring staff

Sponsor staff members in local charity events. This helps to build a community within the library and increases connections with the local community.

Reaching politicians

Many library organizations support efforts to lobby national and state legislators, efforts in which library staff can participate as long as they follow policies about employee involvement in political activities. For publically funded libraries, there are rules that may prohibit some activity during work time or that may prohibit all activity based on the position. The ALA (*http://www.ala.org/offices/cro/ getinvolved/alachaptersfaq*) provides information on advocacy for local chapters that includes tracking state and federal legislation, and includes information on marketing activities for libraries.

When developing grass-roots campaigns to reach stakeholders, keep the message simple and clear but avoid template letters that lack personal context. Voters can be influential, and library users who are passionate about the library are the best advocates. Messages can be delivered in a variety of formats that match the comfort level of patrons.

These include conventional mail, e-mail, phone calls and petitions, which can be paper or online. Change.org (*http:// www.change.org/*) and iPetitions (*http://www.ipetitions. com/*), among other sites, offer free online petitions.

Connecting advocacy, marketing and assessment

Why is it important for librarians to incorporate advocacy into their daily interactions with patrons? "It is often assumed that faculty, students, staff, administrators, and others associated with institutions of higher education understand the inherent value of the academic library's services and resources, yet recent trends of diminishing reference transactions, declining gate counts, and the competition from the web for ubiquitous access to information may suggest otherwise" (Welburn et al., 2010: 92). This statement applies equally to school, public and special libraries. Gate counts and usage reports are a barometer of support for the library, and should be monitored for trends that will support further action to improve library use. Every staff member should understand the connection between library use, advocacy, marketing and support for the library.

Research conducted by Singh (2009) points to a positive relationship between the attitudes of librarians towards marketing and their behavior; so managers need to establish a culture in which marketing is valued. Library managers can encourage positive attitudes about marketing through training and marketing planning that involves all staff. Providing information about the library and the impact the library has on patrons will give librarians "talking points" and instill a sense of belonging and pride in the achievements of their organization. Promoting the strengths of the organization is always a good practice, especially when supporting data validates the strengths that librarians are marketing.

7

Metrics for decisions

Abstract: The purpose of assessment is to measure the impact of library services on the user experience. National standards are evolving to include measures of library effectiveness. Local assessment methodology includes identifying goals, actions and methods to evaluate the success of actions. There are several techniques to evaluate print and digital collections, including: raw use, density use, cost per use, institutional cost ratio, simplified Palmour method, and bibliometrics. Digital collections use data provided by vendors, and many are using standards like COUNTER and SUSHI to make reports more consistent. Google Analytics and Google Alerts are also tools for collecting information that can be used to analyze electronic usage and library services. Usability studies are another method for sampling patron use of resources and they provide detailed information from the perspective of the end-user. Social media, surveys and focus groups are additional methods for gathering information on the patron's experience. Libraries have borrowed ROI techniques from the commercial sector to evaluate services. Impact studies are another way to collect data and identify areas where the library needs to improve the patron's experience.

Key words: assessment, customer service excellence, LibQUAL+®, bibliometrics, digital assessment, COUNTER, Google Analytics, Google Alerts, usability studies, social media, statistics, ROI, impact studies, balanced scorecard.

"We live in a intersecting web of communities, and the work that we do as librarians, when we are at our best, has a positive rippling effect on all of them" (Plutchak, 2012: 12). In an age of information overload every librarian must be an advocate. Fewer and fewer librarians will spend their entire lives at one institution and the ability to demonstrate effectiveness through assessment is an important skill for professionals in every type of library. The goal of all assessment activities is to measure the impact the librarian and library services have on the community served. Administrators are increasingly looking for ways to show that libraries are making a difference to the lives of patrons. Assessment, along with marketing and advocacy, must be a part of the culture of the library and must be integrated into activities.

Collecting quantitative metrics on who the library's users are, where they come from, what their needs are, and what they want to accomplish, combined with qualitative metrics on how much time they are taking for research, whether they are satisfied, and whether they would recommend the library's site, leads to a more complete picture on user needs (Pagano, 2009). These statistics form part of an ongoing process for assessment that develops a culture in which metrics inform decisions on services and collections, and provides important information for advocacy and marketing. It can be difficult to persuade a library to focus on change; metrics assist this transformation process by highlighting changes in user needs and by highlighting expectations that will help convince doubters about the need for change.

However, metrics alone will not make change successful; marketing and advocacy are also important. When the Bill & Melinda Gates Foundation provided support for increasing computer access in the Global Libraries Initiative in five countries (Botswana, Chile, Latvia, Lithuania and Poland), it was clear that an advocacy program would be needed to continue funding after the grant ended. This required a marketing program which included reporting on the impact of improved computer access. The reports included traditional reporting of data that demonstrated increased use of computers and the Internet, as well as non-traditional approaches including desk calendars and video stories (*http://www.youtube.com/tresaistevadels*) (Sawaya et al., 2011). The marketing campaigns undertaken in these countries demonstrate the value of combining assessment and advocacy to influence funding agencies.

Regional and national trends for measuring library performance

Libraries and administrators have developed standards for measuring library performance. The ARL website (*http://www.ala.org/acrl/standards/*) has a list of standards that apply to US academic libraries. In addition, the ALA (*http://www.ala.org/tools/guidelines/standardsguidelines/*) manages a comprehensive list of standards and guidelines for best practices for public, school, special and academic libraries. In the past, these standards focused on the size of the collection, items added, salary figures and expenditures. Increasingly, these standards are being revised to include measures that encompass the user experience.

The UK standard, the Customer Service Excellence (formerly called the Charter Mark), is being employed by libraries to improve service orientation (Broady-Preston and Lobo, 2011). Accreditation acknowledges improvements in patrons' experiences, and highlights the value of the service to stakeholders both inside and outside the library. "Recognizing the increasing symbiotic relationship with models and methodologies derived from services marketing, and employing these in measuring and demonstrating the complex constructs of value and impact in a library service environment may serve to strengthen performance measurement and evaluation in academic libraries" (ibid.: 133).

Standards that measure patron needs can also equalize differences between larger and smaller libraries, and between those with ample funding and those struggling with budget cuts, because they emphasize service rather than collection and budget size. Although qualitative measures of impact on users are more difficult to develop and implement, many libraries are developing methodologies for capturing this data.

The Inspiring Learning for All framework (*http://www. inspiringlearningforall.gov.uk/*), sponsored by the Museums, Libraries and Archives Council in the UK, provides a framework for developing learning-centered programs. It includes a checklist for identifying strengths and weaknesses so that libraries can develop new programs, or improve existing programs that contribute to a learning organization for both patrons and staff. The program advocates five areas that support general learning outcomes (GLO). These include:

1. knowledge and understanding
2. skills
3. attitudes and values
4. enjoyment, inspiration, creativity and activity
5. behavior and progression.

Libraries can build assessments around outcomes like GLO. Fodale and Bates (2011) conducted an impact study of a disadvantaged school in Ireland using the five areas of GLO. The survey included parents and staff, and provided evidence that library activities had a positive impact on the socio-economically disadvantaged children in the area by stimulating their desire to learn, read and spend time in the library.

LibQUAL+® (*http://www.libqual.org/home*) was designed by the ARL as a tool to assist libraries in evaluating the effectiveness of their services through user surveys. There are 22 standard survey questions, with five customizable local items on the long survey that measure user perceptions of service quality on three dimensions: efficacy of service, information control, and library as place. It has been used by libraries for a variety of purposes, including monitoring trends over time (Greenwood et al., 2011; Lane et al., 2012), measuring against accreditation standards (Lewis, 2011), and as a tool for identifying areas of improvement (Bower and Dennis, 2007). User perceptions change over time, which is a problem for academic libraries with large undergraduate populations, so tracking trends after graduation can be revealing. However, a better use for LibQUAL+® may be as a tool for assessing user satisfaction (Thompson et al., 2005) and developing action items for improving service areas.

The Lib-Value project (*http://libvalue.cci.utk.edu/*) is a project developing tools to demonstrate an ROI for academic libraries. "One of the central claims of Lib-Value is that the value of libraries cannot be measured, neither simply by raw usage statistics, nor by the financial drain that a library is on its parent institution. Value must be measured in a balanced fashion, and in support of the parent institution's more global strategic goals" (Fox, 2012: 9).

Local assessment methodology

Assessing the library in terms of collection development or service begins with the identification of what should be studied. This involves developing questions to be answered or goals to be achieved, which are worded in measurable terms. Goals will require action items designed to achieve the goal, and the action items become activities that are measured in the evaluation phase of the analysis. The balanced scorecard methodology was modified for libraries by Bielavitz (2010) into three factors:

- Strategy statement, objective, initiatives; one data collection point.

- Input measures; and three analysis measures.

- Output/lag measure, lead indicator and outcome measure. Output/lag refers to measures with quantifiable results. Lead indicators are signs that point to a cumulative forward movement leading to success. Outcome measures result in a behavioral change in the individuals participating.

All activities should result in one of the three measures. Adding data collection points or input measures creates a clear path from exploration, through implementation, to assessment. Some data will consist of numbers, but other qualitative metrics will require sampling or surveys. For example:

Strategy statement: Library use will improve student grades.

Objective: Identify impact of library use on students.

Initiative: Measure impact of library use on student grades?
   Input measure: collect information on use of the library through library records, collect information on grades through administration, and combine the two sources for analysis.
   Measure: determine correlation.
   Type of measure: outcome.

Strategy statement: Building counts are declining and increasing building use will demonstrate greater engagement with patrons.

Objective: Increase building traffic by 10 percent.

Initiative: Offer half-day workshop to help students write a paper from beginning to end.

    Input measure: number of students who attend.

    Measure: grades received.

    Type of measure: outcome.

Initiative: Scavenger hunt in the stacks using QR codes with prizes donated by local merchants.

    Input measure: number who begin exercise.

    Measure: number who complete hunt.

    Type of measure: Output/lag.

Initiative: Storytelling hour honoring local veterans, highlighting books written by veterans.

    Input measure: number of people who attend.

    Measure: number of books checked out. Publicity generated.

    Type of measure: lead indicator.

Initiative: Video challenge for teens, with prizes for the best video which is played on a local TV station.

    Input measure: number of participants.

    Measure: publicity garnered from local media channels.

    Type of measure: lead indicator.

Strategy statement: Due to inflation and no increase in budget it is necessary to reduce the materials budget by cancelling databases.

Objective: Determine the best method for identifying databases for cancellation that will have the least negative impact on users.

Initiative: Analyze both quantifiable and qualitative measures of database usage.

Input measure: examine database use counts, conduct survey of faculty, conduct focus groups with students and evaluate results.

Measure: lead indicator.

Strategy statement: Contribute to the university's goal of increasing research by partnering with faculty on data management plans on grant proposals.

Objective: Provide advice on data management plans.

Initiative: Determine the success rate for grants for which librarians assisted with data management plans.

Input measure: number of grants librarians worked on, and number that were successful.

Measure: percentage of successful grants.

Type of measure: lead indicator.

Note: in this example, it is impossible to state that a successful grant was directly related to the librarian's involvement, but it is an indicator that could be used for publicity about the program.

These examples demonstrate a disciplined approach to collecting metrics in order to assess programs properly. This approach can be used by any librarian for activities they conduct personally or in collaboration with others. When this approach is used systematically it becomes part of the library culture.

Libraries using the balanced scorecard approach will find it useful in aligning efforts with the institution's mission. Reid identifies six possible benefits to libraries using this method:

- Helps make the case for increased funding.
- Builds customer and stakeholder awareness and demonstrates accountability.
- Provides creative metrics to support the library's critical role within the university.
- Aids in assessment and accreditation.
- Encourages the use of internal controls to promote an ethical environment.
- Improves productivity.

(Reid, 2011: 90–1)

Assessment is one part of the planning process that the University of Texas (UT) is applying in order to create a process of continuous planning using the balanced scorecard methodology. "All participants in the process at UT are committed to providing staff a transparent accountability of the implementation of the strategic initiative recommendations" (Taylor and Heath, 2012: 433). The library evaluates objectives using the balanced scorecard three times a year to ensure that administrators and decision makers are informed about the impact of initiatives.

Collection assessment tools

Librarians are stewards of the library collection, which means making selection and withdrawal decisions. When decisions are made using collection policies using the "just in case" model they are based on the assumption that a library collection includes titles identified in a collection development policy to a specified level, which supports the mission of the institution. It doesn't matter if these titles are never used because they are collected so that they would be available "in case" someone, at some time, wants the title. The number of titles on the shelf is a source of pride for the library and the institution. Whether a library uses "just in case" or patron-initiated "just in time" collection development, librarians have an obligation to ensure that the collections are benefiting users. This is easier to accomplish when patrons are selecting the titles through a "just in time" method, but in both cases assessment though usage reports is important.

Collection usage can be analyzed using a variety of tools. Some libraries are developing their own tools for collecting data from their ILS (Hughes, 2012). This study collected circulation data using a structured query language (SQL) database and application to produce weekly reports by call number that identified trends in subject usage. Other libraries have vendor supplied reports for information on trends; for example, Innovative Interfaces provides Reporter (*http://www.iii.com/products/reporter.shtml*), which supplies trend, summary and cumulative reports, including a pre-populated ARL report.

To make these decisions, librarians are turning to analyzing collections using formulas that include criteria for use, and delivery factors. The particular tool or analysis method selected by a library should be considered in relation to the overall mission of the institution and the needs of the users.

Weeding print collections

Libraries need to make space for user activities and, increasingly, libraries are reducing the size of their collections by withdrawing titles, or moving them into remote storage. This can be one of the most difficult issues librarians face in their careers. Although remote storage frees shelf space in the library, it also eliminates the possibility of browsing, since most off-site storage facilities use formulas for compact shelving that make it impossible to browse a collection. Remote storage facilities store materials by size in order to maximize the amount of material that can be stored in a single container; containers are then located by a new storage number, not a call number. This process reduces some of the costs for maintaining a print collection but it doesn't eliminate all expenses because air handling, electricity, shelving, equipment, staffing and construction costs are still incurred. Most importantly, this process doesn't answer the question, "Why keep a copy no one reads?"

Librarians must be prepared to answer that question with data that demonstrates the best use of funds. All administrators are facing competition for limited funds, so without compelling evidence to allocate revenue on housing little-used library materials librarians will face a difficult challenge. Analyzing collection statistics will provide some information about checkouts, and measuring shelves or counting materials as they are re-shelved will also assist. Other factors include availability though ILL or digital copies, but some aspects are less easily measured and should be considered before removing a title from circulation.

Sometimes material would circulate if it was cataloged differently or moved to a branch library. Caution should be exercised before removing "classic" or rare titles in any field, and, when possible, staff should inspect volumes for signatures or other artifacts that might make a title valuable. Further, there may be local considerations for keeping some titles. In the end, the decision to weed may be more emotional or political, than logical.

Consortium repositories as alternatives to print weeding

Some libraries have sufficient resources to build their own storage facilities, but more money could be saved if several libraries cooperated on a single facility. There are two types of storage facilities: shared storage and collaborative storage. In a shared storage facility, each participating library contributes to the cost of building and managing the facility but there is no sharing of the collections. Each library continues to "own" what they store in the facility.

Collaborative facilities differ because the goal is to reduce duplication at both the facility and the library; title ownership can either be retained by the library or transferred to the facility. "A shared print agreement (also called 'print archives' or 'shared collection management') is a formal program in which multiple libraries coordinate long-term retention of print materials and related services by one or more participants to support preservation and allow space recovery among campus collections" (Kieft and Payne, 2012: 142). Transferring control of a collection to a consortium can be controversial for the library staff and stakeholders. Therefore, librarians must present evidence as to how the change would be beneficial to the institution, and as to how user needs will continue to be met. During this process, librarians must ensure that research will be supported, and ensure that unique or rare material will be retained.

Libraries in the US are beginning to form collaborative repositories to preserve print materials and reduce conservation expenses. The consortia described in Chapter 5 – Open Content Alliance, HathiTrust, Alliance for Information Science and Technology Innovation, Western Regional Storage Trust, LYRASIS, California Digital Library, Council on Library and Information Resources, and Taking Academic Law Libraries Online – are collaborative repositories. Another example of a cooperative repository is that of the Association of Southeastern Research Libraries (ASERL), which has developed a cooperative retention program for print journals. The challenges and opportunities of this developing program are described in a 2012 article by Bruxvoort et al. ASERL's cooperative journal retention policy outlines the decision-making process for governance, defines risks associated with the storage site (remote storage, secured stacks or open stacks) and confirms that ownership of the materials remains with participating libraries.

Analyzing print journals

There are several methods for analyzing the use of print journal collections. Analyzing print journals can be complicated because circulation statistics are likely to under-represent use. Journals are published with several variables; some titles are published with more frequency, some with more or fewer pages, and others with more or fewer articles. The library may have a longer run of a journal title making it harder to deselect. The prestige of a title can also influence the collection decision, as can where the title is indexed and online availability for full text. Evaluating by checkout alone may not be sufficient because libraries don't always circulate journals, and, when they do, patrons may only read a single

When collections are analyzed there are a variety of techniques available. Any method of analysis that involves ranking titles must account for local conditions as the criteria for ranking is determined. The mission of the institution and the needs of the community are of paramount importance in the decision. Depending on these local conditions there are several statistical methods to consider.

Raw use vs. density use

Two methods rank titles based on raw use or by density use, so librarians can make collection decisions based on title ranking. Raw-use ranking (RUR) is determined by linear feet of the title (bound and unbound). It is the total space required for a title if all items were on the shelf. Density-of-use ranking (DUR) takes the raw use number and divides it by the actual linear feet for what is on the shelf, accounting for items off the shelf.

A 1981 study by Mankin and Bastille indicated that the DUR analysis provides a different ranking of titles than RUR analysis. They further determined that there are benefits to collection decisions made with DUR calculations because the amount of linear space needed was smaller and the potential for disappointed users was less, making DUR a better analysis method.

Cost per use

Cost per use (CPU) formulas are probably the most commonly used method for rating the effectiveness of journal usage. The cost per use is determined by dividing the subscription plus management cost, by the total number of times a journal is used:

$$CPU = \frac{cost}{use}$$

Milne and Tiffany (1991a, 1991b) used a method of manually tagging titles to obtain a CPU figure that was used for a serial cancellation project. Their survey accounted for inaccuracies that naturally occur in a manual process by including an adjustment factor for under-reporting and for tracking the number of uses for journal issues during the period of the study, which formed the basis for an estimation of lifetime use. A similar methodology was repeated by Chzastowski at the University of Illinois at Urbana-Champaign, which included ILL usage and which concluded that 91 percent of the existing journals were used two or more times, 24 percent were used one or two times, and only three percent of the journals were unused (Chzastowski, 1991). In both cases the librarians were able to identify titles with usage rates that did not justify retention.

Many library systems with electronic resource management systems provide CPU data as part of a statistical package. These applications provide CPU statistics based on price information from order records and usage statistics provided by vendors.

CPU analysis as a decision tool works well for libraries with good document delivery systems, and discovery methods that can substitute for shelf browsing. It is rarely used as the sole determinant for canceling titles because of the need to take into account other factors including: the importance of a journal to the field of study, undocumented counts of article usage through library reserves or campus courseware systems that may skew counts, or availability in a nearby library; all of which may influence the final decision. As with any cancellation or subscription decision, it is important to consider the immediate needs of users as the major influencing factor in the process. Good communication leads to better understanding of the reasons behind collection decisions.

Institutional cost ratio

The institutional cost ration (ICR) introduced by Hunt (1990) provides a ratio for the cost of a journal subscription against the cost of obtaining articles through ILL. Hunt reported that the Biomedical Library at Lawrence Livermore National Laboratory cut subscription expenses by 40 percent with an eight percent loss of use. This formula has the following criteria:

U = annual use
P = subscription price
L = size of bound journal in linear feet
I = interlibrary loan cost per transaction
M = total cost for managing subscriptions divided by number of subscriptions
S = shelving costs per linear feet

$$ICR = (U * I) / (P + M + (L * S))$$

Chalmers Library model

The Chalmers Library model was proposed by Hasslöw and Sverrung in 1995 and served as the basis for analyzing the journal collection of the Chalmers University of Technology Library for serial cancellation. Their analysis, which involved ranking titles into subject areas representing nine schools, sorted on use from low to high, resulting in a ranking into two quartiles, first and third. The median was identified using the following formula:

First quartile $(n + 1) / 4$
Median $(n + 1) / 2$
Third $3(n + 1) / 4$

Titles in the third quartile represented the lesser used titles which were better candidates for cancelation. Hasslöw and

Sverrung used this data to explain the problem of serial pricing and the complicating effect that a currency change made by the Swedish Government had on the library budget. Their efforts resulted in a six percent budget adjustment with an additional 14 percent increase because of the currency change, plus a guarantee of 11 percent for price increases for the following year. Their combination of the two analysis methods led to a middle ground that impacted users the least.

Simplified Palmour method

Lawrence (1981) used another formula for identifying the cost for storage and weeding which considers the cost per circulation, the expected average number of years between circulation, the discount rate over a planning period, the annual cost for shelving, the cost for deselection and the direct cost per circulation:

U_t = total cost per circulation amortized over planning period t

Y = expected average number of years between circulations

r_t = net percent value factor for a discount rate r over useful life of the storage facility t

C_v = annual cost of shelving the volume

C_w = the one-time cost for deselection

C_u = direct cost per circulation

$$U_t = \frac{C_u r_t}{t} + \frac{C_w + C_v r_t}{t} Y$$

This model includes the cost of deselecting titles for weeding or moving to remote storage and a formula for calculating the value r_t from the interest rate and expected lifespan of a library storage facility. C_u is derived using the facility cost for construction and the reoccurring cost of maintenance to determine the cost of permanent retention. The cost of circulation is based on a formula derived from estimates of retrieval, transportation, shelving, delivery time and ILL costs, among other factors. Although this model includes several new factors, it may be useful for librarians who want to account for expenses incurred in weeding, retrieval for deselected items, future expenses and facility construction.

Bibliometrics: citation analysis and impact factors

Bibliometrics is a field of study that analyzes scholarly literature through citation analysis and content measurement. There is some debate over whether it is better to measure a journal using citation analysis or by impact factors, and there are a variety of ways to measure both. The impact factor was developed by Eugene Garfield, for the Institute for Scientific Information (ISI). ISI, which is now part of Thomson Reuters, provides impact factors for journals indexed in *Journal Citation Reports* (*JCR*). The impact factor for a journal in a specified year is calculated using a formula based on the number of times articles are cited in a date range divided by the total number of citable articles published in that same date range. So, if articles in journal A published between 2009 and 2012 were cited 2000 times in 2012, and there were a total of 4000 citable articles published between 2009 and 2012, the impact factor for journal A for the year 2012 would be .5:

$$\frac{2000}{4000} \quad \begin{array}{l}\text{article citations between 2009–12} \\ \text{total possible articles to cite 2009–12}\end{array}$$

Critics of the impact factor analysis argue that the impact factors in *JCR* are not sufficient indicators of journal quality

(Moed et al., 1999). There is evidence that impact factors may be more useful than citation analysis when evaluating journals with a shorter time lapse between citation counting and publication dates (Abramo et al., 2010). For the purposes of evaluating journal usage, a combination of methods may be more appropriate depending on the type of library and the purpose of the analysis.

Citation scoring method

This model evaluates journal titles based on a combination of citations and impact factors. This formula, proposed by Hye-Kyung Chung (2007), uses citation numbers rather than checkouts, downloads or shelving numbers. There are two use factors in this formula, the national citation score and the local citation score. The national citation score is derived from the impact factor listed in *JCR* for a particular journal divided by the impact factor of all the journals in the same category, and converted to a percentage for the adjusted impact factor. The local citation score is based on impact factors developed by the KDI School of Public Policy & Management in Seoul, Korea, and citations from faculty publications owned by the library that fell within the *JCR* categories. An adjusted local citation score is also calculated for each title. The two scores for each title are then divided by journal cost, which is derived from subscription price, and administrative expense, to provide two different CPU numbers. The national and local scores differed significantly, which highlights the need to consider citations from local researchers when using citations for impact studies.

Journal Usage Factor

The Journal Usage Factor, or Usage Factor (*http://www. uksg.org/usagefactors*), originally sponsored by USKG and now taken over by the COUNTER project, proposes the following formula:

$$JUF = \frac{\text{Total usage over period x of items published during period y}}{\text{Total articles published online during period y}}$$

Since this project is now headed by COUNTER, which is an accepted standard, it has the potential to become the standard for evaluating journal impact if it can be proven to be a statistically meaningful measure and is accepted by researchers, publishers, librarians and research institutions.

Eigenfactor

Another technique for measuring impact is Eigenfactors (*http://www.eigenfactor.org/*), developed primarily for science journals. The data used to analyze journals is derived from *JCR*, with the Article Influence score being calculated from citations over a five-year period. Unlike *JCR* it is freely available over the web.

MESUR: MEtrics from Scholarly Usage of Resources

Another free tool is the MESUR (MEtrics from Scholarly Usage of Resources) project (*http://www.mesur.org/services/motioncharts.html*) which can be used for analyzing journal impact. This impact analysis is based on data collected from citations of more than 100,000 serials from 1996–2006, and includes publisher provided COUNTER usage reports from worldwide institutions. Usage patterns are derived by analyzing logs and inferring relationships between journals based on navigation from one to another. Using this methodology, MESUR has created maps that portray the relationships between research disciplines.

Digital assessment

Analyzing digital content goes beyond looking at e-print usage to analyzing website usage. There is no single tool that will collect information about a library's entire digital footprint, and digital assessment requires a combination of quantitative and qualitative data collection.

Digital collection analysis

Vendors for electronic collections provide detailed statistical data in both raw and report formats that evaluate title usage over time. These statistics are usually downloaded from the vendors and count actual usage on several levels. They provide information on per title use for: the number of sessions or connections; the length of a session; the number of searches; the number of downloads or full-text retrievals; and the number of abstracts. Some provide statistics on customized tags that librarians add. Vendor reports may include statistics generated by web crawlers, search engines and aggregate searches so it is important to verify that computer generated activity has been scrubbed from the data before analysis.

By examining usage reports provided by vendors, librarians can identify trends in usage over time that evaluate publisher performance. Comparing e-book usage from two vendors, ebrary and eBook Collection from EBSCO NetLibrary (formerly), for the University of Nevada, Las Vegas, Tucker (2012) uncovered a significant difference in usage, and because the usage decreased over time this led him to question whether leasing might be more cost-effective than purchasing.

Counting Online Usage of NeTworked Electronic Resources (COUNTER)

COUNTER (*http://www.projectcounter.org/about.html*) is a standard which defines how statistics are reported for e-resources. It was created in 2002 and established Extensible Markup Language (XML) metadata for reporting metrics on journal usage. Release 1 of the COUNTER Code of Practice for Books and Reference Works was released in March 2006. Librarians compiling usage information on databases and full-text resources prefer COUNTER statistics to vendor-supplied statistics because of the uniform reporting specifications. There are also provisions in COUNTER for audits to ensure that COUNTER specifications are being followed. A COUNTER compliant report will include metrics on the number of searches, and downloads or views.

Although COUNTER is a step forward, problems have been identified by librarians. COUNTER was designed for text-based resources and lacks the ability to track the enhanced features of some resources, which means that COUNTER will not measure activity outside the COUNTER environment (Sugarman et al., 2011). Activity for non-text items including visual or auditory files that are manipulated, tagged or annotated by users are excluded from statistics. These activities are outside the scope of COUNTER so librarians seeking information on feature use of resources must look for the data using other tools.

When librarians are compiling reports using non-COUNTER statistics extra care should be taken to understand the methods used by the vendors. Vendors may report data using collection criteria that either are similar to COUNTER or are so different that when multiple vendors are compared the combined statistics are not valid.

Standardized Usage Statistics Harvesting Initiative (SUSHI)

SUSHI is part of the COUNTER initiative and defines the communication between library and vendor for automatic harvesting of usage data into a consolidated knowledge base that supports analytics. It reduces staff time on the manual importing and manipulating of data into reports. Most electronic resource management systems support SUSHI data harvesting. Both the library system and the vendor must support the same version of SUSHI, and configuration for the metadata is necessary for the data exchange. It is not always easy for librarians to find the correct information about SUSHI configuration (Pesch, 2011b) because the information can be hidden on vendor websites, and not all SUSHI providers are registered with the SUSHI Server Registry (*https://sites.google.com/site/sushiserverregistry/*).

Website analytics

Website tracking tools which identify traffic sources can provide interesting clues as to what brings people to the main web page or to a specific web page. Website analytics can also provide some insight into returning traffic. Google Analytics (*http://www.google.com/analytics*) is a free tool provided by Google which provides metrics on web page usage. After registering with Google, the librarian creates a profile for the sites to be tracked. After the profile is configured, a small snippet of code is added to the pages for tacking, which uses data stored in a cookie on the user's computer. Users who refuse to allow cookie tracking are not included in the reports.

Google Analytics provides information on the number of visitors or sessions (new and returning), referral sources, the types of devices people use, browsers, how long visitors stay, frequency, language, location (internal and external sources) and mobile devices. It also provides information on social networking sites. Google supports customization, allows librarians to segment traffic for further analysis by type, location, referral source and type of mobile device, and supports regular expressions for more detailed reports.

One trend to watch is visitor loyalty, which is evaluated by the *frequency and recency* factors. Another report, introduced in 2011, is the *engagement* report, which provides statistics on the number of visits and page views, how much time (in seconds) visitors spend on the site, the number of pages they view per visit, and the depth of that visit, giving clues as to why people come to the site. For example, a low page depth score, combined with few returning visits and a low number of page views would indicate a low number of repeat visitors who might be looking for something specific; whereas a high number of page views and return visits, combined with a higher page depth score would be indicative of someone doing more in-depth research. The bounce rate is not particularly useful for libraries because, often, when a person finds what they are looking for they leave the site to go to a resource.

When analyzing statistics for a particular resource, the time spent on a site can be a useful metric to determine the usefulness of the site. The greater the average time spent on a site, the more interest from the searcher; however, this metric is only useful for pages that are not set as a home page for browsers. If a page is set as the home page on library computers, every time the browser is launched that home page is loaded and counted as a site visit, even if the user immediately leaves that web page for another site, which exaggerates the page count. When this is the case, check the page depth report and the visitor flow report, which give better representations of site usage.

From this discussion it appears obvious that librarians need to understand the library website construction and usage patterns as well as Google Analytics. With this knowledge, Google Analytics can be used as a tool for evaluating particular activities; check the statistics before the activity and after to determine the impact of the change. Each analysis provides a piece of the larger puzzle, which in time begins to develop into a picture of website behavior.

Librarians use Google Alerts (*http://www.google.com/ alerts*) to receive e-mail messages with links when people add a comment to social networking sites that match their query. Librarians create queries which are automatically run against news sites, blogs, video sites, discussion sites, books, or all the previous types. Google Alerts is an easy way to monitor the web for comments about the library or a librarian.

Commercial services like Crazy Egg (*http://www.crazyegg. com/*) provide analytic options that include "heat maps" to identify most-used areas through a visual map. Adobe's SiteCatalyst (*http://www.adobe.com/products/sitecatalyst. html*) also provides analytics with custom reporting features.

Local web server logs

Server logs are another source of information on the use of a locally maintained server. These logs are generated by web servers, maintained by local IT staff and contain information on connections and click-throughs. Logs also include data from the headers that identify more information. A marketing campaign can be evaluated by creating a server alias for links on printed brochures – when people click through using that alias the click-through is counted, providing an easy way to distinguish traffic generated from the brochure. There are several free, open source applications including AWStats (*http://awstats.sourceforge.net/*), or commercial log analyzers that are useful in creating reports on web server logs.

Usability studies

Usability testing software is helpful in capturing the behavior of users as they attempt to use a website. Software that provides information on how the user is interpreting the website is more useful than analytics that show numbers for individual clicks. Librarians can borrow a trick from landscape designers who install sidewalks based on where they see people walking. Patterns of behavior for using a website can be analyzed to identify obscure labels, information that is difficult to find, and other navigation problems. For example, can patrons locate the input box to search for a book? Do they understand where to click to find a listing of available databases? Can they find the page with the circulation policies? This type of testing requires users to perform a specific task. The following list provides some examples of tasks that patrons regularly use:

- What is the library location for a book entitled *Gone with the Wind*?
- Look up an article on wind generation.
- What do you do if you lose your library card?
- Find the library opening hours.

- If you need help from a librarian, where you do go?
- Find an image of the state capitol.
- Where can you find an audio recording of a Mozart piece?
- Where do you go to check out a video camera?

There are several commercial products to assist in data analysis – these record user behavior as people complete assigned tasks and provide reports. Most of the products in Table 7.2 charge on a sliding scale based on the number of web pages to be evaluated. Morae and Silverback run on a

Table 7.2	Software for collecting and analyzing library website traffic

Software	URL	Cost	Features
Loop[11]	http://www.loop11.com	yes	Creates test; uses link; collects video behavior
Chalkmark	http://www.optimalworkshop.com/chalkmark.com	yes	Users design navigation
ethnio	http://ethn.io	free/yes	Locates users and collects data via GoToMeeting or Usabilla
Morae	http://www.techsmith.com/morae.html	yes	Audio/video recorder for capturing behavior
OpenHallway	http://www.openhallway.com	yes	Creates test; uses link to collect audio/video behavior
Silverback	http://silverbackapp.com	yes	Mac app captures audio/video behavior
UserTesting.com	http://www.usertesting.com/	yes	Identifies participants; video and summary report

local computer, while the remainder of the vendors are cloud-based services that store the data on their site.

Usability studies are frequently conducted in a laboratory setting where users are asked to perform a specific task, which is observed and frequently recorded for playback. This measurement includes asking the subject to talk through actions so that the reasoning behind those actions can be captured for analysis. Each activity is timed for later analysis to identify navigation or labeling problems. These studies can be conducted on live sites, prototypes that are not assessable to the public, or by using paper wireframes or schematics that simulate what a user might see on the screen.

The preparation for any usability study includes: identifying the tasks to be performed; identifying the target group for the testing; deciding what type of compensation will be provided (if any); recruiting monitors and observers; and conducting a test to identify potential problems. Volunteer subjects should sign consent agreements that disclose details of the test. During the test it is the responsibility of the observers to record all the necessary data. It may be useful to video the subjects to augment observations.

Usability testing that is outsourced to vendors can involve local patrons, or vendor-supplied "patrons" who perform the test. One vendor, UserTesting.com (*http://www.user testing.com/*), will take the user actions to be analyzed, identify participants that meet the library's requirements (gender, age, income, country and web expertise), video the test (with an option for real-time participation by the librarians) and submit the video with a summary of results to the library. Outsourcing can be a cost-effective alternative for librarians who lack the resources, or the time, to conduct their own studies.

There are a few considerations before contracting with a vendor for web analytics. Verify that the information a vendor will provide is better than what the library can get through a free tool such as Google Analytics. Determine whether the library can host a local solution or whether it requires a cloud-based solution. If the vendor is cloud based, ask about the privacy, security and ownership of the data. Identify the technology that will be used to capture the data; JavaScript and cookies will not work with all library users, so determine which means will provide the best data for the study. Understand how the data will be reported and what options exist for data export so that the librarian can do further analysis offline.

If a library doesn't have the budget to subscribe to one of these services another simple option is to link to a survey in library notices or e-mail correspondence. These surveys should be kept short, with the focus on outcomes or experiences. Consider conducting a pilot with a group of candid library patrons before launching any survey.

Library websites can be also be improved through collaboration with other units in the institution. Many librarians do not have experience or training in building websites so partnering with other units can provide that expertise, and is a channel for engaging the parent institution (Stephenson, 2012). The key to such relationships is the exchange of ideas in an open environment that allows everyone to learn from each other for the purpose of creating an interactive website that meets the needs of users.

Anthropological studies

A new trend in user studies involves hiring applied anthropologists to evaluate library use. Anthropologists undertake user studies using ethnographic research methods and can evaluate physical space and virtual presentations to improve the user experience based on observations, surveys and focus groups (Wu and Lanclos, 2011). The University of Rochester Library hired an applied anthropologist to study undergraduate behavior as it related to research practices (Carlson, 2007). The findings were used to improve library operations and marketing to students and helped librarians get a clearer understanding of students in order to better meet student needs.

Assessing social media

The impact of a social networking program can be measured in several ways. Has the program brought in new patrons? Is circulation increasing? Are building counts increasing? Who is connecting to the social media sites, and are they sharing library comments with others? Start by defining two or three main reasons for using social media. For example, to identify the impact of a Facebook listing of new titles, look for circulation statistics for the period the titles are being promoted.

Advertising the library's social sites through librarian word-of-mouth should result in more fans signing up on the site. However, the numbers shouldn't be the final proof of success; it is also important to evaluate behavior that is generated from the sites, and behavior can be measured through tracking. Re-tweets may indicate interest in a comment sent through Twitter. Click-throughs and time spent on a page are also good indicators of interest. The point of social networking is to generate interest, and targeting specific influential groups is a good way to generate conversations. Look for signs that something is going "viral," which means it is being talked about, re-tweeted, etc.

An easy way to determine the influence of a social network for a library is to advertise a service or benefit for a single day and see how many people take advantage of the offering. This provides information on the number of people who pay attention to the advertising, and the number of people they contact about the offering.

Incentive programs can build momentum for social media site activity. Foursquare (*https://foursquare.com/about/new?from=hp*) gives a library a virtual presence on the web where people can check in and leave comments. Users earn badges by checking in at locations and the person with the most check-ins becomes the mayor. Visitors can add tips to a location so librarians should add tips that will increase library usage, which of course can be counted as evidence of the effectiveness of Foursquare. Another way to use Foursquare is to provide incentives for check-ins by awarding prizes for specific activities, which will increase traffic to the library. A community or university with more than one library could use Foursquare to help familiarize the community with the different libraries and their offerings.

Library blogs should also be evaluated for effectiveness. There are web tools that estimate the value of blogs, including Blog Calculator.com (*http://www.blogcalculator.com/*) which displays a dollar amount based on the number of articles, visitors and other metrics. Klout (*http://klout.com/home*) is another tool for measuring influence. Klout provides a score for individuals, based on metrics gathered from social networks, which estimates the number of people influenced, the amount or degree of influence and the influence of personal networks.

AddThis (*http://www.addthis.com/*) is a toolbar that can be added to any web page, allowing information to be passed across to a social media site with a simple click of the mouse. Libraries are using this on bibliographic pages so that patrons can share the record number through their existing social media channels. AddThis provides reports on the number of shares and clicks resulting from shares for social media channels. It provides data on e-mail, G-mail, Twitter, Facebook, Delicious and Evernote, among other social media sites.

A disciplined approach to evaluating social media sites makes it possible to create measurable activities that will assist with marketing library services. By looking at social networking activity the librarian can identify what works and what doesn't. Each insight will improve social networking activities, which will build a stronger community of advocates.

Assessing services

Evaluating the impact of library activities can take many forms. The quality and quantity of personal contacts with patrons and donors can be a useful metric. Relationship building is an important aspect of all library jobs and it can be evaluated through formal means including surveys and forums, or through "stories" that come from either contacts or librarians. It can also be measured through collaborations where librarians contribute to the success of an endeavor.

Statistics are powerful when presented in a way that connects them with impact. The number of articles provided to a specific group, correlations between library usage and grade point averages or reading scores demonstrate impact.

Fortunately, technology provides enormous amounts of data that can be analyzed for trends that point to impact. In addition to raw data, surveys can also provide meaningful information and, when used in conjunction with data, create a compelling story about the value of the library.

Open-ended surveys will generate more ideas than single-response questions. When people are asked to pick numbers on a scale they may have difficulty measuring the differences. Text-based questions should concentrate on outcomes, not what people think they need. People frequently have trouble identifying what they would like, but have no trouble responding to questions about outcomes. Do not ask about the future, nor "what ifs," because most people can't answer questions about things that haven't occurred, or may just agree without giving the issue much thought. Here are some example questions you might consider:

- What would help you be successful in writing a paper?
- Why do you prefer other locations than the library for studying?
- Why do you buy e-books rather than checking them out from the library?
- What characteristic makes you want to go to a website?
- What characteristics at a service desk make you want to return?
- Why do you come to the library?

Focus groups provide opportunities for direct give and take; however, they can also degenerate into complaint sessions unless they are scripted. Start the meeting by explaining its purpose, with a description of the topic that includes what is under discussion. Do not let people immediately jump to solutions because that limits problem exploration. Listening is critical in forums and everyone should leave the session with a feeling that they were heard. Taking the time to document all comments whether or not they were germane to the discussion reinforces the importance of the discussion.

Social media can be used to solicit input from library patrons, but don't rely on library websites alone. Identify other channels where community members participate and post questions on these sites to get additional input from a wider community than fans and friends of the library.

Return on investment

Return on investment (ROI) is borrowed from the commercial sector to evaluate library services. In the business world, ROI is determined by taking the revenue and dividing it by the cost. For the nonprofit sector, sales are synonymous with desired behaviors. This involves measuring behavior before and after the change is made, or by comparing the behavior of patrons not exposed to the marketing with those exposed to the marketing. Data is collected in a variety of ways: surveys, counting activity and analyzing comments by patrons. Once the data is collected it can be compared against the cost for the service in order to determine the ROI.

Impact studies

Impact studies are part of a marketing plan and the results need wide distribution to be effective. In 2006, the Affiliate Assembly of the American Association of School Libraries surveyed library leaders in states where impact studies were conducted, in order to assess changes that had resulted from the studies. Kaplan (2010) reported that only 22 percent of the impact studies were given to teachers, 17 percent to administrators and only 17 percent to legislators. The survey further revealed that "there does not appear to be an overall effect on teacher or principal behavior toward school library media programs, nor was there any reported evidence of changes in teacher education programs or principal education programs to incorporate information about school library media programs into education curricula" (ibid.: 60). This demonstrates the importance of marketing assessment findings throughout an organization and to stakeholders for the library.

It has always been difficult to evaluate reference services. In a brief history of reference assessment, Logan remarked: "Reference assessment emerged as an exercise to maintain or improve the quality of service ... After many decades of defining, discussing, and experimenting, a universally accepted method of assessment does not exist" (Logan, 2009: 230). Counting reference questions, even when they are categorized, gives no indication of the importance of reference work, and with declining numbers in reference activity there are renewed efforts to evaluate the service.

Jacoby and O'Brien (2005: 328) approached this challenge by asking three simple questions:

1. Do undergraduate students perceive the reference staff as being friendly and approachable?
2. Do they learn something during the course of the reference interaction?
3. Do they feel more confident about their ability to independently find information they are seeking following reference interaction?

They adopted a survey methodology to gather the data for their analysis, and included an option for interviewing. Their results reveal an interesting mix of perceived improvement for locating information with continued confusion about the library: "figuring out how to move from a citation to a library catalog and then from a holding record to a physical item somewhere in the library system was a major challenge" (ibid.: 339).

Impact studies are enlightening, sometimes startling, but always informative. They can illuminate problem areas outside the original search topic, provide evidence of success or failure and suggest new areas for research. Qualitative research is time consuming, and direct research with human subjects must be carried out under proscribed conditions. However, the information gleaned will provide a wealth of information about how the library is being used by patrons, which is worth the extra time and effort.

Assessment is a tool to break old patterns, to remake libraries to improve the user experience. Data is evidence to help change libraries from places where users are trained to places where services are trained to help patrons. Caution must be exercised, however, because data can be used to make the case that users don't understand the library and need to be educated. This should never be the case; patrons know best what they need – the trick is finding the diamonds in the sand.

8

The extensible library

Abstract: A patron centered library is extensible; it remains flexible and reactive to user needs. Technology is a tool, not an end, so librarians explore new technology in a climate where experimentation is encouraged through sound management techniques. Access services, document delivery and ILL operations are being redesigned to improve the user experience. Print-on-demand is being used to meet user needs and provide new services. Reference services are undergoing changes as libraries examine the costs and benefits of the service as they impact users, which includes examining options for virtual reference. Technical services continue to evolve to manage digital information and repurpose data to improve user services. Security is an important feature for libraries that provide access to account information or practice e-commerce. SSL and proxies are important security applications that, when implemented across an institution, can improve the user experience. The catalog, database access, link resolvers, reference managers, Google Scholar and discovery tools improve the user experience and increase use of library resources. RFID, NFC and QR codes are being used to improve services and support mobile computing. The library website has the responsibility for bringing together all the resources and services of the library, and provides the welcome mat for patrons.

Key words: extensible library, sand box, project management, reference services, virtual reference, technical services, electronic resource management, link resolver, OpenURL, databases, discovery tools, single sign-on.

Libraries of the twenty-first century are advocates for the communities they support. The collection is no longer the center of activity because activity is focused on identifying and meeting user needs through engagement, assessment, advocacy and marketing. This chapter will look at technology, library services and organizational issues in the context of a patron centered library.

The extensible library

Extensible is a term in computer science that describes a programming language that expands the capabilities of the software code through the introduction of new routines that do not require the basic code to be rewritten, or change the inherent architecture of the language. One of the fundamental characteristics of extensible code is the ability to share new code with other programmers for new uses. An extensible library is a library that adapts to the changing needs of users and cooperates with other libraries in the development of services and collections. An extensible library can be stretched and reconfigured to create spaces that support the changing activities of users without compromising long-standing values.

The goal of the extensible library is to remove all barriers to information seeking. What are those barriers? Users cited the following in a 2002 report by OCLC:

- Inability to access databases remotely due to password and/or license restrictions.
- Difficulty searching and navigating within the library and its website.
- Costs of copying and printing at the library.

- Shortage of knowledgeable librarians.
- Lack of the customer orientation they have come to expect as consumers.

Librarians should discuss these barriers and ask themselves if any progress has been made since 2002. An extensible library addresses impediments as they arise and develops action plans to move forward to the next set of issues. Change is constant, and the failure to respond to changing expectations will result in a mismatch between the activities of the library and the needs of users.

An extensible library has a climate that encourages behavior that might be considered risky by challenging orthodox thinking about library services. Once the focus moves from the collection to improving the user experience, conventional ideas may become obstacles. Change is persistent and a library that can't adapt to change will face serious questions about relevancy from funding agencies sooner or later. The key to riding the wave of change is agility, and experimentation is the method for learning how to surf the big waves.

Bringing a sand box to the library

Librarians strive for stable and predictable systems. That was the reason librarians invented the classification and metadata standards that are in wide use around the world. It is why librarians came to be respected for their organizational skills. Technology has added something new to the mix. At first it was a welcome partner, and librarians made great strides in efficiencies and capabilities for sharing information, but change didn't end with the improvements everyone wanted, it has continued. Google and other commercial search engines became the preferred search engines for patrons, and technology is being introduced so quickly it is hard to keep up with patrons' expectations. For these reasons, libraries need to release some of the control that has made them successful and create a "sand box environment" where it is safe to experiment.

A sand box is the phrase used for a testing environment that is safe and allows for the possibility of failure. Not all projects will be successful, and open acknowledgement of that fact will assist with a climate that encourages exploration. A sand box includes the tools, resources and staffing support that are necessary to experiment and evaluate experiments. In larger libraries this will include programming support for application development. A process of incorporating user input into the testing environment is also an essential component.

Project management is a great tool for managing sand box experiments. Project management requires a deliberate process that includes three phases: exploration, trial and assessment. Even when an individual decides to experiment with a project, some preparation should go into the process to verify that the project manager has enough time and technical support to be successful, and to guide the exploration process through evaluation to implementation.

In the exploration phase, experimentation is necessary. During this phase, the librarians should identify staff members who can assist with technical support, others who are interested in the project and a process for obtaining patron input. At this point, it is important to facilitate ideas and suggestions because too much control at this early stage could result in a bias towards obstacles instead of possibilities. The object of the exploration phase is to identify a trial project. This includes a proposal that defines the scope and duration of the trial, defines the project leader, when and to whom the project will be reporting, the staff that will be involved, the target population served and measurements for evaluating the success of the trial. It should also include an estimate of time requirements and any necessary funding.

During the trial phase all participants carry out their identified roles. The project leader should remain flexible when problems occur and make any adjustments that seem prudent. Once the trial is complete, the measurements taken during the trial can be assembled and a report produced that will determine if continued development or implementation is merited.

Assessment for a library experiment must include collecting information from the patrons involved in the experiment. This can be done with surveys, one-on-one discussions, focus groups or other participation, but care must be taken to protect privacy. The final report should include an analysis of the assessment, lessons learned and recommendations for future action. Not all experiments will be implemented, but a carefully managed project will be successful because it will result in new information.

The extensible library is a changing library where experimentation is the norm. The locus of control is around the user experience and adherence to the core values of service, collaboration and quality, which will guide the practice and experimentation of librarians (see Figure 8.1).

Leveraging technology

Librarians should never become complacent when it comes to information technology. Here are some basic principles:

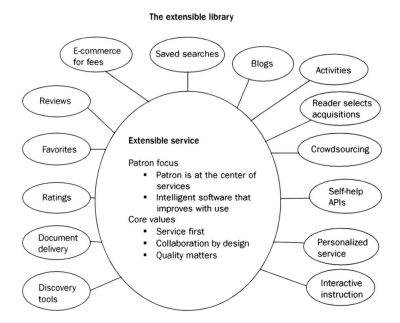

The extensible library

E-commerce for fees

Saved searches

Blogs

Activities

Reviews

Reader selects acquisitions

Favorites

Extensible service

Patron focus

Crowdsourcing

Ratings

- Patron is at the center of services
- Intelligent software that improves with use

Self-help APIs

Core values

Document delivery

- Service first
- Collaboration by design
- Quality matters

Personalized service

Discovery tools

Interactive instruction

Figure 8.1   The extensible library with a focus on service

- *Impact the institution*: never miss an opportunity to integrate library systems with systems in the parent organization. Integrated systems maintain visibility for the library, and make it harder to cut the library budget without harming the parent organization.

- *Impact library efficiencies*: never miss an opportunity to save workers' time with technology support. Any new enterprise system that enables staff to do their work more efficiently will save the institution money, and free staff for other responsibilities.

- *Impact the patron*: never miss an importunity to improve the user experience. Whether it is a seamless way to connect systems, equipment for checkout or mobile application development, any improvement in technology that will attract patrons and impact their lives is a plus.

- *Technology is the means to a goal not the goal itself*: don't believe that technology is *the* answer. Technology requires application and that application must fit the situation in a seamless manner. Technology that must be explained or forced into acceptance will not be successful.

Single sign-on and proxies

Authentication requirements are one of more frustrating aspects of using the library. Patrons frequently report difficulties logging-on to use library resources or accessing their records. Single sign-on is one way to reduce these frustrations. Libraries should work with their parent institution to implement a coordinated system for managing authentication across the institution. When this is accomplished, users have a single login and password that works across all the resources in the institution, reducing the need for users to remember separate logins and passwords and eliminating multiple login prompts as users pass between systems. Three common methods for single sign-on are Athens, Shibboleth and Central Authentication Service (CAS).

Athens (*http://www.openathens.net/*) is an access and identity management service for single sign-on from the UK that is used throughout the world. Shibboleth (*http://shibboleth.net/*) and CAS are other authentication methods for single sign-on to supply credentials that are passed from one system to another. These systems are supported by major database vendors, but, for smaller publishers, the library may need to use a proxy to authenticate users for access.

A proxy is an intermediate application that controls access to resources by first requiring a user to login into the proxy service, which connects to the requested resource. A client connects to the proxy server, requesting a resource or service from a different server, the proxy determines if the user has sufficient privileges for the resource, and, if so, connects the user.

Some proxy servers will hide the requesting client's Internet Protocol (IP) behind another URL so the destination host receives a different IP than is actually being used by the requestor. A rewrite proxy uses this technique because the destination hostname is rewritten, which may cause browsers to display warnings, even when the use is legitimate. Libraries using rewrite proxies that have these issues can eliminate many of these warnings by installing a Secure Sockets Layer (SSL) with Subject Alternate Name (SAN) certificates from SSL providers.

These SAN certificates are supplied by an SSL certificate provider that "vouches" for the authenticity of the certificate. The difference between a SAN certificate and the usual SSL certificate is that the SAN certificate will cover more than one hostname, while a single SSL certificate is authorized for one hostname. A SAN issued for the catalog that has alternate names listing library resources will allow the library catalog certificate to cover the other resources and eliminate browser certificate warnings. Even if a library doesn't use a proxy for resources it will need a certificate if the library does any e-commerce or provides account information.

SSLs are identified by a URL that starts "https," with the "s" signifying secure. All transmissions are encrypted and include a digital signature that binds an identity to a hostname to provide the higher-level security that e-commerce and authentication require. There are a variety of SSL certificates with different levels of security provided by third parties which must be trusted by browsers to be useful for libraries; otherwise, patrons will encounter warnings and other barriers that may cause patrons to avoid using library resources. Before purchasing a certificate, verify that the provider's certificates are trusted. A valid SSL certificate ensures that the patron's identify will be kept private and transmission will be encrypted.

Multiple authentication schemes require: individual troubleshooting for each authentication system, the collection of statistics from each source, and generally increased support requirements from library staff. Establishing Suggested Practices Regarding Single Sign-on, or ESPReSSO (*http://www.niso.org/publications/isq/2011/v23no1/ staines/*), is a NISO project to formulate best practices to standardize terminology and user interfaces for logon, and to facilitate user transparency for determining when and how a user is logged into a particular system. NISO is also working on problems that occur with cross authentication (multiple logins) between different authentication systems in federated searching.

RFID, NFC and QR codes

Libraries have been using barcodes for years as a means of managing inventories and quickly checking out material. Once a library collection is completely barcoded patrons can check out materials without the need for staff intervention. Radio-frequency identification (RFID) is more expensive but has additional features that speed up checkout and inventory processes. RFID uses wireless communication to transfer data from a tag attached to an item. These tags can be read several yards from the device so it isn't necessary to be within line of sight to read the code. A complete shelf can be read quickly without removing the books. There are two reasons why RFID hasn't been widely adopted: cost and standards. The cost for a RFID tag can be prohibitive for large collections, and the manual labor involved for encoding and labeling materials is a major barrier to adoption. However, for smaller libraries or new libraries RFID is more appealing and can save circulation staff time. Two new standards, ISO/IEC 18000-3 Mode 1 and ISO 28560-2, will promote the interoperability of codes between libraries, including fields that can be used to track interlibrary processing (Ayre, 2012).

Near field communication (NFC) is related to RFID. Like RFID, it transmits data via an embedded chip in a tag or sticker; however, the distance is reduced so the reader must touch the item containing the tag. The actual amount of data varies depending on the type of NFC tag used – different tags have different memory capacities. An NFC tag can store from 41 characters to 132 characters. This can be any information including URLs, which a mobile phone can read by touch. Not all mobile devices support NFC technology but there is a growing list of phone manufacturers incorporating the technology (*http://www.nfc-phones.org/*). Within libraries, NFC technology is a supplement to Quick Response (QR) codes and can be used in a similar fashion.

QR codes are two-dimensional codes that can be read through a digital camera using installed software. URLs and other information can be included in the code, which can contain up to 4296 alphanumeric characters. QR codes are being incorporated into librarians' business cards, stack directories (to help people find books) and publicity information. QR codes have been most popular in Japan, where they originated, but they are gaining in popularity in US libraries, where they are being used to link to web pages, blogs, Twitter pages, catalog searches, video tours and individual bibliographic records. Libraries experimenting with QR codes should consider using a QR code generator that tracts usage, or use Google Analytics.

Loughborough University Library used BeeTagg (*http://www. beetagg.com/en/*) for a QR study (Elmore and Stephens, 2012). They assessed QR codes that directed users to popular handouts and found that the QR quotes were used less often than expected (33 times). However, the timing of usage indicated that the codes were used in a "just-in-time" manner when the content was most relevant to the student's needs. Wilson (2012) conducted a statistical analysis of QR code use at the Kuhn Loeb Music Library at Harvard College Library and was disappointed with the low usage, reporting that the numbers were not due to a lack familiarity with the technology, but because students considered QR codes to be a marketing ploy.

Like any other service area, libraries need to introduce new services by highlighting the benefits of the service. Likewise, assessment is an important component to determine if a new service is successful, suggest areas for improvement, or determine when it is time to abandon a service. No technology is guaranteed to be successful; it must meet specific user needs, and over time it will be replaced with something new. It can be difficult identifying when it is time to replace old technology with something new. This requires an assessment of the new technology benefits against consideration of the possible harm that could be done to the existing user population that relies on the current system.

Access services: document delivery/ILL

As the importance of locally owned collections diminishes, access to material becomes important to support the user experience. Consortium agreements for ILLs are increasingly adding standards that embrace practices that require prompt service and a commitment to users (Mak, 2012). The lines between ILLs, circulation and acquisitions are becoming blurred as the emphasis is less on the type of activity and more on the act of supplying needed material to patrons (McHone-Chase, 2010). Workflows are also being re-engineered to expedite material handling by creating online workflows that trigger actions (Moreno, 2012).

Central Florida Libraries created a workflow between interlibrary, digital services and special collections for the purpose of creating a digital collection based on ILL requests (Shrauger and Dotson, 2010). Special collection material requested through ILL was digitized, which increased the library's fill rate. This content was also made available to the general public.

The IT departments in libraries are also impacted by the increasing dependence on technology for electronic requesting and delivery. IT departments are moving towards a service oriented architecture (SOA) model that makes it easier to interoperate applications. This is made possible when databases are directly exposed for queries and modifications through secure application programming interfaces (APIs). "Service oriented architecture assumes change will happen and designs for change at the outset" (Anthony, 2008: 244). With SOA, the service is a self-contained application that does not rely on other applications. It performs a single activity, which maximizes the reusability of code. The application can be reused for different resources and to make connections with other institutions through the Semantic Web.

The library experience for users can be improved by eliminating recalling items from patrons by using ILL to obtain a second copy of the requested item instead of recalling the original book. This has been shown to be a good way to introduce more people to ILL; it increases usage, satisfies the requesting patrons and avoids a conflict with the patron who already has the book (Dethloff, 2012).

Another change that has dramatically improved the user experience is unmediated requesting, which eliminates library staff as the middleman. Clicking on a request button makes the process easier and quicker than filling out a manual form. Ease of use encourages borrowing, and naturally results in increased ILL requests (Mak, 2012).

Patrons who use ILL services require fast delivery (Atwater-Singer, 2011), which can be facilitated through electronic delivery or e-mail. They also appreciate auto-complete forms that can be generated by passing information from one source to another, most commonly using OpenURL resolvers. The automatic renewal of borrowed books, e-mailing or conventional mailing of notices before fines begin accruing and e-commerce options are also conveniences that patrons appreciate.

Although technology is facilitating the ILL process it has also reduced the need for librarians to act as mediators. Their role has changed to focus on workflow and collaboration with other libraries. While some lament this change, others are excited by the possibilities for working with other libraries in a collaborative environment where collections are managed as resources for the benefit of all users.

From the RUSSA guidelines (Reference and User Services Association, 2012), the responsibilities of an ILL librarian include the following:

4.1. Have the ability to work collegially with other groups within and outside the library on issues that directly impact ILL and Doc Del services.

4.2. Be responsible for the fiscal management of the ILL/Doc Del budget, which includes but is not limited to shipping, copyright, borrowing/lending invoices, ILL fee management (IFM), capital equipment, and software costs.

4.3. Have statistical training sufficient to analyze statistical trends within interlibrary loan, document delivery, and shipping to improve overall patron services.

4.4. Possess the ability to evaluate and recommend consortia and commercial agreements.

(Ibid.: 382)

The emphasis here is on collaboration and assessment, reflecting the need for efficient and cost-effective services. The new ILL librarian runs a business center that operates in an efficient and cost-effective manner.

Copyright compliance requires workflow management and the comparison of expenses associated with using staff time for searching out the least expensive option as opposed to a quicker but more costly alternative. According to the Commission on New Technological Uses of Copyrighted Works (CONTU) guidelines, libraries can receive up to five articles published within the last five years from a journal under fair use as specified by US copyright law; payment is required for articles outside this exemption. Until recently there were few alternatives to paying the fee other than subscription, asking the publisher for permission or asking the author for a reprint (Tallman, 1979).

Today, many vendors are offering options to purchase an article on a pay-per-view basis and ILL services are using this to save money (Brown, 2012). Another option is to locate a public domain copy from an institutional repository that was deposited by the author. The final option may be to pay for access through the Copyright Clearance Center (*http://www.copyright.com/*).

Espresso for print-on-demand

The Espresso Book Machine (*http://ondemandbooks.com/*) is hardware that manufactures a paperback on demand from digital copy. The library can then sell the book or make it available for checkout, and orders can be placed online for later pick-up. Patrons and libraries can also upload files to produce their own books. Libraries are using these machines as a variation of patron initiated ordering, and some are even considering the sale of books as a revenue stream. The University of Michigan Library reported that "being able to assist campus departments, faculty, and students with printing special projects, books for classroom use, or general research material is exciting and gratifying, and the UM Library looks forward to continued development and expansion of its book-printing services" (Geitgey, 2011: 61).

Some librarians look at print-on-demand as a vestige of the past, and as more and more materials are being used in a digital format, why bother with print? There are several reasons why an Espresso machine appeals to libraries. Some patrons will use the machine for self-publishing, which is a revenue source for the library. Many patrons still prefer a paper copy of a work over a digital version so they can print a copy instead of reading the online version. Finally, there is another less obvious benefit – publicity. A machine that prints, binds and delivers a book in a few minutes attracts people to the library and impresses potential donors (Anderson, 2010).

Another use for print-on-demand is in scanning materials from special collections to make them available for purchase or loan instead of providing access to the materials. This is a conservation decision to prevent damage to rare materials. Using a Kirtas book scanner (*http://www.i2s-digibook.com/*) in combination with the Espresso machine libraries can scan and produce their own books in an efficient manner that minimizes handling and potential damage to materials through repeated use (Arlitsch, 2011).

Any library considering investing in a print-on-demand solution should first create a business plan. The start-up costs are considerable for both a quality scanner like Kirtas and the Espresso book production machine. Likewise, it would be prudent to analyze local circumstances before deciding to move ahead with what may be perceived as a high-risk venture (Chamberlain, 2012). The final decision will be determined by local circumstances; with the assessment of patron use of the service and publicity as two important factors in a successful implementation.

Reference services

Technology has changed reference activities in very dramatic ways. "The world of online searching in the 1970s and 1980s recognized a distinction between electronic reference and the print oriented reference desk. The expansion of CD-ROM products to include non-bibliographic works blurred the distinction between print and electronic reference" (Straw, 2001: 1). Today, print and offline reference collections are shrinking as a result of being replaced by web-based electronic resources.

The number and complexity of questions posed at reference desks are also declining as more patrons do their research off-campus and find their answers using online resources. After conducting an analysis of reference use at Stetson University, Ryan (2008) concluded that only 11 percent of the interactions required a professional's help, and 89 percent could be answered by trained non-librarians.

It is important to evaluate services in a quantitative manner to uncover the true cost of reference services, but it should not be the sole criteria. Data will point to changing trends in a service and alert librarians to re-evaluate those services. The needs of patrons change over time and a service that isn't cost-effective will starve resources from other areas that would better serve patrons. Data collection is the starting point for an open discussion among librarians about reference staffing levels, and, with additional qualitative measures of impact, will inform decisions about local service levels.

Some libraries have eliminated traditional reference services in favor of modified services that free librarians' time for more engagement with users (Schulte, 2011). When reference services are modified, or when the service desk is eliminated, libraries must identify ways to support users with reference questions. Different techniques have been used, and generally involve a combination of training paraprofessional staff to fill the gap, use of e-mail and help-desk technology. Improvements in communication technology have made it easier for librarians to work with patrons whether or not they come into the library.

Virtual reference services

Everyone is familiar with virtual reference; everyone has used Google (*http://www.google.com/*), Bing (*http://www.bing.com*), Answers (*http://www.answers.com/*), and many others. These services are available at the point of need, and answer questions on the spot. Many of these are thought of as search engines, but in fact they have become a source of information.

Libraries have moved into this space using many different types of technology. These services have been growing in popularity as remote use of library resources has increased. They include 24-hour chat using a consortia arrangement, e-mail and avatars or artificial intelligence (AI) for reference. Each type of service will appeal to different types of users so multiple services may be necessary to fulfill user needs.

The technologies in use include very basic systems such as text messaging, e-mail and online forms, to more sophisticated systems that include cooperatives for chat, avatars and automated chatbots. Librarians are not always comfortable with technology-based reference because of the lack of face-to-face clues. This may be why librarians believe that users are less satisfied with the experience; however, studies indicate that users are more satisfied than the librarians believe they are (Hansen et al., 2009).

When a library decides to introduce some type of virtual reference it is important to market the service. Effective placement and wording of links is important in order to attract users to the service (Mu et al., 2011). However, this alone will not be enough if a user experiences technical difficulties on the first attempt.

Services that require loading client software or that experience frequent outages should be replaced with technology that requires no additional software or plug-ins and is reliable. Another technical consideration is pop-up windows that may be hidden behind other windows, or prevented by the user's browser set-up, which interferes or causes confusion in a reference transaction. The ability to co-browse or push pages to the user's computer is a nice feature if it works reliably with the patron's computer and network.

Libraries may choose a commercial vendor such as QuestionPoint (*http://questionpoint.org/*), LivePerson (*http:// www.liveperson.com/*), LiveHelp (*http://livehelp.com/*),

LibraryH3lp (*http://libraryh3lp.com/*) or Provide Support (*http://www.providesupport.com/*). QuestionPoint includes an option for 24-hour chat using cooperatives (academic, public and Spanish language) manned by participating libraries from around the world.

Factors to consider when evaluating a help desk service include:

- reliability
- hours of availability
- access to transcripts and statistics for analysis and training
- simultaneous users (both staff and users)
- question queuing
- capability to forward questions
- interoperability with other services (e.g., widgets, course management system)
- cost
- web-based interface for patrons
- ability to share service among multiple libraries
- accessibility/accommodation for disabilities
- privacy for staff and users
- customization
- co-browsing/screen pushing
- language support
- user feedback support
- support for a knowledge base (optional).

The final criteria – support for a knowledge base – would seem an important feature to reduce duplication of information, to keep individuals current and to provide a consistent level of knowledge. However, a knowledge base must also have intuitive searching, be comprehensive, have a quick response time, and save time, or it will not be used (Ralph, 2009).

One issue that is of particular importance for public libraries concerns the dangers of chatting with strangers (Connaway et al., 2007). Although librarians follow policies about interacting with patrons, it is possible that parents will block children from using a library chat service as part of the general restrictions they use to protect their children from online predators.

Another criticism of virtual reference is the lack of user involvement in assessment, and too many service options that confuse patrons. In a survey of 46 international university libraries, Pinto and Manso concluded:

> virtual reference services in the university environment need to renew and evolve in line with the emerging technologies that allow a richer feedback from and more active participation of the user community; and secondly, the need to move towards a single point of access for all the products and features associated with this service, such as knowledge bases, book request, OPACs, thematic directories, and FAQs.
>
> (Pinto and Manso, 2012: 64)

Some libraries are concerned about opening their service beyond their local community because they could be overwhelmed with chat questions from non-library patrons. However, there is evidence to suggest that there are fewer chat requests than e-mail questions from non-affiliated patrons (Nolen et al., 2012). Thus, it may be better to include non-affiliates in order to increase transactions, which would offset the expenses that virtual reference entails, including: regular monitoring even when the question level is low, a commitment to pay ongoing vendor costs, and the designation of staff to train, manage and schedule librarians. Like many other service offerings, virtual reference should be available when patrons need the service; closed signs do not encourage patrons to return.

For libraries that do not want the expense of commercial products there are free alternatives; however, these lack many of the features of the vendor products. Instant messaging services are inexpensive: Pidgin (*http://pidgin. im/*), Trillian (*http://www.trillian.im/*) and AIM (*http://www. aim.com/*) are among the top competitors in this category. These are good applications for libraries to use when conducting a pilot to experiment with virtual reference to assess user interest. Ease of use, the relevancy of the answer, speed and reliability are important factors for patrons (Chang and Yang, 2012).

Some libraries are also experiencing with avatars through Second Life (*http://secondlife.com/*). Libraries with a presence in Second Life agree on the importance of selecting human-like avatars that represent the library (Mon, 2012). McMaster University Library (*http://world.secondlife.com/group/ 96d8fc9e-4377-7815-6216-825c0ba9c18b*) and McGill University Library (no longer active) are reporting mixed results. The high technical requirements, participation cost and staff time and training requirements are significant challenges (Buckland and Godfrey, 2010). Libraries considering a presence in Second Life should first identify how participation improved the user experience.

A chatbot is another tool that can be used to answer questions 24 hours a day, including times when the library is closed. It is software programmed to respond to key words and phrases input by users. Chatbots have been used in the commercial sector for many years but there are not many currently in use in libraries (Rubin et al., 2010). The University of Nebraska-Lincoln has been developing a chatbot (*http://pixel.unl.edu*) since 2010 (Allison, 2012). This bot answers routine questions and provides consistent answers through a playful interface that many users enjoy. There are challenges with chatbots which include the handling of spelling variations, homophones and precise matching (Dowd, 2011). The first two issues can be addressed when there is functionality to check spelling, but the last problem can only be addressed through the database, or through programming.

Technical services

Technical services departments have been undergoing a quiet evolution over the last two decades. Numerous cataloging positions were eliminated as departments transitioned from local to cooperative cataloging through large utilities like OCLC. Worries about the quality of shared cataloging have been disappearing along with the large backlogs of uncataloged materials. Cataloging is a labor-intensive activity and, with the availability of records from vendors, combined with perceptions about the reduced value of the catalog versus records available over the web, some (Eden, 2010) are questioning whether certain technical service activities could be diverted to other services. The answer is yes, and no – librarians in technical services are still necessary because there is an urgent need to manage and preserve information in an increasingly complex and transitory web of information.

Not all cataloging is the same; skills for describing rare books are important because special collections are the jewels in all types of libraries and attract visitors and donors to the library. Technical service librarians are moving away from the MARC standards that accentuate the individual towards more flexible metadata that supports linking and interconnections between resources. This opens up new opportunities for high-tech skills that involve creating mash-ups between database information and applications that have a direct impact on the user experience (Thomas, 2007).

These are emerging roles for technical service librarians that require coordinating activities with technical staff to manage records, holdings and access points for massive catalog loads of vendor provided records. Librarians in these roles are also involved in preparing metadata, and managing "harvested" collections that are integrated with MARC records. Technical service librarians will need to be fluent, if not completely skilled, in the language of information technology in order to work with staff both inside and outside the library. Technical service staff members who develop expertise in information technology will be prized for their creative uses of the catalog, their enhancement and/or development of digital collections, their database knowledge and their technology support; all of which directly and indirectly benefit patrons (Gregory et al., 2008).

Technical service librarians also have a responsibility to explore broader, strategic concerns over metadata standards. Librarians who specialize in technical services should develop skills for metadata that go beyond MARC and Resource Description and Access (RDA). They can be leaders and champions for initiatives that promote best practices for identifying the metadata needed to preserve digital information for future use. This includes following and advocating for the use of standard identifiers for authors, institutions, geographic locations and other information necessary for disambiguation.

Technical service librarians are also specially positioned to analyze the collection for usage patterns, to question permanency of access, to evaluate indexing and functionality, to interpret license contracts and to make recommendations that will better align the collection with patron needs. They should work either directly or indirectly with patrons. This connection is essential for the building of collections and services that will meet the changing needs of patrons. User assessment and participation in the development of marketing ideas will prevent technical service staff from becoming siloed into routines that are disconnected from patrons. The goal for all librarians must be centered on improving the patron experience through dynamic services.

Electronic resource management

Electronic resource management (ERM) systems came into existence because of the need to manage large numbers of digital e-journal subscriptions, many through package plans that frequently drop and add individual titles. Management includes tracking the subscription cycle, licensing, statistics, holdings information and reports that include CPU data and holdings overlap. ERM systems must be able to pull information provided by vendors into a single tool that efficiently manages subscriptions that range from single journals to large package plans with a complex mix of full-text and citation-only records. The ERM system should provide a means for collecting and analyzing digital content usage. This tool allows technical service librarians to provide usage information that will inform collection decisions that directly benefit patrons.

Many libraries use an intermediate vendor who prepares an A–Z title list with all the library's titles, which is then loaded into the ERM and updates holding information based on a match point. That match point is critical; titles are often ineffective match points, so ISSN and e-ISSN numbers have become the standard. However, databases which contain older titles that don't have either number must either rely on a title match or use some other identifier. This latter usually requires human intervention to add an unique identifier to the A–Z list so that they will match.

An ERM system should also be able to assist with workflow by providing a means for tracking titles from trial, purchase decision and implementation, to deselection. It should include a feature that can be used by librarians to create custom alerts that trigger follow-up action. Licenses are scanned and linked to records so that information is available to reference and ILL staff. Librarians are using technology to collect data from ERM and other statistical applications to prepare reports that influence purchasing decisions.

Some libraries are developing their own ERMs, either with their own staff or through cooperative projects with other libraries or vendors. Stanford University is working with JIRA (*http://www.atlassian.com/software/jira/*), Eastern Kentucky is using Drupal (*http://drupal.org*), University of South Florida uses Basecamp (*http://basecamp.com*) (Wilson, 2011) and Northwestern University adopted CORAL (*http://erm.library.nd.edu*), which originated at Notre Dame (Gustafson-Sundell, 2011). Many OPAC vendors also sell ERM systems that either can be integrated into their own products or used with other vendors' ILSs.

The implementation of any ERM system, whether "home grown" or commercial, will present challenges to the staff as they examine workflow and develop new communication channels that are necessary when new technology is implemented. Technical service librarians are using wikis and blogs to communicate workflows and decisions. Checklists and LibGuides are additional communication methods used when ERMs are implemented (England et al., 2011). The smooth integration of licensing, statistics, pricing and holdings information, requiring minimal human intervention and providing users with the latest holdings information when they search the catalog, is the goal of an ERM system.

The catalog and discovery tools

In the age of the web, a library catalog can look very old-fashioned to users who are used to finding what they want with a single search. A discovery tool is a tool that assists with the discovery of library resources, or collections that are overlooked because their presence is hidden under menus, not included in the catalog or not recognized because of labels. A discovery tool should reduce the frustration patrons report as they try to find information through the library website.

Discovery tools that search across independent resources provide a convenience that users have indicated is important (Connaway et al., 2011). They also increase the discoverability of local digital collections (Allison, 2010). A single search that displays articles, books, multimedia, graphic and sound files from a variety of sources that match a query saves time.

There are a growing number of choices in discovery tools that include products from traditional ILS vendors and open source projects that provide different display options and features. AquaBrowser (*http://www.serialssolutions.com/en/services/aquabrowser/*) from Serials Solutions, EBSCO Discovery Service (*http://www.ebscohost.com/discovery/*), Encore (*http://encoreforlibraries.com/overview/*)

from Innovative Interfaces, Primo from Ex Libris (*http:// www.exlibrisgroup.com/category/PrimoOverview/*) and WorldCat Local (*http://www.oclc.org/worldcat-local.en. html*) from OCLC are the primary commercial products available at the time of writing.

The commercial products use facets to support post-search limiting so that once results are displayed users can limit their search for a smaller result set with more refined criteria. The facets provide for manipulating results by author, title, tag, publisher, language, date, format, article, availability, etc. Facets eliminate the need for researchers to construct search logic using advanced search forms, which studies reveal are often little used because researchers prefer key word searching (Allison and Childers, 2002). Most of the commercial products also include articles which are integrated into the search results along with books and local full-text collections.

Several of the discovery tools have features which set them apart. AquaBrowser has a facet that graphically displays the relationship between subjects related to the initial query. Encore separates article results into a "sample" facet instead of integrating the results with books. Primo uses a central index that includes global and regional resources, which are integrated with local holdings. BiblioCommons (*http://www. bibliocommons.com/*) provides a new look to the traditional catalog that includes awards, bestsellers, library blogs, reviews, staff picks, book covers, federated searching for articles, library events, readers' advisory and fines' payment into a single site. It is particularly attractive for public libraries and schools because of unique features that address children's needs.

In addition to the commercial products, several libraries have open source discovery projects. Patrons testing VuFind (*http://vufind.org/*), an open source discovery tool, liked the option on bibliographic records for a window overlay with citation information (Emanuel, 2011). Blacklight (*http://projectblacklight.org/*), headed by the University of Virginia, includes material from their institutional repository and articles through Serials Solutions.

Discovery solutions are chasing an elusive audience as they attempt to design interfaces that appeal to librarians accustomed to webPACS and patrons looking for a search option that equals the web search engines they favor. The first-generation discovery tools have made great strides in combining library resources, but the results from user studies indicate that they are far from perfect solutions: "This usability test suggested that while some interface features were heavily used, such as drop-down limits and facets, other features were not used, such as federated search results" (Condit Fagan et al., 2012). Libraries will need to monitor developments in discovery tools and assess how well they are meeting requirements for local users.

Database and full-text sources

Budget considerations play a role in database selection but there are other important factors for decisions. Product value is also important, as measured by: the number of records, amount of full-text availability, currency, depth of back-file accessibility, format inclusiveness, search interface and linking options (Allison et al., 2000). These factors are all evaluated against the cost to determine the favorability of one database over another similar product.

Aggregated databases provide indexing and access to full texts across multiple databases and can gather information from different vendors. They are attractive alternatives for libraries looking for ways to reduce subscription costs when duplicate access from multiple vendors can be canceled. However, these databases historically add and drop titles outside the control of the library, making it impossible to rely on perpetual access or holdings consistency for desired titles (Thohira et al., 2010). As with any decision, local circumstances and the needs of patrons should be the major considerations in determining which databases should be included as part of the library's services.

Reference managers

Reference managing software like Zotero (*http://www. zotero.org/*), Mendeley (*http://www.mendeley.com/*) and RefWorks (*http://refworks.com*) allow library users to easily manage their bibliographic citations and automatically build citations into word processing software. Zotero and Mendeley have free versions. Zotero has unlimited cloud storage for citations and a limited amount of space for attachments, with an option to purchase additional space. Mendeley has cloud storage for citation and attachments, with options to upgrade for additional space. RefWorks provides an option for a library subscription that includes unlimited citations and storage for PDFs. These cloud-based services are replacing single computer versions because of their versatility. They can be accessed from anywhere and have support for citation sharing and social media integration.

Librarians should become familiar with the various reference managers in order to understand their limitations. Important factors to consider include: word processor integration, reliability for capturing citations, and how well the system handles authentication. Not all managers will be able to capture citations from all library applications, and libraries may be using a form of authentication that is not supported by the manager. When authentication fails, the citation that is stored in the manager will not link to the full text.

Link resolvers

OpenURL is designed to link citation databases through library services to full-text journal subscriptions. The linking is accomplished by link resolvers, which parse the elements of an OpenURL to create a list of matching targets defined by the library's knowledge base. This knowledge base consists of information on the library's subscriptions, holdings, coverage dates and vendors, which match against target definitions. Options for services like ILL, help, etc., are additional targets that combine with the full-text matches to form the links presented when a patron clicks on an OpenURL button. This list includes full-text availability for print and digital resources, and additional options designed by librarians to provide help to a researcher using a particular source.

OpenURL is convenient for library users because it connects the citation to the full text, reducing the number of steps, or searches, a patron would normally require to determine if the library provides access to a title. There is evidence that OpenURL linking increases the use of scholarly resources (Yi and Herlihy, 2007). ILL activity among libraries using link resolvers is also higher, perhaps because resolvers are used as a tool for library staff (Williams and Woolwine, 2011). Clearly, if there is a direct relationship between OpenURL technology and an increased use of resources then librarians should work to improve access to and use of resolvers. OpenURL is a tool that impacts users by meeting their needs for immediate access, while supplying the best resources selected for their use by librarians.

Improving OpenURL resolvers

There are two projects underway to improve the accuracy of linking through OpenURL: Knowledge Base and Related Tools (KBART) and IOTA. KBART (*http://www.niso.org/workrooms/kbart/*) is a joint project of NISO and the UK Serials Group. KBART is a framework for vendors that provide title lists for importing into knowledge bases. It is working to improve linking by defining the rules for the exchange of metadata, data format and elements, and addresses problems like title changes or inconsistencies in titles that affect the accuracy of knowledge bases (Pesch, 2011a).

IOTA (*http://www.openurlquality.org/*) is working to develop assessment tools for evaluating the quality of OpenURL sources. The project creates reports that advise vendors on improvements to their OpenURL strings that will increase the number of OpenURL requests that resolve to a correct record. Their tool can assist librarians who work with resolvers to improve the success rate for linking between citations and full-text articles.

Google Scholar

Google Scholar fits a niche outside the constellation of the library because Google is attempting to provide access to a universe collection well beyond the means of a local library. It is easy to use and most children are exposed to it early in their introduction to the web. However, Google does not provide access to library full-text subscriptions, but it does provide indirect access to licensed material when libraries support linking through the Google preferences set by library patrons. Whether or not libraries support Google's activities, the convenience provided by Google to users is undeniable, and it is difficult for libraries focused on user needs to ignore that convenience.

The library's web presence

The library website is the primary means for the library to introduce itself to visitors – the welcome mat. It is important to make a good first impression by applying best practices to the website. An uncluttered site that hides as little as possible under multiple tabs or avoids a navigation that is confusing can be achieved through usability studies. The website should also be accessible to people with disabilities to ensure compliance with W3C Web Content Accessibility Guidelines (WCAG) (*http://www.w3.org/WAI/intro/wcag*), US Section 508 accessibility standards (*http://www.access-board. gov/508.htm*) and the UK Equality Act 2010 (*http://www. homeoffice.gov.uk/equalities/equality-act/*). Other website management issues include regular checking for bad links, spelling errors and browser compatibility. There are free and commercial products that assist with this process. The W3C Committee maintains a list of free tools for checking accessibility at *http://www.w3.org/WAI/RC/tools/complete.* PowerMapper (*http://www.powermapper.com/index.htm*) is a commercial product that checks for these problems and includes a tool for creating maps of the website, which can assist with the identification of overly complex navigation that may hide information from users.

The online catalog can be enhanced with add-on features that empower users to interact with the catalog in ways that take advantage of social networking. Two examples are LibraryThing (*http://www.librarything.com/forlibraries*) and ChiliFresh (*http://chilifresh.com/*). LibraryThing is an add-on to the catalog that integrates social media features such as: tags, reviews, similar books, shelf browse, series, awards, stack maps and mobile options. ChiliFresh integrates reviews that come from local patrons or a wider community, based on the library's preference.

Images have become an important feature for web users and libraries are providing access to digital images. There are commercial and free services that libraries can use to manage and make images available. Pinterest (*http://pinterest.com/*) is a free service that some libraries are using to host book covers, displays and photos from events that will attract and engage users. Pinterest has been used successfully to market the Central Methodist University Library's new acquisitions and DVD collections (Dudenhoffer, 2012). For libraries with large collections of images there are several database-driven products that support authentication for licensed and openly accessible images. Among these are CONTENTdm (*http://www.contentdm.org/*), Content Pro (*http://www.iii.com/products/content_pro.shtml*) and LUNA Imaging (*http://lunaimaging.com/*). ARTstor (*http://www.artstor.org/index.shtml*) also provides the capability to store images as well as providing access to a large database of images.

Loyalty programs

Most people are familiar with loyalty programs in the commercial sector. Public libraries have recognition programs for children, which could be considered as the foundation for a loyalty program, but most libraries take their adult population of users for granted. Using social media sites like Foursquare, the library could formerly recognize the "mayor," and provide promotional tips when people check in at the library. Incentives could be as simple as an annual recognition photo for the patrons with the most check-ins or checkouts, both of which will help build a feeling of community among patrons.

A loyalty program begins with the identification of what loyalty means in the context of the library and the user community it supports. A discussion centered on answering the question, "Who would be impacted if the library closed?" is one way to start. This is the target population for a loyal group. Once a target group is identified, the next questions are: "Why do they need the library?" and "How are they using the library?" This discussion can reveal some obvious areas from which a loyalty program can grow. Incentives can be provided naturally though library services, or they can come from local businesses or inexpensive promotional items. People want to feel special, so creating a path for patrons to express their loyalty is a priority for a library that is patron centered.

Donors are another group that every library is interested in attracting – the need to make them feel special and appreciated is obvious. Libraries should continually demonstrate the value of donor contributions. Consider a periodic letter providing statistics and other facts that demonstrate how their gift is making a difference. The letter can include circulation statistics, volumes purchased or stories from patrons. When possible, honor donors through celebrations or special recognitions; even small honors like a "special" library card with honorary membership to the library can be much appreciated.

9

Digital collections

Abstract: Managing digital material is becoming more important for libraries as they both acquire and create digital information. Libraries are working in collaboration with others to digitize all of the world's digital content. This is a scattered process with overlapping partnerships and no agreement about standards for e-books and other content. As libraries struggle with decisions about e-books and digitization, they are using metadata to create the architecture for information to be preserved for future use, while providing functionality in meeting users' needs.

Key words: e-books, digitization, markup language, born digital, copyright, digital preservation, HathiTrust, Internet Archive, Google Books, institutional identifiers.

Libraries are increasingly collecting and producing digital material. Vendors are beginning to explore creating e-books that are more than an electronic version of a book, that include hyperlinks, video, high resolution graphics, and the ability to interact in ways that are not possible with printed materials. Digital materials have the capability to be non-linear and exploratory, a format that appeals to the Millennial Generation. However, e-books pose some interesting challenges to libraries struggling with questions of support for equipment, formats, access and preservation.

The essence of digital content can be reduced to characters, shapes, colors and textures, which can be searched and displayed using criteria that are far beyond the capabilities of a printed index. In fact, the capabilities are often beyond the imagination of the creators for the objects and it isn't until they are used and repurposed that the true value of a collection is revealed. An image may have different purposes based on the needs of the person viewing the image and that may require different versions of the image in different formats for image manipulation.

For example, should watermarks or scribbles be removed from a digital image? That depends on who is asked. For Charles Cullen, examining papers from Thomas Jefferson, a watermark became a significant clue for interpreting a document (Cullen, 2007). He was examining the original document, but a scholar working with a digital version might also need that information, whereas a casual reader would only be concerned with the writings. Likewise, word semantics create difficulties for searching texts (Sobel and Beall, 2011); should an encoder modernize words or retain the original word and variant spelling? Early English Books Online (*http://eebo.chadwyck.com*) and Eighteenth Century Collections Online (*http://gale.cengage.co.uk/product-highlights/history/eighteenth-century-collections-online.aspx*) have options for variant or fuzzy spellings that attempt to accommodate linguistic variations. Digital material is redefining the nature of information and presenting significant challenges for the creation of knowledge, but the benefits of access and data manipulation also create great potential.

E-formats for e-books

The issue of the long-term preservation of e-books is a concern for libraries that want to maintain long-term access to their electronic collections. This is particularly true for e-books that are born digital without a print version. The Library of Congress (LC) has a website with information on the sustainability of digital formats (*http://www. digitalpreservation.gov/formats/*). The site has information on graphic images, sound files, video, text (a growing list of e-book formats), web archives, data and geospatial formats. It also includes information on which file type is preferred at LC for conservation, which is helpful for libraries developing procedures for managing digital formats.

One of the first questions facing a consumer or librarian is which e-reader device? There is a wide array of e-readers on the market with new devices added each year. As of 2012, there are at least 40 different devices on the market, not including mobile phones or computers. However, all e-readers are not the same as there are variations in e-book formats supported by devices, and not all formats are supported on all devices.

Table 9.1 provides a list of the common file types used by e-books. The epub format is being promoted by the International Digital Publishing Forum as the standard for e-books, but it has been challenged by proprietary standards like those developed by Amazon (azw), Adobe (pdf) and Sony (bbeb). Although e-reader devices do not support all formats, there are utilities that will convert formats from one version to another with some degree of success.

The situation with e-readers is less than ideal for libraries struggling with tight budgets. Currently, the major e-readers are Kindle, iPad, Kobo, Sony and Nook, with additional mobile devices using different operating systems. Each of the five major vendors has library distribution programs and it is not unusual for a library patron to ask if they can access library materials on their e-readers because "the sales person

Table 9.1 E-book formats and associated readers

Format	Description
3gp	Third Generation Partnership Project multimedia container format for mobile phones
aac	Advanced Audio Coding format for audio files
aax	Audible enhanced audiobook file
aa	Amazon audio file format
azw/kf8	Amazon Kindle/Fire format for e-books
bbeb/LRS/ LRF/LRX	Broad Band eBook format used by Sony
bmp	Microsoft bitmap format image
doc	Microsoft Word document
docx	Microsoft Word XML document
epub	Electronic Publication open e-book standard advocated by the International Digital Publishing Forum
gif	CompuServe Graphics Interchange Format
htm/html	HyperText Markup language for web
ibook	Apple
jpeg/jpg	Joint Photographic Experts Group lossy image format
midi/mid/smf	Musical Instrument Digital Interface format for music
mobi/prc	Mobipocket same format as azw with different DRM
mp3	Music format
mp4	A container format for text, graphic, video and audio combinations
oepub	Open e-pub format without DRM
ogg	Open container format for streaming multimedia
pdf	Adobe document format
png	Portable Network Graphics lossless image format
ppt	Microsoft PowerPoint presentation
rtf	Microsoft Rich Text Format for text and graphics
tiff/tif	Tagged Image File Format
txt	Plain text file with limited formatting support
vp8	Google open video codec

wav	Microsoft audio format
webm	Open video format
wma	Windows Media Audio format
xml	Extensible Markup Language format for documents

said I could get all kinds of books from my library." Since many libraries can't afford to purchase multiple e-reader devices for checkout they are opting to subscribe to an e-book distributor. These e-books are stored in the cloud, and library users can either read the book online, or download software to their device before reading. When e-books are downloaded, digital rights management (DRM) controls access to the content.

DRM was developed to stop copyright infringement by prohibiting the copying and illegal redistribution of copies. DRM controls when and how a file can be accessed and can frustrate legitimate file activity such as making copies for back-up purposes. The most common version of DRM for e-books is Adobe's DRM. Apple developed a DRM for Apple e-books called FairPlay, which is only used with Apple devices. Transferring content between devices can be tricky, for example moving e-books protected by Adobe's DRM requires both devices to use the same Adobe ID for activation. Device independence is a priority for libraries in selecting e-books with multiple formats, and different rights management systems make preserving long-term access a challenge. ALA's Digital Content and Libraries Working Group (DCWG) is working with publishers: "the goal is to ensure that publishers are aware of the needs and concerns of libraries and their communities, and the group must persuade them to engage with libraries and strengthen those relationships in order to work toward viable solutions" (Feldman and Wolven, 2012: 5).

E-books in libraries

Patron interest in e-books is increasing and libraries must invest in this new format to meet the expectations of users. While print checkout appears to be declining, the trend for e-print usage is increasing (Shen, 2011). Although e-book popularity is growing as more consumers purchase e-readers, many patrons still don't associate e-books with libraries because of preconceived notions that libraries are print. A 2011 survey from Sunshine Coast Library in Australia highlights this problem. When users were asked if they had knowledge about the e-book and e-audiobook collection, which started in 2010, 62 percent responded that they didn't know about it (Duncan, 2011). This situation could be remedied with an aggressive e-book marketing plan.

E-books are not adequate replacements for all printed books. Although technological advances are improving the readability of e-books, there are many instances where print is better than digital. Users report frustration when they can't download a title to an e-reader device either because the format isn't supported or because they encounter technical issues. E-books do not always reproduce the print version with the same reader experience as printed texts. Some e-books do not support color, which makes illustrations and charts difficult to read. Page numbering is a continuing problem for e-books when they fail to reproduce the page numbers of the print version making them difficult to cite, or for e-books that are born digital that lack any reference points for citation. Searching and locating specific information can be more difficult in e-books, and annotations or notes are often handled awkwardly. Information can be missing in e-book versions when it is too difficult to reproduce the content from the print version. Finally, when the vendor hasn't developed mobile reading software the screen size of some portable devices is an impediment to reading e-print. In cases where there is a small screen application, it can lack features available on the full software version.

Publishers will continue to work on these issues, and most of these problems can be overcome with technology. "The quickening pace of technological change is removing difficulties before most consumers are even aware of them, while at the same time making the library's strategic decisions more challenging than ever. It is impossible to predict what e-reading will look like in ten years, but it is likely that most, if not all, purely technological challenges will be overcome" (Advisory Board Company, 2011: 23).

E-books have a lot to offer in terms of on-demand linking via the web, incorporating multimedia and providing users with interactive applications that enhance learning and comprehension. Reading Life by Kobo (*http://www.kobo books.com/readinglife*) offers several exciting features that make reading a social adventure. Using the app, readers can share passages, engage in conversations and share books.

The portability of e-print, and the ability to carry an entire library on a single device is attractive to library users who are looking for portability. According to *Library Journal's* 2011 survey on e-books, "76% of public libraries believe that e-books have drawn new people into the library" (Miller, 2011: 34). As e-books evolve, libraries will need to adapt to the multiple versions, much like multiple editions of books. Libraries need flexible collection development policies that support e-book options for purchase or lease depending on user assessment.

There are a number of e-book distributors, including: Books24x7, MyiLibrary, OverDrive, EBL, ebrary and eBook Collection. Vendor mergers and acquisitions are also occurring in the e-book market as evident with ProQuest's purchase of ebrary, and EBSCO's acquisition of NetLibrary.

The cost model for each vendor is different, and volatility about perpetual access as titles are moved from one vendor to another combines with confusion about formats and options to create barriers for many librarians.

While librarians hesitate, sales for e-books in the US increased 145.7 percent from March 2010 to March 2011 (Mulvihill and Schiller, 2011). A survey of 265 librarians in that same year revealed that librarians were still reluctant to invest in e-books (Mulvihill, 2011). The survey reported a lack of demand, unacceptable DRMs, unsatisfactory platforms and a fundamental need to "own" the e-books among publishers' reasons for waiting. Given the increase in sales in 2011, it seems that librarians are not keeping pace with users, and a wiser course of action would be to experiment with e-books, and confront the DRM issues with e-book publishers.

There are many purchasing models for experimenting, including the standard title-by-title purchase and package plans from e-book vendors or aggregators. Other models include leasing, pay-per-view or patron initiated acquisition. There is also the question of preservation or perpetual access to complicate the purchasing options.

At a 2012 American Association of Publishers meeting librarians opened a conversation to address these issues. Librarians cited the evidence that library patrons are also buyers (Kelley et al., 2012). Publishers are also seeking collaborations, and the University Press Content Consortium (UPCC) was formed to provide scholarly content at affordable prices. Project MUSE and university presses joined this to create a database with several options that include purchase or subscription. Scholarly publishers may have more reason to work with libraries than other publishers because they are more dependent on libraries for sales.

Larger publishers are adding restrictions and additional charges to the e-book sales to libraries. "Many librarians are protesting the fact that most of the big 6 publishers refuse to sell e-books to the library market. Random House, Inc., a publisher that sells to libraries through distributor OverDrive, Inc., raised its prices by 300% on March 1, sending shock waves through the library community and causing many librarians to rethink their collection decisions" (Hane, 2012: 10).

In February 2011, OverDrive announced that HarperCollins required libraries to purchase a second e-book copy after 26 uses. Josh Marwell, President of Sales at HarperCollins justified the actions "by making the analogy that print books in library collections wear out and need to be replaced" (Ojala, 2011: 36). These developments are troubling for libraries on several levels. Most librarians find analogies to book circulation unrealistic, and point to the fact that print items can circulate more than 26 times without having to be replaced.

Limitations on circulation activity also put consortia at a disadvantage, requiring them to purchase more copies than any individual library would need. In September 2012, representatives from the ALA met with executives from the Big 6 (Penguin, Rosen, Scholastic, HarperCollins, Random House and Hachette) to discuss the e-book situation and find common ground. Undoubtedly these discussions will continue, but while the situation remains unsettled some libraries are looking for alternate ways to provide e-books to their users.

Douglas Country Library in Colorado implemented their own e-book distribution system by reaching agreements directly with publishers and serving e-books through their own platform (Kelley et al., 2011). Whether or not this is the future for libraries, it is clear that libraries should not wait to provide access to e-books; e-books are here today, and there is no evidence this is just a fad that will eventually go away.

E-books for consumers

E-books are becoming more popular among the general population. Pew Research's 2012 survey on e-reading habits demonstrated a growing appetite among consumers for e-books. "One-fifth of American adults (21%) report that they have read an e-book in the past year, and this number increased following a gift-giving season that saw a spike in the ownership of both tablet computers and e-book reading devices such as the original Kindle and Nooks" (Rainie et al., 2012: 3). The survey also revealed that owners of e-books read more than the general population, which is a hopeful trend for increasing the amount of reading in the US. However, one troubling statistic from the survey is that "only 10% said they borrowed it from a library (vs. 14% of all readers)" (ibid.: 60). Librarians must do more to make e-book collections more visible to their communities.

Digitization in libraries

Many libraries are engaged in digitizing texts, either through scanning projects or by creating new, born digital information. In both cases it is important to create best practices that will guide projects. These should address the following: acceptable file format(s), resolution requirements for images, content metadata, interoperability between systems, preservation metadata (necessary for long-term preservation), provenance information, compliance with national standards, usefulness, staffing requirements, long-term conservation, and copyright. Projects that involve scholarly content will have additional requirements for evaluating the merit of the project in comparison with other projects or print copies (Panitch and

Michalak, 2007). Digital collections that will be maintained in perpetuity will have maintenance costs that extend far beyond the end of a project, so libraries need to be prepared for long-term budget implications.

Scanning and photography are two very different methods for digitizing materials. Scanning and OCR text recognition are efficient means for quickly digitizing standard text, while digital photography is better for three-dimensional objects. Handwritten, decorative fonts and non-standard English text usually require manual transcription into machine-readable text.

Digital text formats

Digital text is fundamentally different from print matter because it is structured to include information for computers. Behind the text displayed on the screen is a markup language that provides structural information that can be manipulated. It is the essential architecture for building files that can be preserved and repurposed as technology advances. The America COMPETES Reauthorization Act of 2010 is an important development towards progress in metadata standardization. The Act provides for a "working group under the National Science and Technology Council with the responsibility to coordinate Federal science agency research and policies related to the dissemination and long-term stewardship of the results of unclassified research, including digital data and peer-reviewed scholarly publications, supported wholly, or in part, by funding from the Federal science agencies" (United States, Cong. House, 1011th Congress). In addition to preservation the group will "coordinate the development or designation of standards for research data, the structure of full text and metadata, navigation tools, and other applications to maximize interoperability across Federal science agencies, across science and engineering disciplines, and between research data and scholarly publications, taking into account existing consensus standards" (ibid.). Librarians should participate and make contributions to these efforts which will build on existing practices for metadata.

Extensible Markup Language (XML) is a common markup used throughout the world, and Text Encoding Initiative (TEI) (*http://www.tei-c.org/index.xml*) and Encoding Archival Description (EAD) (*http://www.loc.gov/ead/*) are recognized as versions of XML designed for printed texts (TEI) and archive materials (EAD). There are many other standards for metadata including: Standard Generalized Markup Language (SGML), Portable Document Format (PDF), Dublin Core (DC) and Functional Requirements for Bibliographic Records (FRBR, which is an element set of Resource Description Framework (RDF)) used by librarians for encoding.

RDF is significant for libraries because it defines the structure for linked data that makes the Semantic Web possible, which led to FRBR as the model for library data. RDF uses a three-part or triplet structure that describes content as subject, predicate and object, all of which can be queried separately or together. In the FRBR model this becomes entities, relationships and attributes for describing bibliographic data. There are four objectives in FRBR for assisting users: find, identify, select and obtain (Kincy and Wood, 2012).

Resource Description and Access (RDA) is another RDF element set based on the four objectives of the FRBR model. The Library of Congress implemented RDA in 2013 and other libraries in the US are in the process of adopting the new code. RDA will replace the Anglo-American Cataloging Rules (AACR) that have been used for the past 30 years. RDA was developed to be more user-friendly by the reduction of the number of abbreviations in records, the removal of Latin terms, more explicit descriptions of multimedia and the elimination of limits on the number of author links.

Patrons will also notice differences in authority records which are intended to encourage exploration. "Authority data created in accordance with RDA guidelines contain far more data elements than in AACR2, necessitating the creation of new MARC variable fields in order to accommodate them. Some variable fields may look unfamiliar as they may represent new concepts such as form of work and content type" (ibid.: 28).

RDA will expose data that is useful for machine manipulation and data linking. However, to truly release the power of the Sematic Web, the catalog database should be exposed for application development outside the standard ILS front end. "Linked data empower others to create new ways to integrate data to solve their particular problem" (Miller and Westfall, 2011: 20). By supporting direct queries to catalog databases librarians will be able to expand services and create new applications that exploit catalog information in new and unanticipated ways that benefit patrons.

Markup languages support navigation both inside and outside the document so users can move beyond the linear flow of text. Metadata is the means for defining the content in files and provides a framework for sharing information that is important in the Semantic Web. RDA, TEI, EAD and other metadata schemas are the architectures that make it possible to repurpose information, and a key feature that will enable digital text to be useful into the distant future.

Digital objects, either transcribed or born digital, are created for users and care should be taken to address the needs of users while adhering to standards that will allow the content to be perpetually managed. Tzoc (2011) suggests five important features for XML coded files. These are: autosuggest for displaying alternative searches, tag clouds for displaying subjects, an A–Z list for a collection inventory, a calendar view for displaying creation dates for large collections, and a share feature for embedding content into social media sites. These options take advantage of the extensible characteristic of XML, and by analyzing user trends librarians can create metadata that will assist in the display and functionality of digital content that enhances the user experience.

Managing born digital collections

There are many formats used for today's born digital information including word processing files, spreadsheets, and reports created by proprietary applications. A born digital item is any content that has never existed in a non-digital form. Since this information never existed in analog form, it usually requires a specific application for rendering or display. This type of digital material is being created in unprecedented numbers and poses great challenges to library archives trying to preserve the content for the future.

Archivists must identify the correct rights management for digital content, which requires the untangling of copyright and provenance before determining the level of access that can be provided. Version manifests for digitals files are also important because digital files can be revised through numerous modifications or additions, which potentially makes every digital item a perpetual work in progress. Managing the versions and migrating obsolete formats to newer standards can be difficult, especially if the hardware needed to read the files is no longer available.

Libraries which began experimenting with book digitization projects in previous decades are retooling to support the demands of a new generation of library patrons who are eager for digital material. Workflow is moving out of speciality units and being distributed into other departments as digitization is being embraced as part of the library's mission.

The focus is changing from simply converting printed text to considerations about what material is being requested and how it is being used by library patrons. For example, in 2008 the New York Public Library revamped the Digital Library Program into a new unit, NYPL Labs. The objective of the change was to remove the barriers around the Digital Library Program, which focused on digital projects as a separate service from other departments, initiating a new mission where digitization is part of the normal workflow of the library (Taranto, 2009).

Other libraries are also revisiting workflow as they look for ways to increase the amount of digitization. The University of Maryland was able to increase scanning production for patron requests by distributing work beyond the digitization unit (Gueguen and Hanlon, 2009). A collaborative workflow at the University of Nebraska, involving staff from the music library, ILL and technical services, involves scanning fragile music material that has been requested through ILL. These items are frequently requested so the scans are retained for later use.

Google, Microsoft and OCA digitization projects

There are many digitization projects underway across the publishing, web provider and library communities. Google started their ambitious Google Books project to "remove the barriers between people and information and benefit the publishing community" (*http://books.google.com/google books/issue.html*). To further this goal they joined with the University of Michigan in 2008 to scan that library's entire collection. Other libraries have joined the project (*http:// books.google.com/googlebooks/partners.html*), though this has been slowed by a lawsuit filed by publishers (settled October 2012) and authors (ongoing at the time of writing).

In 2005, Microsoft launched a similar project with the British Library to digitize content from the library's collection. In 2010, the partners announced an open source Research Information Centre (RIC) Framework (*http://ric.codeplex. com/*) to support research collaboration, which is built on Microsoft Office SharePoint.

Yahoo has also entered the digitization race targeting public domain titles and is working with the California Digital Library on the project. The OCA (*http://www. opencontentalliance.org/*) was funded by libraries to support the scanning of items not in copyright that are made available through the Internet Archive (*http://archive.org/ index.php*). Unlike Google, Microsoft and Yahoo are members of OCA.

Litigation and questions around copyright are an impediment to many digitization projects. Authors, publishers and those involved in digitization all have a stake in the outcome of current court actions. Recent discussions at the international level show some promise of reconciling differences between groups. The World Intellectual Property

Organization (WIPO) is considering a proposal for copyright exemptions for disabled readers. WIPO is also convening a conference on DRM as a means for simplifying content access, and the International Federation of Reproduction Rights Organizations (IFRRO) signed agreements with European libraries, authors, publishers and collective management organizations on the digitization and licensing of out-of-commerce works by cultural institutions in Europe (Armstrong, 2012).

The Copyright Clearance Center (*http://www.copyright. com/content/cc3/en.html*) is a rights broker for US and international licensing for in- and out-of-print books, articles, movies, television, images, blogs and digital material. The Center contributes toward the vision of collective licensing where the copyrights of different holders are managed centrally. A new service, "Get it Now," was added to the Center to provide quicker document delivery either through unmediated OpenURL or librarian-mediated ILL options.

Another service, DeepDyve (*http://www.deepdyve.com/*), is a commercial service designed for professionals that provides scholarly articles from associated publishers for rental or a monthly fee, with an option for a group plan for organizations. Articles can be rented but not downloaded or printed.

In the US it is not necessary for authors to register works with the copyright office, unless they plan to pursue their rights through litigation. The Copyright Catalog (1978 to present) (*http://cocatalog.loc.gov/cgi-bin/Pwebrecon.cgi?DB= local&PAGE=First*) is a front-end for searching US copyright records to locate a particular registration. Copyrights can be searched by title, name, key word, registration number, document number and command key word. For records prior to 1978, researchers can use a card catalog at the Library of Congress.

It is difficult to predict the future results of the ambitious projects that are collectively attempting to digitize all the books and articles of the world. Many librarians are skeptical of the commercial vendors' motives and worry about a future where information is too costly for library users. The one certainty in these developments is that technology will continue to change, and eventually the printed book will become as obsolete as manuscripts became after the invention of movable type. The superiority of e-print lies in the ability to create works that interact with users to enhance understanding. Many developments must take place before this happens. E-books today are frequently an imitation of the printed book, but this will change, and librarians need to watch developments and participate in discussions on the future of e-books.

Preservation by digitization and digital preservation

There is a difference between preserving by digitizing, and digital preservation, though in practice the two have become blended. Digitizing creates a copy of a printed item so the print copy will be preserved in a digital format, while digital preservation is the act of preserving a digital item in digital format. HathiTrust, the Internet Archive, Google Books, Portico, LOCKSS, CLOCKSS and WEST are among the examples of preserving by digitization. LOCKSS (Lots of Copies Keep Stuff Safe) (*http://www.lockss.org/*) has a strategy for managing multiple copies so that there will always be at least one copy preserved. The LOCKSS principal is that librarians will preserve access to their subscription e-content through a collaborative network of computers. "The LOCKSS software functions best and most securely with at least seven boxes. More can be added at any time, the public LOCKSS network contains well over 100 boxes" (Seadle, 2010: 711).

The Internet Archive (*http://archive.org/index.php*) is a collaborative effort to provide permanent access to historical digital collections. The Archive includes web pages through the Wayback Machine, the ARPANET collection, the Million Book Project and Children's Library, and includes multimedia collections that are part of the public domain (Edwards, 2004). In addition to the Wayback Machine's efforts to archive web content, the YouTube Time Machine (*http://yttm.tv/*) preserves many YouTube videos and makes them accessible through a timeline for browsing genres. Likewise, Twitter is being archived at the Library of Congress (*http://blogs.loc.gov/loc/2010/04/the-library-and-twitter-an-faq/*) as an effort to capture social communication for historical preservation.

The Million Book Project, Project Gutenberg and the Google Book Project aim to digitize scholarly content and make it available to the masses. The Million Book Project was funded by the National Science Foundation in 2000 and has furthered research in storage, searching, image processing and machine translation (St. Clair, 2008).

CLOCKSS (Controlled LOCKSS) is a joint venture between scholarly publishers and research libraries for the purpose of building a sustainable distributed archive which preserves scholarly publications. CLOCKSS (*http://www.clockss.org/clockss/Home*) preserves "orphaned" content (content no longer available from any publisher) with a Creative Commons License. Portico (*http://www.portico.org/digital-preservation/*), OCA (*http://www.opencontent alliance.org/*) and WEST (*http://www.cdlib.org/services/west/*) work with members to preserve digital content for perpetual access.

HathiTrust (*http://www.hathitrust.org/*) is another member-directed preservation effort of research institutions and libraries working to preserve and make accessible the digital content of member libraries. An important goal of the project is to "stimulate efforts to coordinate shared collection management strategies among libraries, thus reducing long-term capital and operating costs of libraries associated with the storage and care of print collections" (Christenson, 2011: 95). It differs from CLOCKSS and Portico in that it focuses on the collection of member libraries, whereas the former focus on publisher content. "Looking beyond digitized book and journal content, HathiTrust is engaged in pilot projects to support submission and preservation of digital audio materials and digital images such as maps and photographs" (York, 2012: 2).

Google Books (*http://www.google.com/googlebooks/library.html*) is a sometimes uneasy collaboration between Google and libraries with the purpose of digitizing materials from major library collections. There is considerable overlap between Google's digitization projects and those already underway in participating libraries. The bulk of the project concentrates on pre-1923 material, or material outside US copyright law, and many librarians believe the older material may be misleading because more current research isn't freely available on the web. A few libraries are opening their material to the project regardless of copyright status while waiting final litigation from the suit.

Digitization activity is occurring at different levels in an uncoordinated and scattered manner. Digital preservation presents challenges that involve managing a wide variety of formats, storage media and technology which can handle the file formats. "The underlying storage technologies will be replaced on a regular basis, services will be closed down and new ones started, and workflows will be adapted as technology, policies, or processes change. The holdings of the repositories will need to be moved to new storage media (i.e., refreshed), migrated, or just emulated" (Ross, 2012: 50). While many libraries have requirements for preserving the highest quality of a scan in a non-proprietary format for library digitization projects, making derivatives for public access, it is not always possible to enforce that standard on individuals creating digital content outside the library, and who later donate content.

Preserving the content alone is not sufficient to ensure that it will be usable in the future. It is also important to understand the context of the file. This is the Representation Information (RI) that includes enough detailed information to make the file usable. This can be complicated because of connections between elements that exist in multiple files. Other important factors include references to time and geographic location, which can be obscured by semantic changes that take place over time:

> Creation and management of RI networks have some inherent challenges because semantic meaning and world view of a given object are often different from one community to another or even from one user group to another within the same community, and how such differences may result in a failure or misuse of RI networks among communities will remain a matter of concern.
>
> (Chowdhury, 2010: 218)

These problems are not unique to digital information; however, unlike print material with citation standards, the ephemeral nature of digital content frequently lacks citation information, so it is left to curators to fill in the missing pieces of information which will make the files useful to researchers in the future.

Identity management for authors is also a problem in sharing files and making the files interoperable between applications. Until the Open Research and Contributor ID (ORCID) movement (*http://about.orcid.org/*) there were few attempts to standardize or control name variations across geographic or subject specialties. ORCID is creating a scholarly identifier that will be unique to individuals and that allows them to link to external services and import information from those services. Records for authors who are no longer actively involved in research will be more difficult to authenticate since the individual isn't available to validate their record. In such cases, ORCID is planning to use an automated disambiguation process, which is known to be at best 90–95 percent accurate (Fenner et al., 2011). Other efforts to identify unique researchers include ISNI (*http://www.isni.org/*), ResearcherID (*http://www.researcher id.com/Home.action*) and Scopus Author Identifier (*http:// www.info.sciverse.com/scopus/scopus-in-detail/tools/author identifier*), which are publisher sponsored projects.

Institutional Identifiers or I² (*http://www.niso.org/ workrooms/i2*) is one of a number of initiatives being developed to create an institutional identifier that describes journals through the supply chain. This standard is designed to be implemented in library and publishing environments and will include definitions for metadata. The challenge for the project is to provide enough information that every organization in the chain is associated with what is being identified. This is particularly important for digital material that may be released in multiple editions and formats through multiple authorities.

Obsolete technology is of particular concern in the preservation of information, and libraries are struggling with the issue of either preserving the original application and the necessary obsolete hardware, or migrating the application to newer technology. The best way to handle ageing files is to migrate the files to XML or another non-proprietary format before the hardware or software disappears. This can be difficult or impossible to do because of workload issues, and because items may be acquired or donated after the technology used to create it is no longer available. Commercial data retrieving vendors may be the only option for partial recovery using a forensic software package like FTK (*http://accessdata.com/products/digital-forensics/ftk*).

New technology is also being developed to assist with accessing information from obsolete technology using emulation software that allows files created with old technology to be executed on newer platforms. One example is Dioscuri (*http://dioscuri.sourceforge.net/*), which was designed to emulate an x86 computer. Another technique is to reconstruct the obsolete applications, which requires an understanding of the purpose and construction of the original application. Detailed information of the original is used to create a reasonable duplicate of the original on newer technology.

Technology isn't the only consideration for preservation; there are also organizational stability issues, financial questions, management and accountability. The Open Archival Information System (OAIS) reference model was developed to address many of the issues for preservation. OAIS (*http://www.iso.org/iso/catalogue_detail.htm?csnumber=24683*) defines the minimal requirements for an OAIS compliant repository including: preservation, information migration, the role of software in preservation and the exchange of information (McMeekin, 2011). Best practices for trusted digital repositories (TDRs) follow these requirements. However, the OAIS model is probably not the last word for preservation as it may need further elaboration as information is stored in the cloud (Askhoj et al., 2011).

Data curation is the act of preserving raw data documented in articles and other publications, so it can be viewed, or used, by other researchers. Data curation is a new role for libraries which are accustomed to preserving information after it has been published. The general public and researchers are beginning to request data, and libraries are beginning to tackle the issues surrounding data curation. Data curation requires an understanding of the process by which the data was created and the uses for the data. This requires collaboration between librarians, researchers and the community of users who need access to data (Heidorn, 2011).

10

Data repositories, open source and the library

Abstract: Libraries are assuming new roles as publishers and managers of institutional and data repositories. Publishers have different requirements for authors wishing to deposit in institutional repositories, and some are charging author fees before articles are published and/or deposited. Libraries are also publishing e-books and e-journals, sometimes independently of any publisher and sometimes working with publishers that also offer print-on-demand services. Standard numbers like ISBNs, ISSNs, EISSNs and DOIs are important for identifying unique items. Creative Commons Licenses and General Public Licenses are useful for managing access and usage of publicly available resources.

Key words: open source, open access institutional repositories, data repositories, arXiv, Creative Commons Licenses.

Libraries are assuming new roles as publisher and conservator of information that goes beyond print or published material. These new roles include hosting institutional repositories where original and post-published material are made accessible, managing data repositories and publishing their own material as both e-print and print-on-demand.

Changing publishing models

The advent of e-publications has changed much of the publishing field. For-profit publishers are developing new methods for distributing content that include choices for open source deposits. While some publishers prevent authors from depositing in open source repositories, others are searching for a revenue model that supports local institutional repositories.

> For example, green OA, whereby authors publish in a journal and then self-archive either in their own institutional repository or in another OA website, is unpaid access to publisher or society content and, therefore, unsustainable. Gold OA, in which authors pay to publish in a journal that then provides immediate access to all articles, is considered sustainable by publishers, as is a third option, hybrid OA, where authors pay to have their article made available immediately on publication in an otherwise subscription-based journal.
>
> (Campbell and Meadows, 2011: 174)

To recognize the importance of publisher compensation for open access the Compact for Open-Access Publishing Equity (COPE) was formed (*http://www.oacompact.org/compact/*). COPE is a pledge signed by universities to underwrite reasonable publication charges for articles written by its faculty that are published in fee-based open-access journals, and for which other institutions would not be expected to provide funds. The goal of this effort is to expand access to scholarly journals, and it is a compromise that represents forward momentum for aligning the interests of publishers with libraries.

Smaller publishers are also struggling with the long-term content management of their publications and are looking for ways to preserve content for the future economically. This includes turning to outside repositories to manage content. In 2010, JSTOR (*http://about.jstor.org/csp*) launched the Current Scholarship Program to expand their holdings by including recent issues of scholarly journals from publishers. The University of California Press joined the program for several reasons: "JSTOR offers a stable, affordable hosting solution for publishers who do not wish to host their own content or are looking for an alternative hosting solution, and also helps publishers with print-only journals to bring their titles online" (Fritsch, 2011: 79).

The Directory of Open Access Journals (DOAJ) (*http:// www.doaj.org/*) lists scholarly journals that use a peer-review or editorial process to guarantee the content quality. There are no access fees or embargoes on content. DOAJ works directly with publishers who submit the journal content, and some publishers require the authors to pay a fee before accepting the article for inclusion in their publication to offset potential revenue losses because the article is made available through DOAJ. As a consequence, the journals may be free to readers, but the authors (or grant agencies) may have been required to pay a large fee before the article was published.

The Directory of Open Access Books (DOAB) (*http:// www.doabooks.org/doab*) was created to provide access to scholarly e-books. Scholarly publishers provide metadata of their open access books to DOAB, and the metadata is made available to aggregators and libraries for integration into their catalogs. The directory is open to all publishers who publish academic, peer-reviewed books through open access.

The US Government hosts a repository of federal documents at *http://www.fdsys.gov*, which includes all three branches of the government. Information about government publications is provided in XML formats, with options for downloading. It was developed as both a content management system and a preservation repository.

Another large repository is hosted at Cornell University Library (*http://arxiv.org/*), and provides open access to e-prints in physics, mathematics, computer science, quantitative biology, quantitative finance and statistics. This site is not peer reviewed but provides quick dissemination of information, along with links to "also reads."

Managing intellectual property is becoming a priority for the commercial sector, and Bibliogo (*http://info.bibliogo.com/*), which received the 2012 CODiE Award for Best Online Science or Technology Service, provides a tool for life science and engineering researchers that combines access to information while capturing the intellectual property of companies. It manages the research process from beginning to end by providing tools for collaboration, bibliography management and article preparation.

The library as publisher

Librarians have developed expertise in content management and have much to offer in the publishing arena. Librarians understand indexing and metadata, and can assist with building content that is interoperable, making it possible to repurpose content in applications that go beyond the journal. Many libraries are entering the publishing arena at the same time they establish institutional repositories. The two activities are similar, and commercial products like Digital Commons (*http://digitalcommons.bepress.com/*) include features for managing both an institutional repository and publishing e-journals. There are a variety of options from both commercial and open source libraries entering the e-journal or e-book publishing arena. E-books fall into two categories, those that have been digitized from printed texts, and those that are born digital without a previous print version.

E-journal publishing is more complicated than e-book publishing because it involves managing editors, the peer-review process, submissions, archives and subscriptions. Table 10.1 lists a number of providers with support for digital publishing at the time of writing.

Each book, and e-book publisher, has different services and pricing models that librarians should compare before selecting a publisher. A business plan will help identify the most important factors to consider when selecting a publisher, including: requirements for emerging technology adaptions of e-books and audio versions, distribution channels available, marketing assistance and the ROI based on the publisher's fees. Careful attention should be given to contracts that include exclusivity clauses, which will limit the options for additional distribution channels and ultimately reduce sales.

Before entering into e-journal publishing, libraries should identify the level of support that will be offered, how the service will be funded and whether or not the library will be hosting the service on library supported computers. In addition, there are questions about how much training will be given to editors, who will provide technical support, what assistance will be given for content development and whether or not to publish as open access or for paid subscription. In the case of universities that have a press division, it may be advantageous to partner with the press.

Many of the open access e-publications use a Creative Commons License for rights management (*http://creative commons.org/licenses/*). It is not a DRM system that restricts access to information; rather it is intended to protect the

Table 10.1 New opportunities for digital printing

Producer	URL	Format and features	Type
Allen Press	http://allenpress.com/	E-books, books, e-journals, journals: on-demand printing; production tracking; manuscript tracking, peer review; pre-editing; copy-editing and proofreading; composition; 2d tags; illustration processing; author billing; advertising and sponsorship sales support; marketing; book; project management for books; license management.	Commercial
Apple	http://www.apple.com/ibooks-author/	E-books: multimedia: supports only EPUB files and Multi-Touch books; exclusive for iBook format, not exclusive for other formats.	Commercial
AuthorHouse	http://www.authorhouse.com/	Books, e-books, audio books, animation app: print-on-demand; design; production; scanning.	Commercial
Bench>Press	http://highwire.org/publishers/benchpress.dtl	E-books, e-journals: web-based manuscript tracking and management service; configures workflows; integrates with HighWire's online publishing services; reduces time from submission to publication.	Commercial
BioMed Central	http://www.biomedcentral.com/	E-journals: open access only; editorial control; submission to decision management; marketing; collaboration with web-based services such as CrossRef and with aggregators; peer review.	Commercial
Cadmus/Cenveo	http://www.cadmus.com/index.htm	Books, e-books, journals, articles: content, print and distribution services including articles, journals, magazines, books, catalogs; ad management; data conversion; digital art; editorial services; electronic proofing; multimedia; online submission and tracking; page composition and coding; production tracking; project management.	Commercial

CreateSpace and KDP Select (Amazon)	https://www.createspace.com/pub/l/general_value.do?rewrite=true&ref=1159301&utm_id=6031	Books, e-books: publisher option for books; print-on-demand; Kindle; book scanning and production services; DVD, CD and MP3 production; marketing. Create space is not exclusive, KDP is exclusive for a minimum of 90 days.	Commercial
Digital Commons	http://digitalcommons.bepress.com/repository-software/journals/	E-journals, e-books: supports open access or subscription-based journals; custom design; access control; editorial management of workflows; peer-review tracking and referee activity; automatic email reminders; mechanism for anonymous correspondence.	Commercial
DPubS	http://dpubs.org/	E-books, ejournals: organization, presentation and delivery of scholarly journals, monographs, conference proceedings; open-access and subscription or pay-per-view options; managing new publications, defining collections, submitting content and subscription data; viewing content and subscription-data; submission queues.	Open source
IssueManager	http://onlinemagazinepublishing.com/	E-journals: uses WordPress; publish to Twitter, Facebook and LinkedIn; offers both free stories, paid articles with teaser text and community building tools.	Commercial
iUniverse	http://www.iuniverse.com/	Books, print-on-demand; marketing; production; not exclusive contracts.	Commercial
Kobo	http://www.kobobooks.com/KoboWritingLIfe	E-books: convert to epub, supports DRM; not exclusive.	Commercial
Lulu	http://www.lulu.com/	Print books, e-books: cover design, editing, formatting, marketing; exclusive.	Commercial
Mill City Press	http://www.millcitypress.net/publishing	Books, e-books: print-on-demand; design; marketing.	Commercial

Table 10.1 New opportunities for digital printing (*cont'd*)

pub2web	http://www.publishingtechnology.com/products/digital/pub2web.php	E-journals: subscription management for libraries and consortia; in-page editing tool in real time; management tool for tracking; tool to view and edit licenses; registrations and trial access; analytics; supports discovery tools; link resolvers; multiple licensing models; mobile; multiple content formats.	Commercial
PubIt! (Barnes & Noble)	http://pubit.barnesandnoble.com/pubit_app/bn?t=pi_reg_home	E-books: not exclusive; included in NOOK Books program, such as Read in Store, LendMe, Samples, and eGifting.	Commercial
Public Knowledge Product	http://pkp.sfu.ca/	E-journals: includes open source and service plans; editor configure for workflow; online submission and management; subscription module; open access options; indexing, reading tools; e-mail notifications; readers' comments.	Open source/commercial
Smashwords	http://www.smashwords.com/	E-books: provides tools for marketing, distribution, metadata management and sales reporting; free ISBNs; not exclusive.	Commercial
Xlibris	http://www2.xlibris.com/	Books, e-books: not exclusive; print-on-demand; genre services; data entry; marketing; hard, leader and paperback editions.	Commercial

author's rights while encouraging the distribution of information. Creative Commons provides several models for licenses, which cover a variety of situations including commercial use, and includes provisions for derivatives. A Creative Commons License can be added to e-journals, e-books, blogs, presentation slides, photographs, etc., and can provide the terms for redistribution. The Creative Commons website has a license chooser that generates HTML code that can be incorporated into any web-based content (*http://creativecommons.org/choose/*).

ISSNs, EISSNs, ISBNs and DOIs

Standard numbers that identify unique items are becoming increasingly important as more and more information is added to the Internet. ORCID identifiers for authors will soon join with ISBNs, ISSNs and EISSNs to create another reliable way to identify unique content. Standard numbers also play a role in interconnecting applications in the Semantic Web by providing a match point to "join" related information. Any library considering a venture into publishing should obtain either the ISBN or ISSN number for their publication, as well as a DOI for any digital publication.

ISBN numbers have a history that dates back to 1966 when the English retailer W.H. Smith created the Standard Book Numbering (SBN) system which became an ISO standard in 1970. Since then, the size of the number has grown to 13 characters, and additional types were added for print journals (ISSN) and e-journals (EISSN). ISBN numbers are assigned by national agencies around the world. In the US, numbers are assigned by registering with the US ISBN Agency (*https://www.myidentifiers.com/*); in the UK, it is the

Neilson ISBN Agency (*http://www.isbn.nielsenbook.co.uk/ controller.php?page=158*); in Canada, numbers are supplied by Libraries and Archives Canada (*http://www.collections canada.gc.ca/isn/041011-1010-e.html*); and other countries can be found at the International ISBN Agency (*http://www. isbn-international.org/*).

Journals receive ISSN numbers that are maintained at the International Centre (France) (*http://www.issn.org/*). Numbers can be requested from the Centre or from a national library. In the US they are assigned by the ISSN Center at the Library of Congress *(http://www.loc.gov/issn/)*. ISSNs and EISSNs are both considered sub-properties of ISSN-L by the International Centre (*http://issn.org/2-22637-What-is-an-ISSN-L.php*), under an ISO standard for linking multiple versions.

Digital Object Identifier (DOI) numbers were established to provide permanent identification that is unique to all web content. DOI is also used by resolvers to match citations in article databases with full text. DOIs are managed through the International DOI Foundation (IDF) (*http://www.doi.org/*). DOI numbers can be requested through CrossRef (*http://www. crossref.org/index.html*), which is the official DOI registration agency. Every DOI identifies the unique item and provides a persistent URL to its web address. DOIs are assigned to the article level; for example, DOI: 10.1080/19322909.2010.507 972 identifies an article on discovery tools (Allison, 2010), and when entered in a browser as *http://dx.doi.org/10.1080/1932 2909.2010.507972* it will retrieve the full text.

Digital repositories

Many libraries are managing digital repositories for their institutions. These institutional repositories (IRs) are used to store documents authored by individuals at the institution and include copies of articles that are either first published in journals or published originally through the repository. Some repositories are subject-field based, and some collect format-based content. The most common repositories are associated with universities and contain scholarly publications by the faculty. This model includes Gold, where the author pays a fee for archiving a published paper in an IR, and Green, where the author publishes in a journal and then submits the paper into an IR.

A variation on the Gold model is the commercial open access repositories, in which accessing the article is free, but the author must pay a fee for deposit. "These article processing charges can range from hundreds of dollars to several thousand dollars. While authors are assessed these processing charges, typically the funding APC payments come from the same grants that produce the research being documented" (Boissy and Schatz, 2011: 480). Several more traditional publishers are also providing an option to eliminate embargoes on depositing in public IRs if the author pays a processing fee.

Faculty members who publish articles are beginning to accept repositories as a means for providing open access, although not without reservations. A 2011 survey of researchers, from a sample biased towards science researchers, indicated that 63 percent of the researchers had deposited in a repository, with 47 percent doing so voluntarily and another 21.6 percent doing so because of an institutional requirement (Nicholas et al., 2012). A journal article was the type most frequently deposited in an IR. Among this sample, 63 percent of the researchers preferred obtaining information from a subject repository over an IR (52 percent). Not surprisingly, the survey respondents reported concerns about the quality and long-term viability of IRs over subject repositories.

These findings are important for libraries with IRs. First, it is important for repositories to have clear explanations about the quality of IR content and any peer-review process applied to deposits. The quality of deposits is an important factor in the reputation of the repository and may explain why faculty members prefer subject-field repositories over local IRs. Librarians can also provide information about the long-term preservation of materials, provide persistent URLs to faculty contributions, provide assurances about an infrastructure that will support growth, be adaptable as technology changes, and expose IR content so that faculty can repurpose the content on their own sites. This last will help assure faculty that the library is committed to the long-term support and enhancement of content.

Librarians can play an important role in facilitating the implementation of policies that require depositing in the IR. The University of Kansas implemented a policy in 2009 that accomplished two goals: "This policy implemented the two critical elements of open access required deposit in an institutional archive and it created an automatic license that attaches to the work before transfer of copyright to the publisher" (Emmett et al., 2011: 563). The license referred to in the policy is a non-exclusive license to provide open access versions, but it does not transfer copyright. This policy makes the Dean of Libraries responsible for implementing the policy, and liaison librarians were asked to participate in all phases of implementation including education and scholarly communication activities.

Copyright assistance is another area where librarians can provide advice to faculty who are considering deposit. Many faculty members continue to be confused about what is appropriate to deposit, and what comes under fair use, or may even want libraries to pay the fees for public access. Whether or not libraries, authors or research offices will pay these fees will be an institutional decision. It is important for the librarians to take the lead in these discussions, or the lack of clarity will be a barrier to increasing deposits in publicly accessible IRs.

Hosting services and software is available for libraries that establish their own repositories. Many libraries use the open source application DSpace (*http://www.dspace.org/*) for their repository architecture. Fedora (Flexible Extensible Digital Object Repository Architecture) is another digital asset management application that also supports IRs (*http://www.fedora-commons.org/*). Fedora software is integrated with semantic triple store technology and can handle different content formats. There are also commercial options for IRs, including EPrints (*http://www.eprints.org/*) and Digital Commons (*http://digitalcommons.bepress.com/*), both hosted by the vendors.

Whichever product is selected it is important for libraries to engage the community that will be making deposits. Periodic usage reports will encourage additional deposits and provide evidence of the value of a repository to the parent institution. Repositories that allow depositors to link to, and incorporate, their deposits into their personal site will also attract deposits. Marketing that drives traffic to the IR is also an important aspect of managing an IR. Finally, libraries should be careful not to silo their repositories, but to integrate the repository with their other resources.

It's all about the data

Librarians are accustomed to managing all types of books and articles, and, previously, have not been concerned with managing the data used as a source for publications. However, publishers and funding agencies are recognizing the importance of data in an age where data can be made available to the general public through inexpensive technology. The number of US governmental agencies requiring data management plans with options for public availability is growing. Journal publishers are also beginning to request that data be made available with articles, as seen with *Nature* and *Cell*.

Librarians have become involved in this area because of the expertise they bring to managing content, and data is content. There are alternatives to a local repository for data which include a mix of public and private repositories that concentrate on a particular sector of research activity. A local or institutional data repository can fit into this structure by providing redundancy (for long-term preservation), and by collecting information on research activity at the institution, which, when shared with a constituency, demonstrates value to stakeholders.

Data.gov (*https://explore.data.gov/*) was established to expose raw data for the general public. This site provides browse and search functionality for data that was sponsored by the federal government. Databib (*http://databib.org/*) is a collaborative, annotated bibliography of primary research data and is a good source for locating subject repositories.

The Data Preservation Alliance for the Social Sciences (Data-PASS) project (*http://data-pass.org/*) was instituted to archive, catalog and preserve social science research data including: opinion polls, election records, surveys on social issues, social data, government statistics and indices, and GIS data measuring human activity. This type of data is important to preserve, if researchers in the future hope to do comparison analysis.

Another preservation initiative is the Digital Preservation Network (DPN), launched in 2012 (*http://d-p-n.org/*). DPN is a collaborative project of US universities to create redundant nodes that are geographically dispersed. The purpose of DPN is to eliminate a single point of failure that could result in the loss of scholarly material.

A Cal Poly survey of science faculty indicated that faculty believed they were responsible for data management, but a majority didn't believe a data preservation plan was necessary (Scaramozzino et al., 2012). Librarians need to work with faculty to convince them of the necessity and importance of data preservation. However, there may be a larger issue for libraries working to create local registries for their institutions, that of competition with subject or domain registries, or of convincing faculty of the need to deposit – or, at a minimum, register – data with the local institution.

Subject data repositories have been in existence for many years. The Digging into Data website contains a registry of data repositories that includes many library and subject repositories (*http://www.diggingintodata.org/Repositories/ tabid/167/Default.aspx*). As libraries have become more active in developing institutional data repositories they must make accommodations with the subject repositories already using data contributed by researchers from their institutions who prefer to continue to use the familiar repository, by providing connections between the home institution and the subject repository. Researchers recognize the importance libraries have played historically in preserving information and, hopefully, will recognize the expertise that comes with that experience.

The DANS-ABC model can assist institutions in creating a long-term costing model for the preservation and dissemination of data (Palaiologk et al., 2012). This model, as proposed by the authors, divides the cost areas for data preservation into five activities: resource pools, resource cost drivers, activity, activity cost drivers and cost objects. Resource pools include salary and non-salary budget items that relate to data acquisition and management and are specific expenses associated with resource activities in the pool. Specific activities are described in the model and are associated with activity cost drivers that help estimate future costs. When this model is combined with a balanced scorecard, it provides a method for aligning the cost for preserving data with strategic goals and can identify inefficient processes. Given the amount of staff time required for managing a data repository, this model presents an interesting method for estimating the cost for managing data long term.

Metadata for repositories

There are several challenges in preserving digital repositories that involve metadata. The OAIS Reference Model has been helpful in providing a framework for preserving metadata through the Archival Information Package (AIP) that describes the content and the Preservation Description Information (PDI) which contains the information necessary for long-term preservation. It is specific enough to identify the characteristics of the data, including structure and semantic interpretations along with provenance, context and version. The OAIS model is the framework used by Metadata Object Description Scheme (MODS), Metadata Encoding and Transmission Standard (METS) and Preservation Metadata Implementation Strategies (PREMIS) which guide PDI information for collections. These are flexible metadata schemas that are content-independent and can be combined in a variety of ways. That is good news for flexibility, but creates complications when it comes to sharing the metadata.

Web Ontology Language (OWL) is metadata designed to facilitate computer interpretation of content by providing a vocabulary with formal semantics. OWL is managed by the W3C (*http://www.w3.org/TR/owl-features/*) and, like any ontology, is a framework for specifying the hierarchical relationships between elements. What makes OWL different is the focus on elements specific to machine processing, which provides for greater functionality in a Web 2.0 environment.

Closely related to data conservation is the question of support for e-Science. This describes the process that uses computational science, usually in a distributed network that results in massive amounts of data. The most prominent example is the data being generated from the CERN Large Hadron Collider. E-Science preservation creates additional challenges beyond the very large data sets that involve metadata for process description. This metadata must describe the methodology of the experiment in sufficient detail so that another researcher can repeat the experiment. Mayer et al. (2012) propose a contextual model using OWL that contains approximately 240 elements arranged into groups that describe the activities, human resources, software, hardware, tools and processes required to reconstruct the experiment.

The new math of open source

Open source is similar to open access for e-publications because software applications are developed in a shared environment. Open source projects frequently use a collaborative mechanism that helps applications grow over time. Each participant adds to code development contributing part of the total resources available for development. Collaboration is becoming more essential as a means of controlling expenses for libraries, and this is especially true in developing open source code. Although there are examples where open source has failed, there are also examples of where it has succeeded dramatically. The Apache web server has been so successful that it is in common use around the world (*http://www.apache.org/*).

The Open Source Initiative (OSI) (*http://opensource.org/*) is the recognized authority that guides the open source movement. It advocates for the free distribution of source code so the code can be easily modified. Hedgebeth (2007) corrects some misconceptions about open source:

- It is not less secure than commercial software; it includes customer support (in many ways it is built by customers).

- It is different than shareware or freeware because it adheres to community standards and makes the code available in the public domain.

- It will work with commercial software.

- Businesses can build and sell applications using open source code.

- Not all open source code is free.

Open source software usually has a license covering usage. The General Public License (GPL) is used for collaborative licenses to protect software developers' rights, assert copyright and state permissions for distribution and modification. GNU licenses (*http://www.gnu.org/licenses/licenses.html*) cover a variety of circumstances and, like Creative Commons Licenses, are intended to protect the developers while encouraging software sharing. A common characteristic of open source licenses is protection against liability from misuse or potential harm that might arise from use. This is important in software development since technical complications are always possible with implementations.

There are also open source efforts that involve the library community. These include collaborations for developing library catalogs, such as with Evergreen (*http://evergreen-ils.org/*), Koha (*http://www.koha.org/*), PMB (*http://www.extradrm.com/blog/?p=30*) and Kuali Open Library Environment (OLE) (*http://kuali.org/ole*). Kuali is developing an extensible service-centered library system using the OLE reference model (*http://www.kuali.org/ole/modules*).

Selecting an open source solution over a commercial product can be a challenging decision to make. There is the question of resources, requiring programmers both for development and bug fixing, and staff to coordinate programming with other partners in the project. Functionality is also important. Müller (2011) recommends evaluating open source library catalog software against three criteria: licensing, community and functionality. Of these three criteria, evaluation of the community may be the most important because open source either succeeds or fails because of commitment from development partners.

When evaluating the strength of the community it is important to look at what resources each partner is contributing to the project. Here is a simple formula for assessing the value of an open source project:

Local resources + community resources = outcome

The closer the local resource contribution is to 100 percent, the less viable a partnership; the lower the number, the more valuable the alliance. The resources devoted to projects should be considered in whole, not in part. If the local commitment is 50 percent, and each of several other partners is individually less than that, but collectively underwrites the remaining 50 percent, then it is a better solution for the library to contribute 50 percent than to devote the 100 percent needed do a project alone. However, if the combination of members' commitment is less than the 100 percent anticipated resources needed to carry out a project, the participants will encounter delays and obstacles to success.

Free/Libre and Open Source Software (FLOSS) is an international effort to evaluate and associate business methodology to the management of open source (*http:// www.flossproject.org/*). The goals of FLOSS include quantifying the cost and value of open source projects and the identification of best practices into a business model. The final report provides information for any librarian who is considering a major investment in software development and is looking to develop a business plan that may have commercial implications.

When there is a commercial product available it is reasonable to compare it with open source alternatives. The expense of a commercial online catalog will at first appear to be more expensive than an open source alternative; however, the stability of the product, combined with vendor support, and the development cycle for features should also be considered. Normally a commercial product will be more developed and full-featured than open source alternatives, but this is not always the case, so careful comparisons are necessary. Develop a list of functional requirements and rank each product based on "must have," "nice to have" and "optional." Evaluate all products on this scale to determine the functions that will best meet current and short-term needs.

Yang and Hofmann (2010) proposed ten categories for comparing the functionality of two open source catalogs, Koha and Evergreen, against a commercial catalog, Voyager:

- A single point of entry to all library information.
- State-of-the-art web interface.
- Enriched content.
- Faceted navigation.
- Simple key word search box.
- Relevancy.
- Did you mean ...?
- Recommendations and related materials.
- User contribution – ratings, reviews, comments and tagging.
- RSS feeds.

All evaluations of products should stress the features local users are requesting, plus future plans for functionality. It is also important to calculate the ROI, which can be determined on fixed prices for technology (including hardware depreciation) and staffing, with anticipated changes in the same costs calculated over time. Finally, an evaluation of the community behind an open source project should be weighed against the reputation and depth of the commercial vendor. The ability to support any technology will determine the short- and long-term success of that application, and whether or not users will accept and be satisfied with the product.

11

The new professional librarian

Abstract: While the digital culture is challenging librarians by requiring new skills, it is also providing new opportunities in non-traditional jobs in the commercial sector. Library positions are being redefined through reclassifications and reductions to accommodate the higher skill levels needed for knowledge workers. Professional development is available through websites that offer social networking and webinars. The workforce in a patron centered library is empowered through enlightened management that acknowledges limited control, with a flattened hierarchy. Hiring digital natives provides new ways for managers to assess personality as well as skills, both important for changing libraries from collection centered to patron centered approaches. Change management and technology adoption are ongoing issues that can be addressed using analytical techniques including social network analysis, theories of learned helplessness and assessment. Locating and obtaining funding is becoming a more important function for libraries, and responsibility for obtaining funding is becoming more dispersed in the organization.

Key words: non-traditional library jobs, librarian entrepreneurs, virtual reference, knowledge workers, career growth, post-hierarchical library, social network analysis, learned helplessness.

As reported by *Forbes*: "The low pay rank and estimated growth rank make library and information science the worst master's degree for jobs right now" (Smith, 2012: 2). This statement is being echoed by recent graduates struggling to find positions in a weakened economy. However, this writer doesn't share this pessimism because the digital culture is providing new opportunities for those willing to venture beyond traditional library positions to address with confidence and determination the challenges it brings. As librarians change their focus from collections to patrons there are new opportunities to use traditional library skills as knowledge workers.

> But for us to come to a clear understanding of these changes, and what they mean for us as individuals, requires that we think clearly and analytically about our relationship, as librarians, to both our libraries and to the larger communities that we serve. Indeed, I believe that if we do this, we find that while the great age of libraries is coming to an end, the great age of librarians is just beginning.
>
> (Plutchak, 2012: 10)

This statement by Plutchak summarizes the path ahead for those seeking to redefine the role librarians play in every type of library, as well as reshape the image of librarians in society.

Non-traditional jobs for non-traditional librarians

The days when the profession attracted timid book lovers are gone – replaced by a new age that is attracting dynamic and technology-savvy workers into the profession. Catalogers are no longer catalogers, but metadata specialists who understand content and access. Bibliographers are now subject specialists who engage patrons in ways that emphasize the user experience. ILL managers must collaborate with other managers for the rapid exchange of documents. The primary responsibility of technology units is no longer the catalog, but mobile, instruction and user engagement, with an emphasis on collaboration (Erlandson, 2010). Ten years ago, the library technology viewpoint may have been "If you build it, they will come," but this is no longer true. The library of today must be built for users, and there are a growing number of positions for skilled librarians who share this vision.

Many of the traditional jobs that were prevalent in the last decade are being transformed. "At the University of Iowa, the librarian administering the e-journal publishing service is a former serials librarian" (Lawrence, 2010: 238). Digital content is complex content and requires a knowledge worker. It can be challenging to refocus from collections to patrons when the workforce includes staff members who were hired in a print world and now must transition into the digital world. Staff members who are still needed for paper-based workflows can be cross-trained for positions that require technology skills (Michalak, 2012). Cross-training is also a good way to help staff members transition into technology positions, so that they can experience success under less pressure.

New jobs require new skills and Table 11.1 is a list of competencies for librarians entering the profession. These are a combination of skills and talents, both essential in a new environment that places great importance on collaboration and meeting user expectations. Public service librarians will also need expertise in areas relating to their customer base, while technical service librarians will need a high level of competency in computing technology.

Changes in competencies for staff members are occurring along with increased adoption of technology for resources

Table 11.1 Skills and talents required of today's librarian

Skills for librarians	Talents
Advocacy	Adaptability: ability to change
Assessment	Articulation: ability to write and speak clearly
Business practice	Balanced thinking: ability to see possibilities beyond personal opinions
Conflict management	Collaboration: ability to work with others
Content management systems	Commitment to lifelong learning
Copyright	Courage
CSS style sheets	Creativity: ability to see possibilities and alternatives
Data management	Empathy
E-publishing	Flexibility: willingness to change
HTML and XML	Foresight: ability to see ramifications of personal actions
Licensing	Integrity: willingness to "do the right thing"
Marketing	Intuition: ability to read silences
Metadata standards	Leadership: ability to inform and guide
Mobile computing and applications development	Openness: approachability
Multi-lingual	Salesmanship: ability to create enthusiasm
Negotiation	
Open source movement	
Project management	
Public speaking	
Reference managers	
Research and scholarship	
Search strategies	
Spreadsheets	
SQL database	
Statistics	

Teaching	
Understanding of computers	
Word processing	
Writing	

and operations. The biggest impact from digital content comes from reductions in the volume of work in binding, serial check-in and claiming (Glasser and Arthur, 2011). Additional reductions have occurred when libraries move from manual cataloging to processing catalog records from vendors. The University of Pittsburgh redesigned its workflow and outsourced English language cataloging to OCLC, reducing staffing from 70 to 29 (Miller, 2012).

The transition to e-resources has also been difficult for support staff members who must learn new skills as records are retrieved from bibliographic utilities, and when they are asked to manage e-journals that arrive invisibly from aggregate systems and that sometimes disappear just as mysteriously. There are complex authentication systems, link resolvers, ERM systems, federated search engines and statistics to be compiled for reports. Managers in technical services have often responded by reclassifying lower positions into higher positions, or by combining positions to create higher-paying positions, all the while training staff for increased responsibilities (Mitchell et al., 2010). These changes are powered by information technology and automation, which bring the benefit of efficiency but require a higher order of technical skills. This has also changed some fundamental values among technical service units as the emphasis for work moved away from books to information, and as staff members have become less involved in managing collections and more directly aligned with customer service.

New jobs for digital librarians

As libraries look for ways to increase service by outsourcing, there are opportunities for librarians in alternative positions. Virtual reference (VR) services are opening up new opportunities for librarians. Tutor.com (*http://www.tutor. com/libraries/products/virtual-reference*) offers reference services to libraries seeking to outsource reference or supplement local staff. Although there is some debate over the quality of outsourced VR, Hill et al. (2007) reported user satisfaction with the service. VR requires the same skills as face-to-face reference, plus some new talents. The ability to conduct a good reference interview is still a prerequisite for VR, as is a positive attitude.

The VR librarian will also need a good understanding of a broad number of resources, because libraries do not all have the same resources. Likewise, the librarian answering a question from a patron at another library will not be familiar with that library website so flexibility and familiarity with business operations is necessary to navigate through the unknown website to locate information. VR can be more challenging because of a dependence on technology (both the known workstation and the patron's unknown computer set-up) that may create communication problems, which means that librarians need a good understanding of technology. Finally, a VR librarian may need to handle multiple simultaneous questions when queue options are not available. Despite these challenges, VR may be a good choice for some librarians.

New professionals should not limit their job searches to positions in libraries. There are entrepreneurial opportunities emerging from the digital culture. It is expected that there will be fewer hard technology jobs like server administrators in the future because of outsourcing technical support to the cloud, and contracting for specialized services at the point of need (King and Mayor, 2012). Employers will be hiring people who understand processing and workflows, and who are skilled at working with people. Does this sound like librarians? Not that technology skills are less important, they are still essential in a digital world, but librarians who are able to keep current with technology and willing to invest in training will be well-positioned for the job market, not just library positions but other positions where the skills of information management and collaboration are valued.

There is growing activity in self-publishing among writers, especially fiction writers who are frustrated with the slow process of breaking into the publishing world. Self-published or "indie" authors have many options for publishing, and can build a community of readers by independently selling works at lower prices. Tim Cushing writes, "if an author can earn the same or greater income selling lower cost books, yet reach significantly more readers, then drum roll please, it means the authors who are selling higher priced books through traditional publishers are at an extreme disadvantage to indie authors in terms of long-term platform building" (Cushing, 2012: 1).

Librarians who understand publishing as a business, the technology of publishing, e-book formats and marketing could have new careers offering services to authors who want to concentrate on the art rather than the business of self-publishing. This isn't a literary agent job but the post of a consultant who solves problems, connects authors with resources and offers advice. Librarians can assist a new author with social media for advocacy, navigate through e-book formatting and copyright issues, and educate about the differences between e-book publishers.

There are other opportunities for the independent or indie librarian. A librarian blogger can turn a passion into profit by creating a business of supplying information. The following summarizes advice from others (Morell, 2012):

focus on a specialization, develop multiple skills for marketing your expertise, create a business plan or vision, and build multiple streams of income that can include e-journals, books, television or presentations, and other venues that showcase abilities.

Using the web for career growth

The web offers many opportunities for career growth that encompass webinars, social media networks, blogs and a variety of websites that offer practical advice or technical information. LinkedIn (*http://www.linkedin.com/*) provides opportunities for career building through individual and group networking. Members can build networks of like-minded colleagues and join discussion groups that bring professionals together to exchange ideas and advice. Library associations and subject interest groups are also excellent ways to establish connections with other professionals.

In addition to library conferences at the national and regional levels, librarians have opportunities for learning through webinars. Some webinars are sponsored by vendors to educate librarians about features or changes in their products. Infopeople (*http://infopeople.org/*) offers presentations on current topics of interest to librarians. Infopeople is supported by the 1996 Library Services and Technology Act and is administered by the California State Librarian. Encompass Live (*http://nlc.nebraska.gov/NCompassLive/*) is administered by the Nebraska Library Commission and provides webinars on a variety of topics. Many other state libraries offer similar online courses that are either free or low cost.

Table 11.2 lists resources for current information on library and technical developments.

Table 11.2	A sampling of websites that provide current information of interest to librarians

URL to site	Focus area
http://www.apple.com/hotnews/	Apple product information
http://www.bl.uk/blogs/index.html	British Library list of blogs
https://www.cdt.org/	Center for Democracy & Technology
http://www.zdnet.com/	Computer news
http://datamining.typepad.com/data_mining/	Data mining
http://epic.org/	Electronic privacy information
http://embeddedlibrarian.com	Embedded librarianship
http://gizmodo.com/	News about technology, mobiles, etc.
http://www.gameinformer.com/	News about games and gaming
http://www.handheldlib.blogspot.com/	Handheld Librarian blog
http://mobile.engadget.com/	Mobile computing news
http://infopeople.org/	Info people: podcasts and webinars on library topics
http://www.librarytechnology.org/	Information on developments in ILS and related tech
http://blendedlibrarian.org/index.html	Instructional design, technology and librarianship
http://www.thelibrarynews.com/	Library news collected from web sources
http://blogs.loc.gov/loc/	Library of Congress news
http://www.linkedin.com/	LinkedIn: social networking
http://mashable.com/social-media/	Media news
http://www.libsuccess.org/index.php?title=Main_Page	Library best practice wiki
http://nonprofitmarketingblog.com/	Marketing for non-profits
http://www.nonprofit-marketing-blog.com/	Marketing for non-profits
http://technet.microsoft.com/en-us/ms376608.aspx	News on Microsoft product information
http://www.opensourceuniverse.com/	Open source information

Table 11.2	A sampling of websites that provide current information of interest to librarians (*cont'd*)

http://intellogist.wordpress.com/	Patent information
http://www.popgoesthelibrary.com/	Pop culture in libraries
http://www.reddit.com/	Source for what's new and popular online, vote on links
http://informedlibrarian.com/	Selected publications of interest to librarians
http://semanticweb.com/	Semantic Web
http://www.teleread.com/	E-book and publishing information
http://thefutureofink.com/	The Future of Ink – e-publishing

Managing the patron centered library

One of the biggest challenges facing a manager of a patron centered library is the question of control. Libraries were started to control books, to classify, arrange and control the shelf presence. When the web came along there were plans to catalog that as well, but no one is considering that project today – Google took that role. Librarians spend too much time talking about policies, procedures, protecting our users from themselves, and not enough time talking about what users want now and in the immediate future. While librarians tried to explain how the catalog is better than the web, patrons moved on to embrace Google.

A patron centered library requires new tools to help the staff interact with users. Social media can enable librarians to share knowledge with patrons and each other. These sites also provide a channel for workers to connect with each other and with the organization, and to facilitate collaboration with colleagues inside and outside the library. Networked sites can also reduce costs by reducing the need for sending e-mail attachments, printing, or even traveling.

The empowered workforce

The patron centered library has a flattened hierarchical structure so there is less central control and more empowerment for staff. Richard Sweeney terms this "the post-hierarchical library," which is more adaptive to change in order to offer new services as needs arise. "This library is likely to be a flattened organization with empowered cross-functional teams, fewer people, constant learning, reduced operating resources, new knowledge and information infrastructures, and reinvented and reengineered work processes focused on customized service" (Sweeney, 1994: 64). In a patron centered library assumptions are put aside, and work processes are engineered to meet the needs of patrons.

The hierarchical structure of the past developed because of specializations that were required for library operations. Libraries that are siloed by departments are at a disadvantage in a digital culture because they create barriers between skilled individuals. When individuals share their expertise on projects they can be more creative and productive.

In today's environment it is also important for staff to be empowered to make agile decisions based on a solid understanding of priorities and customer service philosophy. This process begins by identifying the fundamentals and the management framework necessary to support those fundamentals. Transparent decision making is the foundation for creating an informed staff that is confident. Once staff members understand the principles behind the rules they can be empowered to decide when it is appropriate to break the rules because it is in the best interest of the patron. Decisions should be pushed to the lowest level in the organization, and cross-departmental committees can be given the responsibility to fully investigate and implement changes. Policies should facilitate customer service, never get in its way.

In order for this to happen, every employee must assume accountability for their work processes and career development. Lifelong learning is not just something librarians need to instill in patrons; they also need to practice it themselves. Although specialization is valued in a patron centered library, so is the generalist who demonstrates flexibility and a motivation to learn as the environment changes.

Hiring the best

Creating a patron centered library requires librarians with people skills, technological competence, the ability to empathize with patrons and flexibility to adapt to change – all important personality characteristics. Recruiting librarians raised in the digital culture is different than for previous generations. Managers should expect to examine candidates' websites, blogs and Facebook profiles. Likewise, Twitter, Klout scores, YouTube and LinkedIn may provide additional insight. A simple résumé is no longer sufficient for applicants applying for jobs. Savvy candidates will demonstrate not only their skills but their personality. Candidates can send a message to potential employers about who they are, revealing aspects of their personality through the social media links they provide in their applications.

Recruiting candidates also requires new methods for advertising. TweetMyJobs (*http://www.tweetmyjobs.com/*) provides a service that distributes job ads through a variety of distribution channels including social media. Metrics are also included for this service that is free for employers with fewer than 25 openings per year. Job hunters can also search the site for positions, and in addition to mobile and tweet listings they can register for e-mail listings.

When candidates arrive for interviews, they should be asked to make presentations that employ some social media. This will demonstrate both speaking ability and the opportunity to show off social media talent. The topics for presentations should be chosen carefully; a new candidate from an accredited library school will have the requisite skills. Ask candidates to make a presentation that will take them out of their "comfort zone" by asking them to redesign a service, solve a problem or issue facing the library, or defend an unpopular practice like library fees.

Recruiting for the future

Librarians have a responsibility to encourage young people to consider a career in librarianship. Summer work programs and internships are good opportunities to bring new ideas into the library and provide work experience. Students can rotate through departments, assist with programs designed to reach peers, or prepare displays. They can also be helpful in planning marketing events, and making connections back into the community.

Managers for the engaged workforce

Millennials who work in an open environment where they trust management will be more energized, and an energized workforce will push new initiatives and projects forward in a creative and problem-solving way. In a 2003 article entitled "What creates energy in organizations?" Cross et al. identified eight management characteristics that produce trust in an energized workforce:

- Do you weave relationship development into work and day-to-day actions?
- Do you do what you say you are going to do?
- Do you address tough issues with integrity?
- Do you look for possibilities or just identify constraints?
- When you disagree with someone, do you focus attention on the issue at hand rather than the individual?
- Are you cognitively and physically engaged in meetings and conversations?
- Are you flexible in your thinking or do you force others to come to your way of thinking?
- Do you use your own expertise appropriately?

(Ibid.: 56)

Engendering trust requires a manager who is willing to delegate tasks with determination. It is difficult to manage a group of staff members with varying technical skills, and managers sometimes rush to complete work themselves rather than taking the time for training. Likewise, when problems arise a knowledgeable manager may direct the actions of the staff member rather than empower the staff member to solve the problem alone. These approaches don't teach staff new skills or give them the confidence to solve work problems. These approaches also send a message that the manager doesn't trust staff to handle problems alone.

A better approach is to ask the question, "How do I make this problem their problem?" By stepping back and looking at the issue in a new way, managers will be surprised at the resiliency, commitment and ingenuity of staff. This doesn't mean that managers can abdicate responsibility for the work of staff – managers are responsible, and will get the complaints when work is not completed well. Managers should monitor situations, ask questions and become involved at appropriate times, not as commanders but as participants looking for the best solutions.

When managers have engaged library workers they may encounter an unexpected problem with workloads. Highly-energized librarians can be drawn into work or service that isn't appropriate. This can be work that is too clerical, goes beyond their expertise, or puts them in a situation where they become embroiled in another area's politics. Managers can support their staff by staying connected with the individual and maintaining ongoing conversations about work activity. The manager may need to intervene when it appears that there is a serious mismatch of expectations. A management team can also organize additional help from other areas in the library that can supply additional assistance, which also works to break down divisions between departments.

Change management

"Effective library management today is change management; effective leadership is visionary leadership" (Miller, 2012: 14). Managing change is probably the greatest challenge facing librarians today. The pace of technological change and the impact it has on behavior makes it difficult to be agile in meeting patron needs. It requires an environment that is conducive to experimentation (see Figure 11.1).

Management control is like gravity; it keeps activities grounded and is invisible, so that people aren't aware of it but feel secure in their actions, while managing conflict. Management must create a path from experimentation to implementation, which is the *framework* for activities:

A climate that encourages experimentation has a small area of overlap between control and empowerment. This is the area for potential conflict and misunderstandings, which is an impediment to risk taking and exploration.

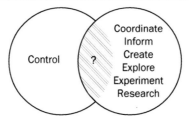

Control ? Coordinate Inform Create Explore Experiment Research

Too much emphasis on controlling the process of exploration creates barriers that prevent innovation and experimentation because people are afraid of "breaking the rules."

Too much control stifles creativity and innovation

Figure 11.1 **Relationship between managerial control and creativity**

- Management of expectations for outcomes – identifies the stages before a project moves to implementation, and post-implementation assessment.

- Management of resource allocation – verifies that the funds or personnel are available for the experiment phase and later implementation. Identifies what resources will be necessary for later implementation and responsibilities of participants.

- Insuring reliable and consistent communication channels – identifies what reports or follow-through is necessary and when.

- Removing barriers – ensures exploration has a fair chance for success.

- Final decisions – determine how to evaluate project outcome and when to go into production.

- Insuring compliance with laws and policies – however, policies that impede innovation should be reconsidered.

When people feel there is a secure climate for experimentation they will be more willing to risk failure. Fear that a project might fail and that the librarian will be criticized are major barriers to experimentation. This criticism doesn't always come from managers, so it is important to manage expectations from the outset to minimize the negative influence of other staff who are skeptical.

Conducting an open discussion about attitudes towards change can be helpful. Table 11.3 is an exercise for identifying an individual's aptitude for handling change. Each individual should respond to the 15 statements, tally the results in the rows, and enter the totals at the bottom of the table.

The ratings from Table 11.3 can be used to place individuals in a continuum of readiness for change in the organization, and Figure 11.2 (see p. 278) highlights where the totaled scores fit on a change adaptability chart.

Organizations that are fortunate to be change oriented are well positioned to take advantage of emerging technology and make adaptations that will improve patrons' experiences. A conservative organization (or individual) will find it difficult to adjust to the inevitable changes that come from the higher organization, or from an outside force. This library will be slow to adopt new technology or change services unless outside influences intervene. There are many reasons why some libraries are conservative, and frank

Table 11.3 Change management survey questions

Please respond to the following statements	Usually	Frequently	Sometimes	Rarely
1. When something new is introduced I understand the reasons behind the change	20	15	10	0
2. I don't mind the frustration that can happen when trying something new	20	15	10	0
3. I make a new process/technology work better through my input	20	15	10	0
4. I learn a new process/technology without much help	20	15	10	0
5. I have the time I need to explore new technology and experiment with ideas for change	20	15	10	0
6. I am often the first to use a new process/technology before many others do	20	15	10	0
7. When I make suggestions for implementing new technology or other changes in operations they are seriously considered or implemented	20	15	10	0
8. I have the resources I need to explore and learn about what is new in libraries	20	15	10	0
9. I am excited by the opportunity to try something new at work	20	15	10	0

10. I'm not worried or afraid if I don't know everything about something new	20	15	10	0
11. When decisions about changes in operations or technology are made in my library my co-workers are on board with the change	20	15	10	0
12. There is always someone I can go to when I have a question or find a problem with new procedures or technology	20	15	10	0
13. Project deadlines for new technology or operations are realistic	20	15	10	0
14. My supervisor is an advocate for change in the library	20	15	10	0
15. My supervisor is flexible and supportive as I learn	20	15	10	0
Totals				

discussions can uncover some of the reasons behind the emotions that are barriers to accepting change.

A nascent library has some support for change but there is sufficient resistance to create conflict between groups, or to discourage individuals working for change. In a nascent organization, the role of management in supporting change should be explored. It may be the case that resistance from staff is being caused by a perception that management isn't supportive, when in fact management is supportive.

Conservative	Nascent	Evolving	Change directed
0–74	75–150	151–225	226–300
High resistance to change among most management and staff This library organization is firmly entrenched in conservative values, and will have difficulty adjusting to mandated change.	High readiness for change among the majority of staff with some outliers who are more comfortable with the status quo This organization will encounter frustration and conflict in adapting to change.	There is some movement towards change but high resistance remains among some Progress will be slow, frustrating and divisive because of different perspectives from staff/ managers regarding the need to change the status quo.	Managers and staff embrace change This is a dynamic organization poised to handle change effectively. These libraries will be leaders in the exploration of innovative technology and services.

Figure 11.2 A change adaptability chart

An evolving library will have many of the same characteristics as a nascent organization but there will be stronger momentum for change. However, in an evolving library there will be opposition from some staff members and/or managers who want to slow progress. It is important to identify those points of opposition and address the reasons behind the resistance. Some staff members who oppose change may be doing so because of a lack of information, or because they perceive that the change is happening too quickly and adversely impacting services.

An honest discussion about these results will be useful for identifying a path forward in order to create an adaptable environment in the library by helping individuals and managers identify areas where both can make improvements. Most discussions around change involve a combination of personal preferences for or against change, concerns over process and perceptions about attitudes from management.

Emotions play an important role in determining how individuals adjust to change. Staff members who are comfortable with current operations can feel threatened when those duties are eliminated or dramatically changed. Managers need to remember that emotions can be contagious, so negative feelings need to be addressed early or replaced by more positive attitudes about change. When work is taken away it should be replaced with equally valued activities that individuals are given time and support to master. Collaboration and team learning can also soften the transition to new practices that in time will feel more natural.

Individuals who fall into the conservative, nascent or evolving quadrants should consider what they can do to improve their readiness for change. Resistance to change, whether passive or direct, is common in library organizations. The introduction of new information technology causes unease because it introduces unknown factors, requires leaning new technology and risks the appearance that a librarian will seem less than competent. *Learned helplessness* is a theory that describes a situation in which an individual experiences a prior failure and responds to a new situation with passive behavior rather than responding with adaptive behavior. In older workers, this can be expressed by feelings of alienation, a loss of identity, anxiety, time pressures, feelings of a lack of ability and a feeling of being too old (Turner et al., 2007).

Martinko et al. (1996) identified several environmental characteristics that influence the degree to which staff adjust to information technology. Among the factors were: attitudes of others in the immediate work area towards the new technology, co-workers' and supervisors' attitudes, prior experiences, and beliefs about the technology's usefulness and accessibility (which could be influenced by the attitudes of managers).

Managers play an important role in facilitating the adoption of new technology by recognizing the emotional impact that change has on staff. Immediate supervisors and higher managers should look for ways to interrupt the learned helplessness feedback loop by creating opportunities for success, and by recognizing successes. Immersion opportunities in a test environment before technology is implemented will also help lessen fears and anxiety when technology is finally implemented. The most important element is a positive climate of exploration that supports staff members as they work through the issues of implementing new technology.

Improving technology adoption

Picking a technology winner five years in advance is like picking the winner of the Kentucky Derby before the horses have been born – it just doesn't work. Some librarians follow technology hype, which is technology that vendor representatives and television commercials launch through publicity campaigns. Curiosity about a new product, desire and social reactions all influence purchase decisions. Hedman and Gimpel (2010) studied the hyped iPhone 3G among a group of 15 participants. They suggest that the adoption of hyped technologies is driven by emotional, epistemic (desire to learn or explore new things) and social value. This has implications both for marketing new library services and encouraging technology adoption among staff members. Typically, librarians focus on training when new technology is introduced – it may be just as important to address emotional and social issues.

The social aspect of technology adoption is often overlooked when a new product is introduced. One of the emerging theories that explains the process of technology adoption is the Social Influence Model of Technology Adoption proposed by Vannoy and Palvia. In this model,

> social influence results at the confluence of four related phenomenon: social computing action, or actions performed through use of technology such as web browsers, cell phones and file sharing software, social computing consensus, or agreement from all people that it is right to carry out the action, social computing cooperation, or participating in a way that is in the best interests of the group, and social computing authority, or recognizing that the authority imposed by the group supersedes traditional authority.
>
> (Vannoy and Palvia, 2010: 151)

One of the important features of this model is the placement of social influence as a precursor to technology adoption and the recognition of the importance of social computing authority, which is the judgment by the group that supersedes other authority. In the case of a library implementing new technology this model highlights the need for staff buy-in that coincides with the introduction of new technology. Many technology trials fail because of a lack of support or acceptance on the part of staff. For this reason, it is important for management to create a social infrastructure that will provide backing for innovation.

Social network analysis

Social connections influence every aspect of our lives so it isn't surprising that they factor in technology adoption. Research into social influence is uncovering some interesting findings. Peers and supervisors play an important role in the adoption and non-adoption of new technology, while information technology departments do not impact adopters but do impact non-adopters (Eckhardt et al., 2009). Although the reasons behind the influences are still unclear, more attention should be given to the how and why of social influence on the acceptance or rejection of technology and change.

Social network analysis is a graphic way of depicting the number and strength of connections between people. Using this technique, it is possible to draw a map of the connections between staff members. This map does not focus on the decision makers; rather, it looks at the interconnection between individuals and where influence resides.

Sempra Energy (Chen, 2007) analyzed the social network of the information technology unit in their organization using six factors: task, grapevine, decision map, innovation, client needs and strategy. Looking at task areas they mapped the intersections for key people. For the grapevine, they looked for the workers most frequently in the know about rumors, news and other organizational issues. For the decision map, they identified workers consulted for input and opinions; and for innovation, they looked for the workers with whom new ideas and technology were discussed. For client needs, they asked workers with whom they discussed client needs and requests; and for strategy, they looked for the workers engaged with discussions about strategy and outside technology. Before a link was made, the researchers required a match between individuals listing a connection, and the frequency of contact had to be at least monthly. By creating a map the company uncovered interesting characteristics: some people were surprised when their reported connects did not share the connection, and gaps were uncovered that pointed to areas for improvement.

Suciu and Petrescu-Prahova (2011) identified different areas for collecting social networking information that would reveal patterns for information sharing, including: knowledge awareness, accessibility, engagement and safety. Conducting a social analysis can reveal important characteristics of an organization and highlight areas where collaboration between departments is disrupted. It can also highlight areas of power concentration that might weaken innovation, and areas of isolation, and also bright spots where collaboration and innovation are exemplary.

In the example in Figure 11.3, an imaginary library is analyzed for three content areas: who is contacted to discuss

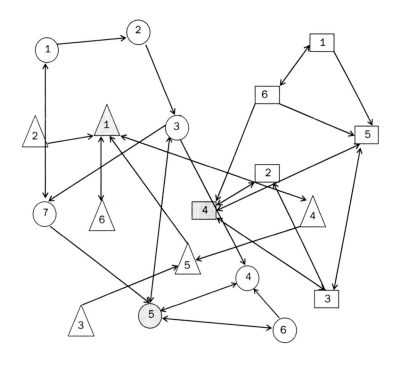

Key: ◯ Discuss ideas

▢ Go to for information and help

△ Go to for information about patron needs

Figure 11.3 Sample network analysis map

an idea, who is contacted for answers (seen as informed), and who is contacted to get information about patron behavior. Librarians 1, 4 and 5 are better connected in the three areas and should be included as prime actors when considering issues for which their contact strengths apply. Using this approach (rather than selecting members based solely on position or after asking for volunteers) might improve staff engagement in the process and improve acceptance of change.

Encouraging a climate of assessment

Assessment is an important factor in charting a path for change, and creating a culture of assessment isn't easy for most librarians who might be skeptical of data. However, in the absence of data, the alternative is to make decisions based on assumptions and beliefs which frequently don't keep pace with change. Data from usage studies depend on variables that include individual differences between people, and analyze conditions that change over time. Studying web metrics is like surfing, each wave is different and the person who waits to catch the perfect wave will miss many opportunities. It is important to carry out continual assessment and experimentation with the actions suggested through the data until the data changes again. In the digital culture, nothing is perfect and nothing is permanent.

A good place to begin creating an environment in which assessment is accepted as a core responsibility is to start a discussion on assessment by asking librarians what information they need to do their job better. Most will be able to present questions that can be answered by data; follow this discussion by introducing analytic tools. Demonstrate how these tools reveal actionable items from the data and demonstrate impact. When leaders are committed to the power of assessment, the values will trickle downward. If supervisors are requesting evidence of impact from subordinates, the subordinates will become more creative in finding ways to demonstrate the impact of their accomplishments.

Finding money

During this current recession all types of libraries have experienced budget cuts or flat budgets, and it is unlikely that there will substantial increases in the near future. Budget management is becoming an important skill for librarians. Librarians can supplement budgets with grants and donations but these are not useful for funding ongoing operations. Stretching diminishing funds requires a process of strategic reallocation based on priorities that focus on patron needs. Every position that becomes available should be re-evaluated in light of those priorities. Staff should be moved into positions that use their strengths, and ineffective personnel can't be ignored. Departmental budgets need justifications that align with the library's priorities, which will cause some departments to face difficult choices.

While fund-raising is a primary activity for library directors, some libraries are creating development officer positions to assist with fund-raising. Gift solicitation, which has traditionally been a requirement for special collection librarians, is now becoming more important. Cultivating donors is an art and requires librarians with sensitivity and insight into the personality and interests of potential donors in order to match the donor's values to those of the library. Cuillier and Stoffle (2011) highlight the importance of annual campaigns, capital campaigns, friends' groups, endowments and grants as important funding sources. They also suggest alliances with athletic departments and e-commerce areas including print-on-demand, services for corporations, journal hosting, cafes and fee services as revenue ideas.

Libraries can also raise money by recovering the cost for services like ILL or other programs. E-commerce can provide an economical and efficient way to collect fines and sell images and other items. Westerville Public Library entered into a partnership with Innovative Interfaces which resulted in a successful implementation of e-commerce for collecting fines, creating convenience for patrons. Their motto is: "We must always remember that to accomplish what we have never done, we have to do things we've never attempted" (Kline and Barlow, 2006: 152–3). The Steely Library at Northern Kentucky University operated a fee-based research assistance program in 2008 to support a fund-raising campaign for the university. This service was deemed successful because it introduced the development department to new resources and expertise from the library, and made new connections with the department (Brooks, 2010).

One often overlooked source of income for libraries is the library facility itself. Sharing the space with vendors and student-run businesses can also generate funds (Bulpitt, 2000). Other ideas include selling supplies, photocopies, in-house printing and digital or print copies of special collection images.

Budgeting for the patron centered library may require new approaches. When budgets are allocated based on previous expenditures it can be difficult to locate funds for new projects or experiments. A zero-based budget (ZBB) requires every line item to be approved, rather than the traditional method for justifying only changes. For libraries, a less drastic approach using a modified zero-based budget (MZBB) could help identify funds that can be reallocated for new projects. Hong Kong Libraries used this approach for budgeting for acquisitions with a starting base of 95 percent to protect existing collections (Chan, 2008). This approach was successful in redistributing funds to cover emerging institutional priorities.

There is no single answer, no simple formula, and each library will have a different environment in which to consider reallocating funds or uncovering new sources of revenue. Nothing will be accomplished without setting goals for raising funds, or seeking ways to become more cost-effective. The future is never certain, but with the support of engaged and skilled librarians it can be fruitful.

12

Whither the library?

Abstract: The architecture of libraries is changing as collections are emphasized less and user engagement becomes more central to library missions. Assessment is providing the information necessary to identify space needs for user activity. New libraries are being built incorporating a philosophy that stresses flexibility, the user experience and environmental sustainability. Libraries are rising from non-library structures, repurposed to house collections and services that mesh with local communities. High-capacity repositories are being used to house lesser-used collections and make room for user spaces. Attention is being given to the needs of those with disabilities, as libraries strive to build friendly environments for lifelong learning. This includes making room for learning commons that are conducive to exploration and support research activities that will result in student achievement. Special collections are assuming new importance as a means for publicity and for attracting patrons into the library.

Key words: buildings, architecture, construction, remodeling, sustainable building, building use studies, disability accommodations, learning commons, special collections, preservation.

Libraries are unusual places; they attract a variety of people for multiple purposes. They are a place for reflection, inspiration, learning, gatherings, research, and a place of solitude. It is difficult to create spaces for all these activities, but a patron centered library can accommodate these areas by reducing the footprint used to house collections. "The library can be a context for knowledge integration as well as a repository of knowledge" (Harley et al., 2001: 29). This can be accomplished though flexible buildings, in which consideration is given to aesthetics and function. High technology can blend into spaces to create inviting areas for collaboration and inspiration. One example is the Assen Public Library in the Netherlands, opened in 2012, that features a 175" interactive video wall and 46" touch tables (*http://www.youtube.com/watch?v=hMv93vpU3Xg*). This attraction welcomes people inside the library, where there are spaces designed for multiple uses.

The library as architecture

The patron centered library must be as dynamic as the librarians associated with the library. "The automation of manual handling, the use of sorting robots, compact shelving, RFID technology and the emergence of extended self-issue/-return service points have all brought staff out from behind the desk; they have changed our libraries from places where the storage and display of resources governed the premises to ones dominated by users and user facilities" (Latimer, 2010: 30). Future libraries will be constructed using a model of maximum flexibility, much like hotels and convention centers, with mobile walls (demountable) that can be easily repurposed. If flexibility is important in building design, so are the spaces designed for lifelong learning.

The library needs learning centers where programs and spaces are designed to meet patrons' needs for mastering research. This includes free Wi-Fi, plenty of electrical outlets, self-service checkouts and conveniences like beverage and snack availability. A survey of academic respondents with new library buildings completed between 2002 and 2009 reported an increased number of computer labs, snack bars, general use classrooms, auditoriums, and centers for tutors, writing and copying (Stewart, 2011). Many of these spaces are new to the libraries and reflect a refocusing towards collaboration, patron requests and technology use.

New construction must also address concerns over utility expenses, with an eye to reducing environmental impact. Exposing interiors to daylight and providing natural ventilation when possible improves conditions for patrons while saving energy costs. This is of concern to libraries because they are consuming increasing levels of electricity for computers and other equipment with corresponding increases in energy bills. "Typically a modern office building uses about 30 percent of its total energy consumption for electric lighting. However, in a public library the lighting figure can approach 45 percent" (Edwards, 2011: 196). Architectural designs that take advantage of natural conditions can reduce energy costs by using solar energy, by the placement of reading areas to avoid afternoon glare and by mixing natural with mechanical solutions for heating and ventilation.

Schlipf (2011) discusses several building conditions that can adversely influence the patron's experience and complicate library operations. These include excessive noise caused by architectural features such as peaks and atriums that reflect sound for great distances. Courtyards, which are attractive but confuse patrons and disrupt traffic patterns, and water features, which introduce hazards for children and create additional maintenance costs and potential water damage to materials and equipment, should be avoided.

The library entrance is important and should welcome patrons into the building by setting a mood or delivering an image that excites. Portable furniture will encourage patrons to be creative and provide possibilities for them to create their own space, either for collaboration or solitude. Signs need to be clear, consistent and strategically placed to help patrons find their way around the building. Artwork can also provide inspiration and create ambience; and provides opportunities to showcase patron art.

Increasing building traffic begins with an understanding of patron motivation for using the library, which requires an analysis of space use, function and aesthetics. Libraries are not spiritual centers, but they can be inspiring given the proper attention to aesthetics. Several new buildings represent different approaches to creating exciting spaces that will attract patrons.

Forrest Library (*http://www.hale.wa.edu.au/Our-School/ library/Pages/default.aspx*) at Hale School in Wembley Down, Western Australia, created spaces that addressed patrons' needs for collaborative and individual space, with interesting areas outside the building. The Bibliothek der Hochschule für nachhaltige Entwicklung Eberswalde (FH) (*http://www.hnee.de/Einrichtungen/Hochschulbibliothek/ Geschichten-und-Bilder/Bilder-des-Gebaeudes/Bilder-des- neuen-Bibliotheksgebaeudes-E2494.htm*) was designed as a square, which would have made it unremarkable, except that the outside is covered in imprints of photographs depicting the library contents to draw people inside.

The Anythink Wright Farms Library in Colorado (*http:// www.anythinklibraries.org/location/anythink-wright-farms*) includes a computer lab, a teen area and a large area for children, and is situated adjacent to a park that includes outdoor seating, reading areas and a children's play area. The Anacostia Neighborhood Library in Washington DC (*http://www.dclibrary.org/anacostia*) has an open floor plan with few walls, and was built with environmental considerations. The Mission Bay Library in San Francisco (*http://sfpl.org/index.php?pg=0100001201*) is an example of blending library and community needs, sharing the building with others, including space for community activities, senior housing and retail outlets. The Bibliotecca comunale degli Intronati di Siena in Italy (*http://www. bibliotecasiena.it/*) is an unusual example where a medieval street was repurposed into a library in order to generate a retreat for local citizens, saving resources through the reuse of existing structures.

Lemieux Library and McGoldrick Learning Commons at Seattle University (*http://www.seattleu.edu/library/*) combines a reading room, cafe, multimedia lab and lounge, with a learning commons. The most radical approach was taken by the University of California Merced Library (*http:// ucmercedlibrary.info/*), which was built on a new model. This library houses 93,000 volumes, over 630,000 e-books, 56,000 e-journals, and has access to millions of volumes from other University of California campuses, with purchasing accomplished through patron-driven acquisitions (Advisory Board Company, Education Advisory Board, University Leadership Council, 2011). There are no librarians – subject or catalogers; circulation is automated through RFID, and reference services is outsourced.

TU Delft Library in the Netherlands (*http://www.library. tudelft.nl/en/*) represents a departure from traditional public libraries. It has a grass roof to conserve energy, and provides study spaces, project rooms and comfortable chairs dispersed throughout the library. It was designed to maximize the patron experience with open spaces and flexibility for rearrangement, and access to nearby support staff.

Another interesting new library building is the Joe and Rika Mansueto Library at the University of Chicago (*http://mansueto.lib.uchicago.edu/*). This award-winning repository/library hybrid was built underground with a "grand reading room" that rises above the surface under a glass dome. The bulk of the repository is high density storage/retrieval managed through an automated system. It presents a marriage between a storage facility and a quiet study area. This not a multi-purpose use library, but it does fill a particular niche for efficient access to volumes that would normally be housed at a high-capacity storage facility.

For some libraries in America, renovating a former big box store is more practical than new construction. Retail stores have been located for strategic convenience and they have large footprints with load capacity that can accommodate library operations. "McAllen, Texas, purchased an empty Wal-Mart store in 2006 for its new library ... for $39/square foot (sf). Bedford, Texas, purchased a vacated Food Lion for their new library in 2007 ... for approximately $60/sf" (Lesneski, 2011: 399). The McAllen Public Library (*http://www.mcallenlibrary.net/default.aspx*) is now open, demonstrating a remarkable transformation from a big box store to a library. It received the International Interior Design Association (IIDA) and the Buildings and Equipment Section of the Library Leadership and Management Association (LLAMA) 2012 Library Interior Design Competition Award for Public Libraries over 30,000 sq ft.

Creating exciting spaces will frequently mean repurposing stack areas. Compact shelving can double the storage capacity of an area but requires floors that can handle the weight, and reduces the number of people who can browse the collection. Using compact storage also squeezes more books into a given area, producing concerns about preservation, and may create an unpleasant environment for patrons. A better solution may be to build a storage facility designed to house large numbers of volumes that can be efficiently retrieved for delivery.

Remote storage has two economies, it frees valuable building space for user centered activities, and it provides for more compact storage than is practical in existing stack areas. Preservation, however, is a major concern in high-capacity storage facilities. Some libraries with storage facilities are locating their conservation labs inside or near the storage facility (Mook and Walker, 2004). The advantages of on-site conservationists include the ability to scan or microfilm brittle materials, and to provide "first-aid," and identify and remove deteriorating items (due to mold, insects, etc.) that could spread to nearby books.

Another way to increase space efficiency is to remove or reduce the number of computers in public areas. This can only be accomplished if there is room available somewhere in the library for supporting activities that require multimedia and other high-end devices that patrons need. Likewise, this solution requires a population of library patrons who can bring their own devices to use on the library's Wi-Fi, or it requires mobile devices available for checkout from the library. Wireless technology can dramatically change a space from one filled with rows of computers wired to the network into an open expanse with furniture that can be easily moved and combined by patrons to meet impromptu needs. However, it is important to note that all devices eventually need access to electricity for charging, so charging spaces or electrical outlets interspaced through the library is as important as Wi-Fi.

Sharing facilities among libraries may be an additional way to maximize efficiency. Dedrick identified several trends from a survey of shared facilities that existed over periods of time ranging from 10 to 25 years: "In terms of the types of institutions involved in joint ventures, the most common pattern was a community college and a university or college (typically a university branch library)" (Dedrick, 1994: 438–9). Although budgeting was generally not consolidated (with 75 percent of respondents), those surveyed highlighted positive aspects, including: receiving increased acquisition budgets, better discounts from vendors and garnered efficiencies in staffing. Although a shared facility approach might not work in all instances, it could prove beneficial to smaller libraries struggling with increasing acquisitions costs and reduced staffing.

Accommodations for disabled patrons

No discussion of architecture is complete without a discussion of accommodations for patrons with disabilities. Since the 1990 Americans with Disabilities Act, libraries have worked to improve services to this group. Although disabled patrons comprise a minority of the library population, the needs of disabled patrons are important and can't be neglected. Accommodations must be made for the visually impaired, those in wheelchairs and those with service dogs. This includes facilities that meet standards for aisle width to accommodate wheelchairs, computer equipment for the visually impaired and staff to help when needed.

A 2011 survey that solicited participation via an Academic Health Sciences libraries' listserv suggests improvements have been made in some areas (Willis, 2012). Libraries have made progress in reducing physical barriers and using adaptive technology, and 32 percent reported offering services to learning disabled, which appears to be a growing concern among libraries. In addition, 62 percent of the libraries reported creating instructional pages using HTML web pages instead of PDFs, which are more difficult to work with for screen readers. One problem, revealed by the survey, is the lack of captioning on videos for hearing impaired patrons. Respondents to the survey (56 percent) indicated that they weren't seeing increases in demands for services; however, this could change as veterans returning from duty in the Middle East with disabilities enter library communities.

Barker (2011) lists some common barriers for disabled patrons, including: vertical obstacles, inadequate wheelchair clearance under fixtures, slopes, access hazards, surfaces that impede wheelchairs, and general clutter that can be hazardous to wheelchairs and the visually impaired. In addition, staff members need to be trained in working with disabled patrons who need assistance because some patrons may require physical contact. For example, it is customary to let a blind person hold on to your elbow as you lead them. Understanding accommodations for disabled patrons will inspire more sensitivity to their needs.

For the visually impaired, many libraries use JAWS reading software (*http://www.freedomscientific.com/*), or ZoomText magnification on computers (*http://www.aisquared.com/zoomtext/*). Kurzweil (*http://www.kurzweiledu.com/products.html*) has been a long-standing tool in libraries for assisting patrons with reading books. New tools include POET Compact (*http://www.baum.ro/index.php?language=en&pagina=produse&subpag=poetcompact*), which works like a photocopy machine only it reads text. Window-Eyes (*http://www.gwmicro.com/Window-Eyes/*) is another software application for reading text aloud. The Windows and Apple operating systems also have built-in speech recognition software for reading aloud, and Dragon speech recognition software (*http://www.nuance.com/dragon/index.htm*) also transcribes speech into text.

Some patrons may need special equipment for enlarging text or accommodations for using computer mice. Clearly Superior (*http://clearlysuperiortech.com/*) manufactures trackball mice with large, high-density balls that are easier for those with hand mobility problems. Other solutions for visual difficulties include magnifiers, adjusting the font size on monitors or the monitor stands. All-in-one computers have become popular because they don't have CPU units and therefore save space. However, the monitors may not have the same degree of adjustability as regular desktop computers, making them more difficult to read for those with bifocal correction. In one instance, flipping the monitor upside down lowered the monitor enough to accommodate bifocal patrons.

For the hearing impaired, videos should be captioned and telecommunication devices or sign language interpreters may be necessary depending on the situation. MAGpie (*http://ncam.wgbh.org/invent_build/web_multimedia/tools-guidelines/magpie*) is a free application for captioning video. These captioned videos can be played, and the captions decoded, on a variety of devices including BlackBerry smartphones.

The facility as a learning commons

The learning commons is a popular re-branding of media centers and other spaces that have been redesigned to include multimedia, projectors, large monitors and other equipment that will engage patrons in learning. It differs from an information commons, which is usually considered a place to go for information or facts, in that a learning commons is a place that facilitates the learning process. This requires a blending of information resources, information tools and instruction capabilities with spaces that facilitate collaboration (Beagle, 2012).

Ideally, a learning commons will include space for personal learning that provides opportunities for developing competencies that help individuals achieve their goals and aspirations. "It is about creating a culture of learning by fostering habits of mind conducive to learning how to learn. These habits include curiosity, a desire to make sense of the world, empathy for others, value of self, the need to take charge, and a sense of community" (Loertscher and Koechlin, 2011: 23). In a learning commons, individuals build skills for selecting and using resources that will last a lifetime.

Learning is an active process that begins with hands-on research using current technology in an attractive facility, which is supported by experienced librarians. Research support services, such as writing and tutoring centers, can be seamlessly integrated with reference services to create a dynamic environment for learning (Seeholzer and Salem, 2010). Step by step, patrons experience success and build confidence in their abilities to conduct research and acquire knowledge, thereby avoiding or breaking the cycle of learned helplessness.

In academic libraries, a learning commons will often include collaborations with other units on campus. These can take the form of tutoring, classrooms and other student services designed to increase student achievement. The University of Guelph-Humber Library Reference Services and Humber College's Writing Center collaborated on efforts to improve the quality of research papers by providing support for an integrated process that includes research and writing (Palomino and Gouveia, 2011). Libraries should provide spaces for formal and informal collaborations between librarians and teachers that support learning.

Collaboration between faculty and librarians can result in better library curriculum integration. The College of New Jersey undertook a program across their three-year chemistry seminar using an integrated librarian model that follows students from freshman through junior class standing (Tucci, 2011). Librarians formed stronger relationships with the faculty, and through that partnership the librarians were directly involved with student learning as an integral part of the curriculum.

Public libraries are also creating exciting spaces that encourage learning and bring patrons into the library. The Chicago Public Library has a digital media lab called YOUmedia (*http://youmediachicago.org/*). Within this facility teenagers can access books and use media creation tools and applications, either individually or in teams, to create projects that promote critical thinking, creativity and skills that will continue to attract them to the library.

As libraries rush to redesign space for more collaboration and designate work areas that have no regard to noise levels, it is important to remember there are many patrons who seek out the library for quiet study and reflection (Massis, 2012). There are a variety of methods to separate space based on activity. Segregating the quiet areas to specific floors is one way to control noise. Another method is to situate book stacks or compact shelving strategically, to buffer the noise between areas. Whatever method is used, providing separate areas for quiet and noisy activities is imperative.

The facility as a play space

Maker-spaces, or Fabriken, are laboratories inside libraries where patrons can explore new technology to create things.

"Incorporating maker-spaces into library service can have a life-altering impact on community members, who then have the tools, access, and training necessary to tinker with and remake their world" (Britton, 2012: 20). What makes these places special is the unusual equipment patrons can use.

This equipment can vary from 3D printers and Espresso Book Machines to full-scale kitchens – any equipment that supports exploration for a given community. Multimedia equipment can also make a library special. The TFDL Digital Media Commons at the University of Calgary (*http:// library.ucalgary.ca/dmc*) offers patrons high-end Apple hardware, editing suites, touch tables, gaming PCs, gaming consoles and software and staff to support the exploration and creation of animation, soundscapes, graphics design and digital video.

Maker-spaces are designed for collaboration in an environment of mutual learning, where patrons are partners and are fully involved in both teaching and learning. Peer-to-peer learning takes place as patrons explore new technology together, and teach each other along the way (Nilsson, 2011). The Westport Public Library offers a maker-space with a Maker-in-Residence to assist patrons in using a 3D printer which prints objects from digital files (*http://www. westportlibrary.org/services/maker-space*).

Collecting information on facility use

It is as important to conduct periodic assessment for library space utilization as it is for any other service. Unobtrusive observation can be an important way to discover current use patterns. The areas of space in the university library and adjoining areas at Indiana University – Purdue University

Indianapolis were analyzed to identify usage patterns for carrels, tables, soft chairs and group study rooms based on time-sensitive changes in the percentage of area capacity (Applegate, 2009). Observation can be a great way to discover usage patterns, as was found at Purdue, where they discovered that study carrels were used more at the end of the semester, some areas were preferred based on gender and usage dropped between fall and spring. Their data suggested that library usage was directly related to academic schedules.

Oregon State University Valley Library conducted a three-phase analysis of student use of the library and library resources (Bridges, 2008). This study began with a survey, was followed by focus groups with non-library users, and ended with another survey of infrequent users. The results from the surveys indicate a correlation between academic college and library use. Focus groups and survey methodology were also used to analyze teen usage of an Eastern Canadian public library (Howard, 2011). The study found evidence that a lack of relationships with library staff, a lack of attractive facilities, a lack of programs directed towards teen interests and a website that did not appeal to their generation were among the barriers to library use.

Mixed qualitative and quantitative methods will provide more information on library use than a single method. While surveys provide good quantitative data they can miss important information that is revealed through the discussions that occur in focus groups. Collecting information from patrons who are not using the library facility can illuminate problems in services and suggest possible actions that can increase gate counts. For example, hire students to go to student hang-outs and conduct a video survey, asking participants why they use that space instead of the library.

Special collections: the jewels of the library

In an era in which the general collection is becoming less important, special collections are assuming a more prominent role in libraries. Frequently, special collections are built around themes that resonate with the local community. These collections contain rare materials that are not available in other libraries, and because they are not subject to the usual lending process they provide a unique attraction to bring patrons into the building. Most special collection material is in the public domain and can be used for digital exhibits, which, combined with the possibilities for physical exhibits and programs, will attract patrons into the library.

Like all the other areas in libraries, special collection staff members are being asked to assume new roles. They are becoming less the security guard and more the tour guide, employing social media and other technology to market and advocate for special collections. Digital exhibits will bring patrons into special collections, where librarians will be the educators and guides to the world of rare and unusual artifacts. This can result in new partnerships with members of the community; for example, Harris and Weller (2012) report on a series of successful outreach activities at the University of Illinois at Chicago (UIC) that contributed to city-wide projects and resulted in new people coming to the library. UIC special collections staff also participate in the "Ask a Librarian" service and receive the largest portion of inquiries made to the service.

Special collections can also support classroom activities by embedding the library into the curriculum (Aurand, 2011). Student projects based on special collection material can be used as part of an exhibit, or added to a website for supplementary value. Students and volunteers can also assist with digitization projects by scanning or researching special collection materials.

Special collections require environmental conditions that preserve the materials. The Society of American Archivists published guidelines for facilities that house special collection or archival materials (Pacifico et al., 2009). Security for these collections must also be higher than general reading areas in the library, demanding a clear line of vision for observing patrons using the collection. Among other practices, pencils should be provided for note-taking to prevent patrons from using their own ink or other writing implements that could damage materials.

Many libraries will not have the expertise in-house to evaluate and plan for special collection facilities. The National Endowment for the Humanities (NEH) offers two different grants to fund expert consultants to assist libraries in preservation management. The first, Sustaining Cultural Heritage Collections (*http://www.neh.gov/grants/ preservation/sustaining-cultural-heritage-collections*) "helps cultural repositories plan and implement preservation strategies that pragmatically balance effectiveness, cost, and environmental impact. Projects should be designed to be as cost-effective, energy efficient, and environmentally sensitive as possible, and they should aim to mitigate the greatest risks to collections rather than to meet prescriptive targets." A second grant from the NEH, Preservation Assistance Grants for Smaller Institutions (*http://www.neh.gov/grants/ preservation/preservation-assistance-grants-smaller- institutions*) assists smaller libraries with preservation planning for significant humanities collections.

The future of the library

Libraries are moving into the future at an uncomfortable pace for many librarians trained in the pre-digital world. Libraries no longer have substantial budgets to support collections that are based on assumptions and speculation about potential use. Point-of-need acquisition through patron and ILL acquisition is becoming the norm for collection development. Mobile computing will become ubiquitous, and libraries must find ways to deliver content and services to mobile users in a seamless manner that integrates with their experiences with other technology.

Libraries will continue to economize and become more segregated into libraries (with great resources) and smaller institutions (more agile and efficient) which will collaborate on document delivery – not necessarily free to the smaller libraries but a more economical and supportable way to meet patron needs. "This could most effectively be accomplished through a small number of print repositories, with very good security, climate control, and the like, with costs and access shared across a network of libraries" (Council on Library and Information Resources, 2008: 26). For this to happen, there must be a transformation in the manner by which libraries are evaluated, away from collection size to the value of services.

What will happen to libraries when Google completes the book project? No one will argue with the goal of digitizing all print material, but there are questions about the standards Google is using for metadata, scanning and OCR processing (Dougherty, 2010). Licensing and copyright questions continue to beset the project, while digital publishers also struggle with many of the same issues. As libraries conduct their own digitization projects with high standards, and build open repositories containing scholarly material, it may be possible for libraries to win the digitization war even after losing the search engine battle. This must be a collective action by thousands of libraries, each contributing items to a global digital library.

Collaboration will aid libraries in sustaining collections and services for patrons. "This spirit of cooperation, be it with publishers through cataloging-in-publication data and electronic data interchange, or with Google through the digitization of millions of books, has helped libraries remain in the mainstream of the process of cultural exchange and information flow, and has helped librarians to perpetually test and debate the library's appropriate priorities" (Dillon, 2011: 31).

When libraries collaborate on standards and inter-operability they have power and influence; when they stand alone they create silos that do not work for the benefit of their patrons nor contribute to the good of all. After all, libraries exist to preserve information, provide access to information and support learning through dynamic spaces, which is a mandate that can compete with commercial producers that rely solely on business models. Libraries as community learning centers will endure as vibrant spaces for lifelong learning.

Conclusion

Technology doesn't solve problems, it creates opportunities for problem solving. This is true for all technological advances. For example, some time ago humans decided to wear clothing but they quickly discovered a problem – clothes get dirty, so they either threw them away or took them to the river and washed them against a rock. That worked, but it was hard on the clothes and back-breaking labor. Someone got the idea for a washboard, which saved some time and labor, and was a little easier on the clothes, but it wasn't perfect. Along came the hand-cranked washer, then the automatic washer, and, finally, dry cleaning. All of the advances saved time and labor but none of them solved the original problem – clothes get dirty.

All technology is like this; it doesn't solve the problem, and waiting for a perfect solution will keep people washing clothes on rocks. A librarian who is waiting for the perfect solution will be left behind, with few professional options; and for the lucky few who have a position – they will be running a library that looks more like a museum. This book describes the technological and social factors impacting today's librarians, and discusses how librarians can adapt to those dynamics by focusing on patron needs. This is only possible in an organizational culture that encourages imagination and minimizes impulses for control and order.

Technological change is messy and it is time to see the opportunities in the mess; failure to revise libraries today will compromise the future of libraries. The report, "Redefining the academic library," identifies four key drivers for change: unsustainable costs, viable alternatives (e.g., Google), declining usage, and new patron demands as transformational influences on libraries (Advisory Board Company, Education Advisory Board, University Leadership Council, 2011). One does not need to be a clairvoyant to prepare for the future; what is needed is a willingness to step outside the comfortable box of tradition without abandoning the values that libraries have held since their beginning. It is a great time to be a librarian – social evolution and information technology are providing a framework for librarians to build upon the vision of the participants from the White House conferences, by continuing to build libraries for the common good.

> The work of the Conference is not finished; it is just beginning. The Conference was a clear demonstration of the power of participatory democracy: a gigantic town meeting where people expressed their views and laid plans to transform the consensus into policy and law. Shaping its results into a new mission for library and information services for the 1980s and beyond calls for the continuing participation and involvement of all concerned.
>
> (White House Conference on Library and Information Services, 1979: 11)

This work will never be finished.

References

Abram, S. (2006) MILLENNIALS: deal with them! (cover story), *Texas Library Journal* 82(3): 96–102.

Abramo, G., D'Angelo, C. and Di Costa, F. (2010) Citations versus journal impact factor as proxy of quality: could the latter ever be preferable? *Scientometrics* 84(3): 821–33. Print.

Accenture (2012) *Always On, Always Connected: Finding Growth Opportunities in an Era of Hypermobile Consumers*, p. 20. Accenture. Print. Web. Available from: *http://www.accenture.com/SiteCollectionDocuments/ PDF/Accenture_EHT_Research_2012_Consumer_ Technology_Report.pdf*.

Advisory Board Company, Education Advisory Board, University Leadership Council (2011) *Redefining the Academic Library: Managing the Migration to Digital Information Services*, p 80. Washington, DC: The Advisory Board Company. Print.

Albanese, A. (2008) U. of Chicago's daring new library, *Library Journal* 133(11): 17. Print.

Allison, D.A. (2010) Information portals: the next generation catalog, *Journal of Web Librarianship* 4(4): 375–89. Print.

Allison, D.A. (2012) Chatbots in the library: is it time? *Library Hi Tech* 30(1): 95–107. Print.

Allison, D.A. and Childers, S. (2002) Index relativity and patron search strategy, *Portal Libraries and the Academy* 2(1): 145–53. Print.

Allison, D.A., McNeil, B. and Swanson, S. (2000) Database selection: one size does not fit all, *College and Research Libraries* 61(1): 56–64. Print.

Alter, A. (2012) Your e-book is reading you, *Wall Street Journal Abstracts* June: 1. Print.

American Library Association (ALA) Office for Research & Statistics and the Information Policy Access Center at the University of Maryland (2011) Public library funding and technology access study 2010–2011. Web. Available from: *http://www.ala.org/research/sites/ala.org.research/files/content/initiatives/plftas/2010_2011/plftas11-execsummary.pdf*. Accessed 9 October 2012.

American Library Association (ALA) (2012) PRIMO; peer-reviewed instructional materials online, *ACRL – Association of Research Libraries*. Web. Available from: *http://www.ala.org/acrl/aboutacrl/directoryofleadership/sections/is/iswebsite/projpubs/primo/*.

Anderson, J. and Rainie, L. (2012) *The Future of Apps and Web* (p. 27). Washington, DC: Pew Internet & American Life Project. Print.

Anderson, K. and May, F.A. (2010) Does the method of instruction matter? An experimental examination of information literacy instruction in the online, blended, and face-to-face classrooms, *Journal of Academic Librarianship* 36(6): 495–500. Print.

Anderson, K.J., Freeman, R.S., Hérubel, J.-P.V.M., Mykytiuk, L.J., Nixon, J.M. et al. (2002) Buy, don't borrow: bibliographers' analysis of academic library collection development through interlibrary loan requests, *Collection Management* 27(3): 1. Print.

Anderson, R. (2010) The Espresso Book Machine: the Marriott Library experience, *Serials* 23(1): 39–42. Print.

Anthony, S.K. (2008) Implementing service oriented architecture at the Canada Institute for Scientific and

Technical Information, *Serials Librarian* 55(1): 235–53. Print.

Applegate, R. (2009) The library is for studying: student preferences for study space, *Journal of Academic Librarianship* 35(4): 341–6. Print.

Arlitsch, K. (2011) The Espresso Book Machine: a change agent for libraries, *Library Hi Tech* 29(1): 62–72. Print.

Armstrong, T. (2012) Steps to global licensing success, *Publishing Research Quarterly* 28(1): 23–6. Print.

Askhoj, J., Sugimoto, S. and Nagamori, M. (2011) Preserving records in the cloud, *Records Management Journal* 21(3): 175–87. Print.

ASM International (2012) Single-atom transistor may be the beginning of quantum computing, *Advanced Materials & Processes* 170(4): 16. Print.

Association of American Publishers (2010) BookStats distribution channels highlights, *The Association of American Publishers*. Web. Available from: *http://publishers.org/bookstats/distribution/*. Accessed 2012.

Association of College and Research Libraries (ACRL) (2000) *Information Literacy Competency Standards for Higher Education* (pp. 2–3). Chicago, IL: Association of College and Research Libraries. Print.

Atwater-Singer, M. (2011) Interlibrary loan satisfaction survey at the University of Evansville, *Journal of Interlibrary Loan, Document Delivery & Electronic Reserves* 21(5): 227–33. Print.

Aurand, M. (2011) Teaching and learning with collections: the library as a site for exploration and inspiration, *Art Documentation: Bulletin of the Art Libraries Society of North America* 30(1): 12–20. Print.

Ayre, L.B. (2012) Library RFID systems for identification, security, and materials handling, *Library Technology Reports* 48(5): 9–16. Print.

Ballestro, J. (2012) Losing your control: acquisitions and outsourcing, *Technical Services Quarterly* 29(2): 113–21. Print.

Barker, D. (2011) On the outside looking in: public libraries serving young people with disabilities, *APLIS* 24(1): 9–16. Print.

Beagle, D. (2012) The emergent information commons: philosophy, models, and 21st century learning paradigms, *Journal of Library Administration* 52(6): 518–37. Print.

Bell, J.C. (2011) Student affect regarding library-based and web-based research before and after an information literacy course, *Journal of Librarianship & Information Science* 43(2): 120–30. Print.

Bernholz, C.D. and Pytlik Zillig, B.L. (2011) Comparing nearly identical treaty texts: a note on the treaty of Fort Laramie with Sioux, etc., 1851 and Levenshtein's edit distance metric, *Literary & Linguistic Computing* 26(1): 5–16. Print.

Bielavitz, T. (2010) The balanced scorecard: a systemic model for evaluation and assessment of learning outcomes? *Evidence Based Library & Information Practice* 5(2): 35–46. Print.

Blackburn, F. (2010) Something for everyone: learning and learning technologies in a public library, *Australian Library Journal* 59(3): 118–26. Print.

Blackburn, H. (2011) Millennials and the adoption of new technologies in libraries through the diffusion of innovations process, *Library Hi Tech* 29(4): 663–77. Print.

Boissy, R.W. and Schatz, B. (2011) Scholarly communications from the publisher perspective, *Journal of Library Administration* 51(5): 476–84. Print.

Boissy, R.W., Taylor, T.N., Stamison, C.M., Henderson, K.S., Okerson, A. et al. (2012) Is the "big deal" dying? *Serials Review* 38(1): 36–45. Print.

Bosch, S., Henderson, K. and Klusendorf, H. (2011) Periodicals Price Survey 2011. Under pressure, times are changing, *Library Journal Archive* April. Web. Available from: *http://www.libraryjournal.com/lj/home/890009-264/periodicals_price_survey_2011_under.html.csp*.

Bower, T. and Bradford, D. (2007) How to get more from your quantitative LibQUAL+™ dataset: making results practical, *Performance Measurement & Metrics* 8(2): 110–26. Print.

Brabham, D.C. (2010) Moving the crowd at Threadless, *Information, Communication & Society* 13(8): 1122–45. Print.

Bradshaw, S., Millard, C. and Walden, I. (2011) Contracts for clouds: comparison and analysis of the terms and conditions of cloud computing services*, *International Journal of Law & Information Technology* 19(3): 187–223. Print.

Bridges, L.M. (2008) Who is not using the library? A comparison of undergraduate academic disciplines and library use, *portal: Libraries & the Academy* 8(2): 187–96. Print.

Britton, L. (2012) The makings of maker spaces, *Library Journal* 137(16): 20–3. Print.

Broady-Preston, J. and Lobo, A. (2011) Measuring the quality, value and impact of academic libraries: the role of external standards, *Performance Measurement & Metrics* 12(2): 122–35. Print.

Brooks, A.W. (2010) Library research on campus: examining a fee-based library service within university walls, *Journal of Academic Librarianship* 36(4): 347–50. Print.

Brown, H.L. (2012) Pay-per-view in interlibrary loan: a case study, *Journal of the Medical Library Association* 100(2): 98–103. Print.

Bruce, C., Hughes, H. and Somerville, M.M. (2012) Supporting informed learners in the twenty-first century, *Library Trends* 60(3): 522–45. Print.

Bruxvoort, D., Burger, J.E. and Sorensen Sutton, L. (2012) Like a snowball gathering speed: development of ASERL's print journal retention program, *Collection Management* 37(3): 223–36. Print.

Buckland, A. and Godfrey, K. (2010) Save the time of the avatar: Canadian academic libraries using chat reference in multi-user virtual environments, *Reference Librarian* 51(1): 12–30. Print.

Bulpitt, G. (2000) Income generation from library buildings: the UK experience, *Liber Quarterly: The Journal of European Research Libraries* 10(2): 117. Print.

California Digital Library (2012) *WEST: Western Regional Storage Trust.* Web. Available from: *http://www.cdlib.org/west/.* Accessed 2012.

Campbell, R. and Meadows, A. (2011) Scholarly journal publishing: where do we go from here? *Learned Publishing* 24(3): 171–81. Print.

Carlson, S. (2007) An anthropologist in the library, *Chronicle of Higher Education* 53(50): 34. Print.

Chamberlain, E. (2012) Investigating faster techniques for digitization and print-on-demand, *New Review of Academic Librarianship* 18(1): 57–71. Print.

Chan, G.R.Y.C. (2004) Purchase instead of borrow, *Journal of Interlibrary Loan, Document Delivery & Electronic Reserves* 14(4): 23–37. Print.

Chan, G.R.Y.C. (2008) Aligning collections budget with program priorities: a modified zero-based approach, *Library Collections, Acquisitions & Technical Services* 32(1): 46–52. Print.

Chang, J.-J. and Yang, C. (2012) Viable or vital? Evaluation of IM services from patrons' perspectives, *Electronic Library* 30(1): 70–88. Print.

Chen, C. (2007) Social networks at Sempra Energy's IT division are key to building strategic capabilities, *Global Business & Organizational Excellence* 26(2): 16–24. Print.

Chowdhury, G. (2010) From digital libraries to digital preservation research: the importance of users and context, *Journal of Documentation* 66(2): 207–23. Print.

Christenson, H. (2011) HathiTrust: a research library at web scale, *Library Resources & Technical Services* 55(2): 93–102. Print.

Chung, H.-K. (2007) Evaluating academic journals using impact factor and local citation score, *Journal of Academic Librarianship* 33(3): 393–402. Print.

Chzastowski, T.E. (1991) Journal collection cost-effectiveness in an academic chemistry library: results of a cost/use survey at the University of Illinois at Urbana-Champaign, *Collection Management* 14(1): 85–98. Print.

Coffman, S. (2012) The decline and fall of the library empire (cover story), *Searcher* 20(3): 14–47. Print.

Colburn, S. and Haines, L. (2012) Measuring libraries' use of YouTube as a promotional tool: an exploratory study and proposed best practices, *Journal of Web Librarianship* 6(1): 5–31. Print.

Collins, T. (2012) The current budget environment and its impact on libraries, publishers and vendors, *Journal of Library Administration* 52(1): 18–35. Print.

Condit Fagan, J., Mandernach, M., Nelson, C.S., Paulo, J.R. and Saunders, G. (2012) Usability test results for a discovery tool in an academic library, *Information Technology & Libraries* 31(1): 83–112. Print.

Cone, Inc. with AMP Agency (2006) *The 2006 Cone Millennial Cause Study* (p. 22). Cone, Inc. Print.

Connaway, L.S. and Radford, M.L. (2010) Virtual reference service quality: critical components for adults and the net-generation, *Libri* 60(2): 165–80. Print.

Connaway, L.S., Dickey, T.J. and Radford, M.L. (2011) "If it is too inconvenient I'm not going after it": convenience as a critical factor in information-seeking behaviors, *Library & Information Science Research* 33(3): 179–90. Print.

Connaway, L.S., Radford, M.L. and Dickey, T.J. (2007) On the trail of the elusive non-user: what research in virtual reference environments reveals, *Bulletin of the American Society for Information Science & Technology* 34(2): 25–8. Print.

Consonni, C. (2010) Non-users' evaluation of digital libraries: a survey at the Università Degli Studi Di Milano, *IFLA Journal* 36(4): 325–31. Print.

Council on Library and Information Resources (2008) *No Brief Candle: Reconceiving Research Libraries for the 21st Century.* Washington, DC: Council on Library and Information Resources. Print.

Cousins, N. (1954) The need for continuity, *ALA Bulletin* 48(9): 474–5. Print.

Cross, R., Baker, W. and Parker, A. (2003) What creates energy in organizations? *MIT Sloan Management Review* 44(4): 51–6. Print.

Cuillier, C. and Stoffle, C.J. (2011) Finding alternative sources of revenue, *Journal of Library Administration* 51(7): 777–809. Print.

Cullen, C.T. (2007) Is there a digital purgatory? *Journal of Library Administration* 46(1): 75–88. Print.

Currie, L., Devlin, F., Emde, J. and Graves, K. (2010) Undergraduate search strategies and evaluation criteria: searching for credible sources, *New Library World* 111(3): 113–24. Print.

Cushing, T. (2012) Traditional publisher ebook pricing harming authors' careers, case studies. *Techdirt.* Web. Available from: *http://www.techdirt.com/blog/casestudies/*

articles/20120728/19122219866/traditional-publisher-ebook-pricing-harming-authors-careers.shtml. Accessed 9 August 2012.

Dedrick, A.J. (1994) Shared academic library facilities: the unknown form of library cooperation, *College & Research Libraries* 55(5): 437–43. Print.

Dethloff, N. (2012) Replacing recalls with interlibrary loan: The University of Houston's QuickLoan service, *Journal of Access Services* 9(1): 18–27. Print.

Dillon, D. (2011) Why libraries persist: hermits, clouds, Confucius, bubbles, and Hortense Foglesong, *Journal of Library Administration* 51(1): 18–36. Print.

Dougherty, R.M. (2011) Library advocacy: one message, one voice, *American Libraries* 42(5): 46–50. Print.

Dougherty, W.C. (2010) The Google Books Project: will it make libraries obsolete? *Journal of Academic Librarianship* 36(1): 86–9. Print.

Dowd, J. (2011) I just want my website to talk to me: implementation and trial of a chatbot at the University of Wolverhampton, *SCONUL Focus* 51: 35–42. Print.

Dudenhoffer, C. (2012) Pin it! *College & Research Libraries News* 73(6): 328–32. Print.

Duncan, R. (2011) Ebooks and beyond: update on a survey of library users, *APLIS* 24(4): 182–93. Print.

Eckhardt, A., Laumer, S. and Weitzel, T. (2009) Who influences whom? Analyzing workplace referents' social influence on IT adoption and non-adoption, *Journal of Information Technology* 24(1): 11–24. Print.

Eden, B.L. (2010) The new user environment: the end of technical services? *Information Technology & Libraries* 29(2): 93–100. Print.

Editorial (2004) Information quality underpins business quality, *Records Management Society Bulletin* 122: 23–5. Print.

Edwards, B.W. (2011) Sustainability as a driving force in contemporary library design, *Library Trends* 60(1): 190–214. Print.

Edwards, E. (2004) Ephemeral to enduring: the Internet archive and its role in preserving digital media, *Information Technology & Libraries* 23(1): 3–8. Print.

Elmore, L. and Stephens, D. (2012) The application of QR codes in UK academic libraries, *New Review of Academic Librarianship* 18(1): 26–42. Print. Web.

Emanuel, J. (2011) Usability of the VuFind next-generation online catalog, *Information Technology & Libraries* 30(1): 44–52. Print.

Emmett, A., Stratton, J.M., Peterson, A.T., Church-Duran, J. and Haricombe, L.J. (2011) Toward open access: it takes a "village," *Journal of Library Administration* 51(5): 557–79. Print.

England, L., Fu, L. and Miller, S. (2011) Checklist manifesto for electronic resources: getting ready for the fiscal year and beyond, *Journal of Electronic Resources Librarianship* 23(4): 307–26. Print.

Erlandson, R.J. (2010) Digital culture: the shifting paradigm of systems librarians and systems departments. In E. Iglesias (ed.) *An Overview of the Changing Role of the Systems Librarian: Systemic Shifts.* Oxford: Chandos Publishing. Print.

Feldman, S. and Wolven, R. (2012) Digital working group pushes for expanded ebook access, *American Libraries* (supplement May/June): 4–6. Print.

Fenner, M., Garcia-Gómez, C. and Thorisson, G.A. (2011) Key issue collective action for the open researcher and contributor ID (ORCID), *Serials* 24(3): 277–9. Print.

Fodale, F. and Bates, J. (2011) What is the impact of the school library on pupils' personal development? A case study of a secondary school in Northern Ireland, *School Libraries Worldwide* 17(2): 99–113. Print.

Fogden, F. (2011) Negotiation of contracts. Planning for the unknown with boilerplate clauses, *Legal Information Management* 11(1): 27–31. Print.

Foster, A.L. (2008) Libraries welcome food amid the books, *Education Digest* 74(2): 56–7. Print.

Fox, B.-L. (2011) Librarians' Picks, *Library Journal*: 22–7. Print.

Fox, R. (2012) Digital viability, O*CLC Systems & Services* 28(1): 6–13. Print.

Frey, S.M. and Fiedler, R. (2001) Working outside the org chart. In T.P. Mackey and T.E. Jacobson (eds.) *Teaching Information Literacy Online*. London: Facet. Print.

Fritsch, D. (2011) It's time to join forces: new approaches and models that support sustainable scholarship, *The Serials Librarian* 60(1–4): 75–82. Print.

Gardner, T. and Inger, S. (2012) *How Readers Discover Content in Scholarly Journals: Comparing the Changing User Behavior between 2005 and 2012 and its Impact on Publisher Web Site Design and Function*. Abingdon: Renew Training. Print.

Geitgey, T. (2011) The University of Michigan Library Espresso Book Machine experience, *Library Hi Tech* 29(1): 51–61. Print.

Glasser, S. and Arthur, M.A. (2011) When jobs disappear: the staffing implications of the elimination of print serials management tasks, *Serials Librarian* 60(1–4): 109–13. Print.

Graduate School of Library and Information Science at Simmons College (2012) Open access statements, *Open Access Directory*. Web. Available from: *http://oad.simmons.edu/oadwiki/Open_Access_Statements*.

Greco, A.N., Wharton, R.M. and Estelami, H. (2007) The changing college and university library market for university press books and journals: 1997–2004, *Journal of Scholarly Publishing* 39(1): 1–32. Print.

Greenwood, J.T., Watson, A.P. and Dennis, M. (2011) Ten years of LibQual: a study of qualitative and quantitative survey results at the University of Mississippi 2001–2010, *Journal of Academic Librarianship* 37(4): 312–18. Print.

Gregory, J.M., Weber, A.I. and Dippie, S.R. (2008) Innovative roles for technical services librarians: extending our reach, *Technical Services Quarterly* 25(4): 37–47. Print.

Griffey, J. (2010) Chapter 5: social networking and the library, *Library Technology Reports* 46(8): 34–7. Print.

Gross, M. and Latham, D. (2007) Attaining information literacy: an investigation of the relationship between skill level, self-estimates of skill, and library anxiety, *Library & Information Science Research* 29(3): 332–53. Print.

Gross, M. and Latham, D. (2009) Undergraduate perceptions of information literacy: defining, attaining, and self-assessing skills, *College & Research Libraries* 70(4): 336–50. Print.

Gueguen, G. and Hanlon, A.M. (2009) A collaborative workflow for the digitization of unique materials, *Journal of Academic Librarianship* 35(5): 468–74. Print.

Gustafson-Sundell, N. (2011) Think locally: a prudent approach to electronic resource management systems, *Journal of Electronic Resources Librarianship* 23(2): 126–41. Print.

Hane, P.J. (2012) A librarian ebook revolution? *Information Today* 29(5): 10. Print.

Hansen, D., Johnson, M., Norton, E. and McNonough, A. (2009) Virtual provider pessimism: analysing instant messaging reference encounters with the pair perception comparison method, *Information Research* 14(4): 9. Print.

Hargittai, E., Fullerton, L., Menchen-Trevino, E. and Thomas, K. (2010) Trust online: young adults' evaluation of web content, *International Journal of Communication* 4: 468–94. Print.

Harlan, M.A., Bruce, C. and Lupton, M. (2012) Teen content creators: experiences of using information to learn, *Library Trends* 60(3): 569–87. Print.

Harley, B., Dreger, M. and Knobloch, P. (2001) The postmodern condition: students, the web, and academic library services, *Reference Services Review* 29(1): 23–32. Print.

Harris, M.H. (1995) *History of Libraries in the Western World*. Metuchen, N.J.: Scarecrow Press. Print.

Harris, V.A. and Weller, A.C. (2012) Use of special collections as an opportunity for outreach in the academic library, *Journal of Library Administration* 52(3): 294–303. Print.

Hasslöw, R. and Sverrung, A. (1995). Deselection of serials: the Chalmers University of Technology Library method, *Collection Management* 19(3): 151–70. Print.

Hawes, S.L. (2011) Playing to win: embedded librarians in online classrooms, *Journal of Library & Information Services in Distance Learning* 5(1): 56–66. Print.

Hedgebeth, D. (2007) Gaining competitive advantage in a knowledge-based economy through the utilization of open source software, *VINE: The Journal of Information & Knowledge Management Systems* 37(3): 284–94. Print.

Hedman, J. and Gimpel, G. (2010) The adoption of hyped technologies: a qualitative study, *Information Technology & Management* 11(4): 161–75. Print.

Heidorn, P.B. (2011) The emerging role of libraries in data curation and e-science, *Journal of Library Administration* 51(7): 662–72. Print.

Herrera, G. and Greenwood, J. (2011) Patron-initiated purchasing: evaluating criteria and workflows, *Journal of Interlibrary Loan, Document Delivery & Electronic Reserves* 21(1): 9–24. Print.

Hill, J.B., Madarash-Hill, C. and Allred, A. (2007) Outsourcing digital reference: the user perspective, *Reference Librarian* 47(2): 57–74. Print.

Hill, T. (2012) The inevitable shift to cloud-based book publishing: the next step in the digital transformation of book publishing may be closer than you think, *Publishing Research Quarterly* 28(1): 1–7. Print.

Holman, L. (2011) Millennial students' mental models of search: implications for academic librarians and database developers, *Journal of Academic Librarianship* 37(1): 19–27. Print.

Howard, V. (2011) What do young teens think about the public library? *Library Quarterly* 81(3): 321–44. Print.

Hricko, M. (2010) Using microblogging tools for library services, *Journal of Library Administration* 50(5): 684–92. Print.

Hughes, M. (2012) Assessing the collection through use data: an automated collection assessment tool, *Collection Management* 37(2): 110–26. Print.

Hunt, R.K. (1990) Journal deselection in a biomedical research library. A mediated mathematical approach, *Bulletin of the Medical Library Association* 78(1): 45–8. Print.

Hunter, K. and Bruning, R. (2010) The global economic crisis: what libraries and publishers can do and are doing, *Serials Librarian* 59(2): 147–58. Print.

Hussong-Christian, U. and Goergen-Doll, K. (2010) We're listening: using patron feedback to assess and enhance purchase on demand, *Journal of Interlibrary Loan, Document Delivery & Electronic Reserves* 20(5): 319–35. Print.

Huvila, I. (2011) The complete information literacy? Unforgetting creation and organization of information, *Journal of Librarianship & Information Science* 43(4): 237–45. Print.

Jacobson, T.B. (2011) Facebook as a library tool: perceived vs. actual use, *College & Research Libraries* 72(1): 79–90. Print.

Jacoby, J. and O'Brien, N.P. (2005) Assessing the impact of reference services provided to undergraduate students, *College & Research Libraries* 66(4): 324–40. Print.

Jaeger, P.T., Bertot, J.C., Thompson, K.M., Katz, S.M. and DeCoster, E.J. (2012) The intersection of public policy and public access: digital divides, digital literacy, digital inclusion, and public libraries, *Public Library Quarterly* 31(1): 1–20. Print.

Jay, M., Simpson, B. and Smith, D. (2009) CatQC and shelf-ready material: speeding collections to users while preserving data quality, *Information Technology & Libraries* 28(1): 41–8. Print.

Jones, D. (2011) On-demand information delivery: integration of patron-driven acquisition into a comprehensive information delivery system, *Journal of Library Administration* 51(7): 764–76. Print.

Kairis, R. (2003) Consortium level collection development: a duplication study of the OhioLINK central catalog, *Library Collections, Acquisitions, & Technical Services* 27(3): 317. Print.

Kanter, R.M. (1994) Collaborative advantage: the art of alliances, *Harvard Business Review* 72(4): 96. Print.

Kaplan, A.G. (2010) School library impact studies and school library media programs in the United States, *School Libraries Worldwide* 16(2): 55–63. Print.

Kelley, M., Schwartz, M., Barack, L. and Berry III, J.N. (2012) Librarians reach out to publishers at conference, *Library Journal* 137(7): 14–15. Print.

Kelley, M., Warburton, B. and Lee, M. (2011) Douglas County libraries buys own e-content, *Library Journal* 136(19): 11–13. Print.

Kesselman, M.A. and Watstein, S.B. (2009) Creating opportunities: embedded librarians, *Journal of Library Administration* 49(4): 383–400. Print.

Kieft, R.H. and Payne, L. (2012) Collective collection, collective action, *Collection Management* 37(3): 137–52. Print.

Kincy, C.P. and Wood, M.A. (2012) Rethinking access with RDA (resource description and access), *Journal of Electronic Resources in Medical Libraries* 9(1): 13–34. Print.

King, J. and Mayor, T. (2012) IT skills: jumping the chasm, *Computerworld* 46(11): 16–21. Print.

Kline, J. and Barlow, D. (2006) Integrated ecommerce in the library: a software development partnership between innovative interfaces and the Westerville Public Library, Ohio, *Journal of Library Administration* 44(3): 137–55. Print.

Knoke, D. and Yang, S. (2008) *Social Network Analysis* (p. 132). Los Angeles, CA: Sage. Print.

Kotler, P. and Lee, N. (2008) *Marketing in the Public Sector: A Roadmap for Improved Performance* (p. 332). Upper Saddle River, NJ: Pearson Education, Inc. Print.

Krabill, B. (2009) Tweeting in the stacks: why public libraries should embrace Twitter, *Florida Libraries* 52(2): 14–15. Print.

Kyrillidou, M. and Morris, S. (2011) *ARL Statistics 2008–2009* (p. 167). Washington, DC: Association of Research Libraries. WorldCatWeb. Print.

Landis, C. (2010) *A Social Networking Primer for Librarians.* New York: Neal-Schuman Publishers. WorldCatWeb. Print.

Lane, F.C., Anderson, B., Ponce, H.F. and Natesan, P. (2012) Factorial invariance of LibQUAL+® as a measure of library service quality over time, *Library & Information Science Research* 34(1): 22–30. Print.

Langan, K. (2012) Training Millennials: a practical and theoretical approach, *Reference Services Review* 40(1): 24–48. Print.

Latimer, K. (2010) Redefining the library: current trends in library design, *Art Libraries Journal* 35(1): 28–34. Print.

Lawrence, G.S. (1981) Cost model for storage and weeding programs, *College & Research Libraries* 42(2): 139–47. Print.

Lawrence, J.C. (2010) Libraries as journal publishers, *Journal of Electronic Resources in Medical Libraries* 7(3): 235–40. Print.

Lesneski, T. (2011) Big box libraries: beyond restocking the shelves with books, *New Library World* 112(9): 395–405. Print.

Lewis, J.S. (2011) Using LibQUAL+® survey results to document the adequacy of services to distance learning students for an accreditation review, *Journal of Library & Information Services in Distance Learning* 5(3): 83–104. Print.

Library Journal (2011) *Ebooks The New Normal: Ebook Penetration and Use in U.S. School (K-12) Libraries* (p. 101). NA: Library Journal. Print.

Lin, Y. and Ranjit, K.M.E. (2012) Using social media to create virtual interest groups in hospital libraries, *Grey Journal (TGJ)* 8(1): 35–42. Print.

Liu, Z. and Luo, L. (2011) A comparative study of digital library use: factors, perceived influences, and satisfaction, *Journal of Academic Librarianship* 37(3): 230–6. Print.

Loertscher, D.V. and Koechlin, C. (2011) Personal learning environments in the learning commons, *Teacher Librarian* 39(2): 23–6. Print.

Logan, F.F. (2009) A brief history of reference assessment: no easy solutions, *Reference Librarian* 50(3): 225–33. Print.

Louv, R. (2008) *Last Child in the Woods: Saving our Children from Nature-Deficit Disorder* (p. 390). Chapel Hill, NC: Algonquin Books of Chapel Hill. Print.

Lowry, C.B. (2011) Year 2 of the "Great Recession": surviving the present by building the future, *Journal of Library Administration* 51(1): 37–53. Print.

LYRASIS (2012) LYRASIS – advancing libraries together, *LYRASIS*. NA. Web. Available from: *http://www.lyrasis.org/*.

Mak, C. (2012) Add to cart? E-commerce, self-service and the growth of interlibrary loan, *Interlending & Document Supply* 40(1): 26–30. Print.

Mangold, W.G. and Smith, K.T. (2012) Selling to Millennials with online reviews, *Business Horizons* 55(2): 141–53. Print.

Mankin, C.J. and Bastille, J.D. (1981) An analysis of the differences between density-of-use ranking and raw-use ranking of library journal use, *Journal of the American Society for Information Science* 32(3): 224–8. Print.

Mantel, B. (2011) Future of libraries, *CQ Researcher* 21(27): 625–51. Print.

Marshall, M.E. (2011) Implications for a medium sized publisher using SERU: a shared electronic resource understanding, *Information Standards Quarterly* 23(4): 18–21. Print.

Martin, J.W. and Hughes, B. (2012) Small p publishing: a networked blogging approach to academic discourse, *Journal of Electronic Resources Librarianship* 24(1): 17–21. Print.

Martinko, M.J., Zmud, R.W. and Henry, J.W. (1996) An attributional explanation of individual resistance to the introduction of information technologies in the workplace, *Behaviour & Information Technology* 15(5): 313–30. Print.

Massis, B.E. (2012) In the library: quiet space endures, *New Library World* 113(7): 396–9. Print.

Matthew, V. and Schroeder, A. (2006) The embedded librarian program, *EDUCAUSE Quarterly* 29(4): 61–5. Print.

Mayer, R., Rauber, A., Neumann, M.A., Thomson, J. and Antunes, G. (2012) Preserving scientific processes from design to publications, *Lecture Notes in Computer Science* 7489: 113–24. Print.

McGlone, T., Spain, J.W. and McGlone, V. (2011) Corporate social responsibility and the Millennials, *Journal of Education for Business* 86(4): 195–200. Print.

McHone-Chase, S. (2010) Examining change within interlibrary loan, *Journal of Interlibrary Loan, Document Delivery & Electronic Reserves* 20(3): 201–6. Print.

McLoughlin, C. and Lee, M.J.W. (2008) The three p's of pedagogy for the networked society: personalization, participation, and productivity, *International Journal of Teaching and Learning in Higher Education* 20(1): 10–27. Print.

McMeekin, S.M. (2011) With a little help from OAIS: starting down the digital curation path, *Journal of the Society of Archivists* 32(2): 241–53. Print.

Mellon, C.A. (1986) Library anxiety: a grounded theory and its development, *College & Research Libraries* 47(2): 160–5. Print.

Mellon, C.A. (1988) Attitudes: the forgotten dimension in library instruction, *Library Journal* 113(14): 137–9. Print.

Mestre, L.S., Baures, L., Niedbala, M., Bishop, C., Cantrell, S. et al. (2011) Learning objects as tools for teaching information literacy online: a survey of librarian usage, *College & Research Libraries* 72(3): 236–52. Print.

Michalak, S.C. (2012) This changes everything: transforming the academic library, *Journal of Library Administration* 52(5): 411–23. Print.

Miller, E. and Westfall, M. (2011) Linked data and libraries, *Serials Librarian* 60(1–4): 17–22. Print.

Miller, J.L. (2011) The library student liaison program at Eastern Washington University: a model for student engagement, *College & Undergraduate Libraries* 18(1): 1–15. Print.

Miller, R. (2011) Dramatic growth, *Library Journal* 136(17): 32–4. Print.

Miller, R. (2012) Damn the recession, full speed ahead, *Journal of Library Administration* 52(1): 3–17. Print. Academic Search Premier. Web. Accessed April 2013.

Milne, D. and Tiffany, B. (1991a) A cost-per-use method for evaluating the cost-effectiveness of serials: a detailed discussion of methodology, *Serials Review* 17(2): 7. Print.

Milne, D. and Tiffany, B. (1991b) A survey of the cost-effectiveness of serials: a cost-per-use method and its results, *Serials Librarian* 19(3): 137–50. Print.

Mitchell, A.M., Thompson, J.M. and Wu, A. (2010) Agile cataloging: staffing and skills for a bibliographic future, *Cataloging & Classification Quarterly* 48(6): 506–24. Print.

Moed, H.F., Van Leeuwen, Th.N. and Reedijk, J. (1999) Towards appropriate indicators of journal impact, *Scientometrics* 46(3): 575–89. Print.

Mon, L.M. (2012) Professional avatars: librarians and educators in virtual worlds, *Journal of Documentation* 68(3): 318–29. Print.

Mook, C.A. and Walker, B. (2004) Providing access and preservation services to collections in remote storage facilities, *Journal of Access Services* 2(3): 53–8. Print.

Morell, K. (2012) Tips from bloggers-turned-entrepreneurs, *Open Forum: Powering Small Business Success.* Web. Available from: *http://www.openforum.com/articles/tips-from-bloggers-turned-entrepreneurs/.*

Moreno, M. (2012) Streamlining interlibrary loan and document delivery workflows: tools, techniques, and outcomes, *Interlending & Document Supply* 40(1): 31–6. Print.

Mu, X., Dimitroff, A., Jordan, J. and Burclaff, N. (2011) A survey and empirical study of virtual reference service in academic libraries, *Journal of Academic Librarianship* 37(2): 120–9. Print.

Müller, T. (2011) How to choose a free and open source integrated library system, *OCLC Systems & Services* 27(1): 57–78. Print.

Mulvihill, A. (2011) Librarians face ebook acquisition obstacles, *Information Today* 28(5): 13. Print.

Mulvihill, A. and Schiller, K. (2011) Social reading heats up with ebooks (cover story), *Information Today* 28(7): 1–34. Print.

Myers, K. and Sadaghiani, K. (2010) Millennials in the workplace: a communication perspective on Millennials' organizational relationships and performance, *Journal of Business & Psychology* 25(2): 225–38. Print.

Newspapers (2008) Murdoch to axe 20+ staff, *Library & Information Update* 7(9): 5. Print.

Nicholas, D., Rowlands, I., Watkinson, A., Brown, D. and Jamali, H.R. (2012) Digital repositories ten years on: what do scientific researchers think of them and how do they use them? *Learned Publishing* 25(3): 195–206. Print.

Nicholas, D., Williams, P., Huntington, P., Fieldhouse, M., Gunter, B. et al. (2008) The Google generation: the information behaviour of the researcher of the future, *Aslib Proceedings* 60(4): 290310. Print.

Nilsson, E.M. (2011) The making of a maker-space for open innovation, knowledge sharing, and peer-to-peer learning. In S. Sonvilla-Weiss and O. Kelly (eds.) *Future Learning Spaces* (pp. 293–8). Web. Available from: *https://www.taik.fi/kirjakauppa/images/5c577177ec71cfcd563ca848dab6222a.pdf#page=294*.

Nolen, D.S., Powers, A.C., Zhang, L., Xu, Y., Cannady, R.E. et al. (2012) Moving beyond assumptions: the use of virtual reference data in an academic library, *portal: Libraries & the Academy* 12(1): 23–40. Print.

OCLC (2002) OCLC white paper on the information habits of college students: how academic librarians can influence students' web-based information choices. Web. Available from: *http://www5.oclc.org/downloads/community/information habits.pdf*. Accessed 2012.

O'Connor, L. and Lundstrom, K. (2011) The impact of social marketing strategies on the information seeking behaviors of college students, *Reference & User Services Quarterly* 50(4): 351–65. Print.

Ojala, M. (2011) Challenging ebook lending policies, *Information Today* 28(4): 1–3. Print.

Okerson, A. and Schonfeld, R.C. (2004) Non-subscription costs of print and electronic periodicals on a life-cycle basis, *IFLA Conference Proceedings*: 1–12. Print.

Pacifico, M.F., Wilsted, T. and Society of American Archivists (2009) Task force on archival facilities guidelines. In *Archival and Special Collections Facilities: Guidelines for Archivists, Librarians, Architects, and Engineers* (p. 191). Chicago, IL: Society of American Archivists. Print.

Pagano, J. (2009) Developing a metrics-based online strategy for libraries, *Program: Electronic Library & Information Systems* 43(3): 328–41. Print.

Palaiologk, A., Economides, A.A., Tjalsma, H.D. and Sesink, L.B. (2012) An activity-based costing model for long-term preservation and dissemination of digital research data: the case of DANS, *International Journal on Digital Libraries* 12(4): 195–214. Print.

Palomino, N.E. and Gouveia, P.F. (2011) Righting the academic paper: a collaboration between library services and the writing centre in a Canadian academic setting, *New Library World* 112(3/4): 131–40. Print.

Panitch, J.M. and Michalak, S. (2007) The scholarly work of digital libraries, *Journal of Library Administration* 46(1): 41–64. Print.

Perdue, J. and Van Fleet, J.A. (1999) Borrow or buy? Cost-effective delivery of monographs, *Journal of Interlibrary Loan, Document Delivery & Information Supply* 9(4): 19. Print.

Pesch, O. (2011a) Standards that impact the gathering and analysis of usage, *Serials Librarian* 61(1): 23–32. Print.

Pesch, O. (2011b) Perfecting COUNTER and SUSHI to achieve reliable usage analysis, *Serials Librarian* 61(3): 353–65. Print.

Petit, J. (2011) Twitter and Facebook for user collection requests, *Collection Management* 36(4): 253–8. Print.

Pinto, M. and Manso, R.A. (2012) Virtual references services: defining the criteria and indicators to evaluate them, *Electronic Library* 30(1): 51–69. Print.

Pitcher, K., Bowersox, T., Oberlander, C. and Sullivan, M. (2010) Point-of-need collection development: the Getting it System Toolkit (GIST) and a new system for acquisitions and interlibrary loan integrated workflow and collection development, *Collection Management* 35(3): 222–36. Print.

Plutchak, T.S. (2012) Breaking the barriers of time and space: the dawning of the great age of librarians, *Journal of the Medical Library Association* 100(1): 10–19. Print.

Poore, M. (2011) Digital literacy: human flourishing and collective intelligence in a knowledge society, *Australian Journal of Language & Literacy* 34(2): 20–6. Print.

Porter, B. (2011) Millennial undergraduate research strategies in web and library information retrieval systems, *Journal of Web Librarianship* 5(4): 267–85. Print.

Poulin, E.T. (2011) Fanbase to the rescue, *American Libraries* 42(5): 44. Print.

Powell, A. (2012) Navigating the new norm: vendor, publisher, and librarian strategies to cope with the changing information industry, *Journal of Library Administration* 52(5): 370–95. Print.

Power, J.L. (2009) An interview with the frontline, *Journal of Access Services* 6(4): 516–22. Print.

Prensky, M. (2001) Do they really think differently? *On the Horizon* 9(6): 1–6. Print.

Pulizzi, J. (2012) The rise of storytelling as the new marketing, *Publishing Research Quarterly* 28(2): 116–23. Print.

Pupeliene, J. (2011) The management of the library's financial resources when implementing an open environment, *IATUL Annual Conference Proceedings* 21: 1–7. Print.

Rainie, L., Zickuhr, K., Purcell, K., Madden, M. and Brenner, J. (2012) *The Rise of e-Reading* (p. 67). Washington, DC: Pew Research Center's Internet & American Life Project. Print.

Ralph, L. (2009) If you build it they may not come: the case of QuestionPoint, *Electronic Journal of Academic & Special Librarianship* 10(2): 1–12. Print.

Ralph, L. and Stahr, B. (2010) When off-campus means virtual campus: the academic library in second life, *Journal of Library Administration* 50(7): 909–22. Print.

Reference and User Services Association (2012) Guidelines for interlibrary loan operations management, *Reference & User Services Quarterly* 51(4): 381–2. Print.

Reid, M.M. (2011) Is the balanced scorecard right for academic libraries? *Bottom Line: Managing Library Finances* 24(2): 85–95. Print.

Reviews, News, and More (2011) 10 more that will inspire, *Library Journal*: 16–17. Print.

Richtel, M. (2012) Wasting time is new divide in digital era. Web. Available from: *http://www.nytimes.com/2012/05/30/us/new-digital-divide-seen-in-wasting-time-online.html?smid=pl-share.* Accessed 2012.

Robinson, C.K. (2012) Peter Drucker on marketing: application and implications for libraries, *Bottom Line: Managing Library Finances* 25(1): 4–12. Print.

Ross, S. (2012) Digital preservation, archival science and methodological foundations for digital libraries, *New Review of Information Networking* 17(1): 43–68. Print.

Rubin, V.L., Chen, Y. and Thorimbert, L.M. (2010) Artificially intelligent conversational agents in libraries, *Library Hi Tech* 28(4): 496–522. Print.

Rudasill, L.M. (2010) Beyond subject specialization: the creation of embedded librarians, *Public Services Quarterly* 6(2): 83–91. Print.

Ryan, S.M. (2008) Reference transactions analysis: the cost-effectiveness of staffing a traditional academic reference desk, *Journal of Academic Librarianship* 34(5): 389–99. Print.

Sawaya, J., Maswabi, T., Taolo, R., Andrade, P., Grez, M.M. et al. (2011) Advocacy and evidence for sustainable public computer access experiences from the global libraries initiative, *Library Review* 60(6): 448–72. Print.

Scaramozzino, J.M., Ramírez, M.L. and McGaughey, K.J. (2012) A study of faculty data curation behaviors and attitudes at a teaching-centered university, *College & Research Libraries* 73(4): 349–65. Print.

Schaupp, L.C. (2010) Web site success: antecedents of web site satisfaction and re-use, *Journal of Internet Commerce* 9(1): 42–64. Print.

Schlipf, F. (2011) The dark side of library architecture: the persistence of dysfunctional designs, *Library Trends* 60(1): 227–55. Print.

Schroeder, R. (2012) When patrons call the shots: patron-driven acquisition at Brigham Young University, *Collection Building* 31(1): 11–14. Print.

Schroeder, R. and Howland, J.L. (2011) Shelf-ready: a cost-benefit analysis, *Library Collections, Acquisitions, & Technical Services* 35(4): 129–34. Print.

Schulte, S.J. (2011) Eliminating traditional reference services in an academic health sciences library: a case study, *Journal of the Medical Library Association* 99(4): 273–9. Print.

Seadle, M. (2010) Archiving in the networked world: LOCKSS and national hosting, *Library Hi Tech* 28(4): 710–17. Print.

Seeholzer, J. and Salem, J.A. (2010) The learning library: a case study of the evolution from information commons to learning commons at Kent State University Libraries,

College & Undergraduate Libraries 17(2/3): 287–96. Print.

Sharp, S. and Thompson, S. (2010) "Just in case" vs. "just in time": e-book purchasing models, *Serials* 23(3): 201–6. Print.

Shen, J. (2011) The e-book lifestyle: an academic library perspective, *Reference Librarian* 52(1): 181–9. Print. Web.

Shrauger, K.J. and Dotson, L. (2010) Scan by numbers: interlibrary loan lending statistics shape digital initiative, *Journal of Interlibrary Loan, Document Delivery & Electronic Reserves* 20(3): 135–48. Print.

Shumaker, D. (2013) The embedded librarian: exploring new, embedded roles for librarians in organizations of all types, *The Embedded Librarian*. Web. Available from: *http://embeddedlibrarian.com/*. Accessed 2013.

Sin, S.-C.J. and Kim, K.-S. (2008) Use and non-use of public libraries in the information age: a logistic regression analysis of household characteristics and library services variables, *Library & Information Science Research* 30(3): 207–15. Print.

Singh, R. (2009) Does your library have an attitude problem towards "marketing"? Revealing inter-relationships between marketing attitudes and behaviour, *Journal of Academic Librarianship* 35(1): 25–32. Print.

Small, G.W., Moody, T.D., Siddarth, P. and Bookheimer, S.Y. (2009) Your brain on Google: patterns of cerebral activation during Internet searching, *The American Journal of Geriatric Psychiatry* 17(2): 116–26. Print.

Smith, F. (2007) 24-hour service at Georgia Southern University: 1989–2007, *Journal of Access Services* 5(1): 69–83. Print.

Smith, J. (2012) The best and worst master's degrees for jobs, *Forbes*. Web. Available from: *http://www.forbes.com/*

sites/jacquelynsmith/2012/06/08/the-best-and-worst-masters-degrees-for-jobs-2/2/;.

Sobel, K. and Beall, J. (2011) Humanities research, book digitization, and the problem of linguistic change, *Journal of Library Innovation* 2(2): 3–15. Print.

Spiteri, L.F. (2011) Using social discovery systems to leverage user-generated metadata, *Bulletin of the American Society for Information Science & Technology* 37(4): 27–9. Print.

Spitzform, P. (2011) Patron-driven acquisition: collecting as if money and space mean something, *Against the Grain* 23(3): 20–4. Print.

Stagg, A. and Kimmins, L. (2012) Research skills development through collaborative virtual learning environments, *Reference Services Review* 40(1): 61–74. Print.

St. Clair, G. (2008) The million book project in relation to Google, *Journal of Library Administration* 47(1): 151–63. Print.

Stephenson, K. (2012) Sharing control, embracing collaboration: cross-campus partnerships for library website design and management, *Journal of Electronic Resources Librarianship* 24(2): 91–100. Print.

Stewart, C. (2011) Building measurements: assessing success of the library's changing physical space, *Journal of Academic Librarianship* 37(6): 539–41. Print.

Straw, J.E. (2001) From magicians to teachers: the development of electronic reference in libraries: 1930–2000, *Reference Librarian* 35(74): 1. Print.

Suciu, A. and Petrescu-Prahova, M. (2011) Social networks as a change management strategy for performance excellence and innovation, *Journal for Quality & Participation* 34(1): 16–20. Print.

Sugarman, T., Krueger, S. and Kelly, L. (2011) Evaluating usage of non-text resources: what the COUNTER statistics don't tell you, *Serials Librarian* 60(1–4): 83–97. Print.

Susman, T.M., Carter, D.J. and the Information Access Alliance (2003) *Publisher Mergers: A Consumer-Based Approach to Antitrust Analysis* (p. 33). Print.

Sweeney, R.T. (1994) Leadership in the post-hierarchical library, *Library Trends* 43(1): 62–94. Print.

Sweeney, R.T. (2005) Reinventing library buildings and services for the Millennial Generation, *Library Administration & Management* 19(4): 165–75. Print.

Sze, L. (2012) Taking ideas to the next level, *Public Libraries* 51(3): 10–12. Print.

Tallman, J.E. (1979) One year's experience with CONTU guidelines for interlibrary loan photocopies, *Journal of Academic Librarianship* 5(2): 71. Print.

Tapscott, D. (2009) *Grown Up Digital: How the Net Generation is Changing Your World*. New York: McGraw-Hill. Print.

Taranto, B. (2009) It's not just about curators anymore: special collections in the digital age, *RBM: A Journal of Rare Books, Manuscripts, & Cultural Heritage* 10(1): 30–6. Print.

Taylor, A. (2012) A study of the information search behaviour of the Millennial Generation, *Information Research Information Research* 17(1): 508. Print.

Taylor, J. and Davies, C. (2011) Change management in technology outsourcing contracts, *Communications Law: Journal of Computer, Media & Telecommunications Law* 16(4): 148–51. Print.

Taylor, M. and Heath, F. (2012) Assessment and continuous planning: the key to transformation at the University of Texas Libraries, *Journal of Library Administration* 52(5): 424–35. Print.

Taylor, P., Parker, K., Kochhar, R., Fry, R., Funk, C. et al. (2012) *Young, Underemployed and Optimistic: Coming of Age, Slowly, in a Tough Economy* (p. 67). Washington, DC: Pew Research Center. Print.

Terras, M. (2010) Should we just send a copy? Digitisation, usefulness and users, *Art Libraries Journal* 35(1): 22–7. Print.

Thohira, M., Chambers, M.B. and Sprague, N. (2010) Full-text databases: a case study revisited a decade later, *Serials Review* 36(3): 152–60. Print.

Thomas, D. (2007) The mashed-up librarian: new roles in technical services, *Feliciter* 53(5): 234–6. Print.

Thompson, B., Cook, C. and Kyrillidou, M. (2005) Concurrent validity of LibQUAL+™ scores: what do LibQUAL+™ scores measure? *Journal of Academic Librarianship* 31(6): 517–22. Print.

Thompson, S. (2010) User-driven purchasing: a pilot project to test an alternative pricing model for Springer e-book collections, *Serials* 23(2): 135–39. Print.

Tonkery, D. (2011) Publishing industry sales, *Searcher* 19(9): 36–8. Print.

Top, E. (2012) Blogging as a social medium in undergraduate courses: sense of community best predictor of perceived learning, *Internet & Higher Education* 15(1): 24–8. Print.

Torbert, C. (2008) Collaborative journal purchasing today: results of a survey, *Serials Librarian* 55(1): 168–83. Print.

Tucci, V.K. (2011) Faculty/librarian collaboration: catalyst for student learning and librarian growth, *Science & Technology Libraries* 30(3): 292–305. Print.

Tucker, J.C. (2012) Ebook collection analysis: subject and publisher trends, *Collection Building* 31(2): 40–7. Print.

Turner, P., Turner, S. and Van De Walle, G. (2007) How older people account for their experiences with interactive technology, *Behaviour & Information Technology* 26(4): 287–96. Print.

Tyler, D.C. (2011) Patron-driven purchase on demand programs for printed books and similar materials: a chronological review and summary of findings, *Library Philosophy and Practice* Paper 635: 108–27. Print.

Tyler, D.C., Melvin, J.C., Xu, Y., Epp, M. and Kreps, A.M. (2011) Effective selectors? Interlibrary loan patrons as monograph purchasers: a comparative examination of price and circulation-related performance, *Journal of Interlibrary Loan, Document Delivery & Electronic Reserves* 21(1): 57–90. Print.

Tyler, D.C., Xu, Y., Melvin, J., Epp, M. and Kreps, A.M. (2010) Just how right are the customers? An analysis of the relative performance of patron-initiated interlibrary loan monograph purchases, *Collection Management* 35(3): 162–79. Print.

Tzoc, E. (2011) Re-using today's metadata for tomorrow's research: five practical examples for enhancing access to digital collections, *Journal of Electronic Resources Librarianship* 23(1): 43–55. Print.

United States, Cong. House, (2010) America COMPETES Reauthorization Act of 2010: America creating opportunities to meaningfully promote excellence in technology, education, and science Reauthorization Act of 2010. 1011th Congress, 2nd session. Washington: GPO. Web. Available from: *http://www.gpo.gov/fdsys/pkg/BILLS-111hr5116enr/pdf/BILLS-111hr5116enr.pdf;*. Accessed 2012.

University College London (2008) Information behaviour of the researcher of the future: a ciber briefing paper, *JISC*. Web. Available from: *http://www.jisc.ac.uk/media/documents/programmes/reppres/gg_final_keynote_11012008.pdf*. Accessed 2012.

Van Dyk, G. (2011) Interlibrary loan purchase-on-demand: a misleading literature, *Library Collections, Acquisitions, & Technical Services* 35(2): 83–9. Print.

Vannoy, S.A. and Palvia, P. (2010) The social influence model of technology adoption, *Communications of the ACM* 53(6): 149–53. Print.

Van Orsdel, L.C. and Born, K. (2009) Reality bites, *Library Journal* (April): 36–40. Print.

Van Scoyoc, A.M. (2003) Reducing library anxiety in first-year students, *Reference & User Services Quarterly* 42(4): 329. Print.

Vattulainen, P. (2005) Maintaining access to print materials – a Finnish model, *Liber Quarterly: The Journal of European Research Libraries* 15(1–4): 310–19. Print.

Wallin, M., Kelly, K. and McGinley, A. (2012) Using mobile technology to deliver information in audio format: learning by listening. In M. Ally and G. Needham (eds.) *M-libraries 3: Transforming Libraries with Mobile Technology* (pp. 57–64). London: Facet Publishing. Print.

Walsh, R.T. (1994) *The National Information Infrastructure and the Recommendations of the 1991 White House Conference on Library and Information Services.* [Washington, DC?]: The Commission. Print.

Wan, G. (2011) How academic libraries reach users on Facebook, *College & Undergraduate Libraries* 18(4): 307–18. Print.

Ward, S.M., Wray, T. and Debus-López, K.E. (2003) Collection development based on patron requests: collaboration between interlibrary loan and acquisitions, *Library Collections, Acquisitions, & Technical Services* 27(2): 203. Print.

Waters, R.D., Burnett, E., Lamm, A. and Lucas, J. (2009) Engaging stakeholders through social networking: how nonprofit organizations are using Facebook, *Public Relations Review* 35(2): 102–6. Print.

Weiler, A. (2005) Information-seeking behavior in Generation Y students: motivation, critical thinking, and learning theory, *Journal of Academic Librarianship* 31(1): 46–53. Print.

Welburn, W.C., Welburn, J. and McNeil, B. (2010) *Advocacy, Outreach, and the Nation's Academic Libraries: A Call for Action* (p. 210). Chicago, IL: Association of College and Research Libraries. Print.

Wells Fargo (2011) What's your negotiation style? *Wells Fargo Conversations*. Web. Available from: *https://www. wfconversations.com/create_wealth/business_assets/ assessment/whats_your_negotiation_style/*. Accessed 26 June 2012.

Werth, E.P. and Werth, L. (2011) Effective training for Millennial students, *Adult Learning* 22(3): 12–19. Print.

White House Conference on Library and Information Services (1979) *The White House Conference on Library and Information Services, 1979: Summary*. Washington, DC: National Commission on Libraries and Information Science: Supt. of Docs., U.S. Govt. Print. Off., 1980.

Williams, J.A. and Woolwine, D.E. (2011) Interlibrary loan in the United States: an analysis of academic libraries in a digital age, *Journal of Interlibrary Loan, Document Delivery & Electronic Reserves* 21(4): 165–83. Print.

Williams, K. (2012) Informatics moments, *Library Quarterly* 82(1): 47–73. Print.

Willis, C.A. (2012) Library services for persons with disabilities: twentieth anniversary update, *Medical Reference Services Quarterly* 31(1): 92–104. Print.

Wilson, A. (2012) QR codes in the library: are they worth the effort? *Journal of Access Services* 9(3): 101–10. Print.

Wilson, K. (2011) Beyond library software: new tools for electronic resources management, *Serials Review* 37(4): 294–304. Print.

Worley, K. (2011) Educating college students of the Net generation, *Adult Learning* 22(3): 31–9. Print.

Wu, M.M. (2011) Building a collaborative digital collection: a necessary evolution in libraries, *Law Library Journal* 103(4): 527–51. Print.

Wu, S.K. and Lanclos, D. (2011) Re-imagining the users' experience: an ethnographic approach to web usability and space design, *Reference Services Review* 39(3): 369–89. Print.

Yang, S.Q. and Hofmann, M.A. (2010) The next generation library catalog: a comparative study of the OPACs of Koha, Evergreen, and Voyager, *Information Technology & Libraries* 29(3): 141–50. Print.

Yi, H. and Herlihy, C.S. (2007) Assessment of the impact of an open-URL link resolver, *New Library World* 108(7): 317–31. Print.

York, J. (2012) HathiTrust: the elephant in the library, *Library Issues* 32(3): 1–4. Print.

Young, N.J. and Von Seggern, M. (2001) General information seeking in changing times, *Reference & User Services Quarterly* 41(2): 159. Print.

Zickuhr, K. (2010) *Generations 2010* (p. 3). Washington, DC: Pew Research Center. Print.

Zickuhr, K., Rainie, L., Purcell, K., Madden, M. and Brenner, J. (2012) *Libraries, Patrons, and e-Books* (p. 80). Washington, DC: Pew Research Center's Internet & American Life Project. Print.

Index

CPSIA information can be obtained at www.ICGtesting.com
Printed in the USA
BVOW04s0542101013

333383BV00006B/46/P

9 781843 347361